A Physicist Examines Hope in the Resurrection

A Physicist Examines Hope in the Resurrection

*Examination of the Significance of the Work of
John C. Polkinghorne
for the Mission of the Church*

John Wilson

Foreword by Vaughn Baker

WIPF & STOCK · Eugene, Oregon

A PHYSICIST EXAMINES HOPE IN THE RESURRECTION
Examination of the Significance of the Work of John C. Polkinghorne for the Mission of the Church

Copyright © 2016 John Wilson. All rights reserved. Except for brief quotations in critical publications or reviews, no part of this book may be reproduced in any manner without prior written permission from the publisher. Write: Permissions, Wipf and Stock Publishers, 199 W. 8th Ave., Suite 3, Eugene, OR 97401.

Wipf & Stock
An Imprint of Wipf and Stock Publishers
199 W. 8th Ave., Suite 3
Eugene, OR 97401

www.wipfandstock.com

PAPERBACK ISBN: 978-1-5326-0514-7
HARDCOVER ISBN: 978-1-5326-0516-1
EBOOK ISBN: 978-1-5326-0515-4

Manufactured in the U.S.A.　　　　　　　　　　　　　　NOVEMBER 21, 2016

New Revised Standard Version Bible: Catholic Edition, copyright 1989, 1993, Division of Christian Education of the National Council of the Churches of Christ in the United States of America. Used by permission. All rights reserved.

Scripture quotations from The Authorized (King James) Version. Rights in the Authorized Version in the United Kingdom are vested in the Crown. Reproduced by permission of the Crown's patentee, Cambridge University Press.

Scriptures and additional materials quoted are from the Good News Bible © 1994 published by the Bible Societies/HarperCollins Publishers Ltd UK, Good News Bible© American Bible Society 1966, 1971, 1976, 1992. Used with permission.

Scripture taken from *The Message*. Copyright © 1993, 1994, 1995, 1996, 2000, 2001, 2002. Used by permission of NavPress Publishing Group.

Theology and Science, © 2009, 2010, 2011, 2012, 2013, 2014, 2015, 2016 by the Center for Theology and the Natural Sciences.

Zygon: Journal of Science & Religion © 2006, 2007, 2008, 2010, 2011, 2012, 2013, 2014, 2015, 2016 by the Joint Publication Board of *Zygon: Journal of Science & Religion*

To Marsha.

Contents

Foreword by Vaughn Baker | *ix*
Preface | *xi*
Acknowledgments | *xv*
Abbreviations | *xvi*
Introduction | *xix*

1	Evangelism in the Contemporary World	1
2	Enquiry in Religion and Science	18
3	Kenosis	47
4	Christology	62
5	Eschatology	79
6	Announcement of the Kingdom	102
7	Resurrection	110
8	Foundation for Christian Hope	136
9	Meaning	150
10	Hope	162
11	Theodicy, Divine Action, and the Trinity	190
12	In Conclusion	204

Bibliography | *225*
Index | *231*

Foreword
by Vaughn Baker

IN HIS BOOK: *A Physicist Examines Hope in the Resurrection: Examination of the Significance of the Work of John C. Polkinghorne for the Mission of the Church*, John Wilson ably weaves the work of Jürgen Moltmann and N. T. Wright with the work of John Polkinghorne on eschatological hope in the resurrection. He goes further to include the work of Craig Hill in support of a fresh, illuminating exposition of eschatology.

Sharing Polkinghorne's background of both physics and theology, Wilson examines in a critical and yet sympathetic manner the use of divine *kenosis* as the means by which to understand the relationship between God and world. Here the author addresses the problem for how one would interpret and commend Christian faith in the contemporary world. In doing so, it discusses evangelism in the contemporary world, examines the work of John C. Polkinghorne in religion and science and asks whether Polkinghorne's work provides insight for evangelism. Second, it examines his contributions to theology and to the religion and science dialogue for evangelism.

Wilson's hypothesis is that Polkinghorne develops carefully reasoned arguments that significantly respond to changes in scientific worldview in the contemporary period. His argument includes a "bottom-up critically realistic approach to knowledge, kenosis, and a well-argued defense of the resurrection." Polkinghorne's work succeeds in answering the concern Newbigin raises regarding the necessity for evangelism to answer the questions science asks, sees reason as important, and offers potential for richer evangelism.

In a time when new concepts of God are emerging, particularly ones that may be called "open and relational," a work such as *A Physicist Examines Hope in the Resurrection* continues the discussion of religion and science in a stimulating way. It also examines and employs emergent models of God which seek to be faithful to the biblical witness of divine agency while at the same time articulating dynamic concepts of God and creation. The audience for this book includes those in the church concerned with evangelism, seminary evangelism and theology faculty, evangelists, pastors, church staff who have responsibility for evangelism, and those interested in the subject of religion and science.

Vaughn Baker

Preface

THIS WORK ADDRESSES THE problem for how one would interpret and commend Christian faith in the contemporary world. In doing so, it discusses evangelism in the contemporary world, examines the work of John C. Polkinghorne in religion and science and asks whether Polkinghorne's work provides insight for evangelism. Second, it examines his contributions to theology and to the religion and science dialogue for evangelism.

Scholars with extensive training in both science and religion are in a good position from which to respond to the impact of science on faith. One such scholar is Polkinghorne who retired as a respected theoretical physicist at Cambridge University to pursue episcopal ordination in the Church of England and proved adept in responding to questions in religion and science.

Polkinghorne began life in 1930 in the British Channel seaside resort Weston-super-Mare.[1] Polkinghorne excelled in and fell in love with mathematics, and he received a Major Scholarship to Trinity College Cambridge.[2]

Polkinghorne entered Trinity College October 1949, concentrated on quantum physics, and studied the core course under professor of mathematics Paul Dirac who held Newton's Lucasian Chair of Mathematics. He went to the Fresher's Sermon at Holy Trinity Church his first Sunday at Trinity and heard Rev. L. F. E. Wilkinson preach on Zacchaeus. When Wilkinson issued the invitation for people to come forward and commit their lives to Christ, Polkinghorne did. He considers that Sunday his time of Christian conversion and refers to those days at Cambridge as his days of evangelicalism. During his student days at Cambridge he began regular practice of prayer and the study of Scripture which he continued his entire life.[3]

Polkinghorne graduated in 1952 and remained at Cambridge to work towards a PhD in theoretical physics of particles and began work on the

---

1. See Polkinghorne, *Physicist to Priest*, 4–6.
2. Ibid., 10–14.
3. Ibid., 23–29.

recently discovered renormalization theory. He won the coveted Trinity Research Fellowship Prize, became a Fellow of Trinity for the initial presentation of his work, finished his PhD the summer of 1955, and prepared to go to Caltech.[4] Throughout his career, Polkinghorne worked alongside well-known physicists such as Paul Dirac, Richard Feynman, and Murray Gell-Mann.[5]

Polkinghorne returned to Cambridge University which later appointed him to the professorship of mathematics in 1968, and one of his students, Brian Josephson, later won a Nobel Prize. Polkinghorne served a spell as the United Kingdom representative on the CERN Council.[6]

The Christian faith always held a central place for Polkinghorne and he participated in Christian community throughout his life. As he neared his fiftieth year, he decided that exploration in particle physics belonged to younger physicists, and after conversation with his wife turned to ordination as a priest in the Anglican Church,[7] resigning in 1979 as professor of mathematical physics in Cambridge University to pursue training for the Anglican Priesthood.[8]

Polkinghorne notes Ridley Hall principal Keith Sutton suggested he begin reading theology in Jürgen Moltmann's *The Crucified God* (1972). Its insight significantly affected Polkinghorne so that the idea of the crucified God became central to Polkinghorne's thought as he pursued ordination.[9]

Polkinghorne received Anglican ordination as priest at Trinity Chapel in 1982, following which he served in parish ministry.[10] Trinity Hall called looking for a new dean of Trinity Hall Chapel. Polkinghorne accepted the position of dean of Trinity Hall Chapel which marked his return to Trinity College Cambridge University where he took on the responsibilities for conducting chapel worship, pastoral care in the college community, and the position of Director of Theological Studies.[11]

---

4. Ibid., 31–36.

5. Paul Dirac, Richard Feynman, and Murray Gell-Mann were all Nobel Laureates in physics.

6. Polkinghorne, *Physicist to Priest*, 45–54. The CERN Council consists today of representatives from 21 European states who meet regularly to discuss particle physics research and associated subjects. CERN is located on the Franco-Swiss border near Geneva, Switzerland. See http://council.web.cern.ch/council/en/Welcome.html.

7. Polkinghorne, *Way the World Is*, 1–2.

8. Ibid., frontispiece.

9. Polkinghorne, *Physicist to Priest*, 81–87.

10. Ibid., 89–100.

11. Ibid., 101–10.

The Anglican Church occupied an important part of Polkinghorne's life from childhood and took on an even greater part when he retired as a physicist. He carried his extensive record of publication over to theology, and as he matured, he turned to the subject of eschatological hope.[12]

In 1989, Polkinghorne became the fortieth president of Queens' College Cambridge.[13] Less than a year following retirement as president of Queens' College Cambridge Polkinghorne received notice of his nomination to the queen for the award of Knight Commander of the Order of the British Empire, and early in 2002, he received notice of the award for the 2002 Templeton Prize.[14]

Polkinghorne went from a young man who loved math to become a member of the Royal Society, an Anglican priest, president of Queen's College Cambridge, Knight Commander of the Order of the British Empire, and the 2002 recipient of the Templeton Prize. Following retirement as a physicist, he published extensively in religion and science, and has achieved significant recognition for his work.

Polkinghorne demonstrates the methodical approach to investigation of questions in the religion and science dialogue, and we would expect such an approach from one of his stature in physics.

---

12. Eschatological hope represents the promise to the Christian through the death, burial, and resurrection of Jesus that all Christians reside with God following death for all eternity.

13. Polkinghorne, *Physicist to Priest*, 119–30.

14. Ibid., 165–72.

Acknowledgments

I EXPRESS GREAT APPRECIATION to Dr. Vaughn W. Baker and Dr. William J. Abraham and to the members of Polycarp for their support and encouragement of my work. I especially express appreciation to Dr. C. William Bridges for his assistance in putting together the final work. I am grateful for the support of the University of South Africa and Professor Nico Botha and for the University of South Africa's financial support for this project. I especially express my love to my wife, Marsha, for her ceaseless love and support.

Abbreviations

Biblical

Old Testament (OT)

Gen	Genesis
Deut	Deuteronomy
Exod	Exodus
1–2 Sam	1–2 Samuel
Ps	Psalm
Pss	Psalms
Isa	Isaiah
Jer	Jeremiah
Ezek	Ezekiel

New Testament (NT)

Matt	Matthew
1–2 Cor	1–2 Corinthians
Gal	Galatians
Eph	Ephesians
Phil	Philippians
Col	Colossians
1–2 Thess	1–2 Thessalonians
1–2 Tim	1–2 Timothy
Heb	Hebrew
Jas	James
1–2 Pet	1–2 Peter
Rev	Revelation

General

CERN	The European Organization for Nuclear Research
KJV	The Authorized (King James) Version of the Bible
NRSV	New Revised Standard Version of the Bible
NRSV–NT	New Revised Standard Version New Testament of the Bible
NRSV–OT	New Revised Standard Version Old Testament of the Bible
SPCK	Society for Promoting Christian Knowledge

Introduction

NOTING THE IMPORTANCE OF the need for evangelism to reach people in contemporary times, Arthur R. Peacocke comments on Leslie Newbigin's *Foolishness to the Greeks* (1986): "No-one concerned with the future of the Christian, or indeed any other religion, can avoid facing up to the impact of science on faith. This encounter is identified by Newbigin as the crucial point at which the gospel is failing to have any impact on 'Western' men and women."[1]

Polkinghorne develops carefully reasoned arguments that significantly respond to changes in scientific worldview in the contemporary period. His argument includes a bottom-up critically realistic approach to knowledge, kenosis, and a well-argued defense of the resurrection. Polkinghorne's work succeeds, answers the concern Newbigin raises regarding the necessity for evangelism to answer the questions science asks, sees reason as important, and offers potential for richer evangelism.

The heart of the problem for evangelism in the contemporary world is whether or not evangelism responds contextually to the contemporary world. Polkinghorne provides the means to do so which is the heart and core of this work. Further, he offers hope both for the present and the future which the evangelist sometimes omits in the message.

I approached research for this work from an archival standpoint. I had the goal to thoroughly research the religion and science dialogue before examining Polkinghorne's work in order to establish my religion and science worldview. I began with the work of Ian G. Barbour and Arthur R. Peacocke along with the five extensive volumes on religion and science from the Vatican City State's Vatican Observatory Publications. Other important resources included peer-reviewed material in *Theology and Science* and *Zygon: Journal of Science & Religion*. I added work from various philosophers and theologians including but not limited to William J. Abraham, Ian G. Barbour, David J. Bosch, John F. Haught, Craig C. Hill, Alister E. McGrath,

---

1. Peacocke, *Theology*, 1.

Jürgen Moltmann, Wolfhart Pannenberg, Arthur R. Peacocke, Alvin Plantinga, Robert J. Russell, Richard Swinburne, and N. T. Wright. Whenever a particular author referenced what I considered an important work for his or her argument, I examined it as well. Through this in-depth examination of sources, I gained important insight into the religion and science dialogue including its important subjects and conclusions.

After completing this archival research, I critically examined the work of Polkinghorne chronologically in order to understand how his thought changed and matured. As in the general archival work, I examined references which appeared important for his conclusions.

Chapter 1 discusses the role of evangelism in the church. In doing so, it examines its decline in effectiveness in recent years and the benefit of Polkinghorne's work for response to questions from contemporary culture. Evangelism to be successful in the contemporary world requires a message that does not overlook today's concerns and that does not avoid difficult questions. It addresses catechesis and discipleship.[2]

Chapter 2 examines the thought of Polkinghorne beginning with critical realism and continues with discussion of his bottom-up approach. He discounts a top-down approach as he says it has the weakness of indeterminism with gaps in knowledge. His approach has importance for the insight it provides to his work. Importantly, Polkinghorne's approach commends itself well to a scientist. It also serves well the evangelistic mission to commend Christian faith in the contemporary world.

Polkinghorne offers a virtually flawless discussion of the relevant physics.

Chapter 3 explains kenosis which Polkinghorne refers to throughout his work. Kenosis refers to the kenotic hymn in Phil 2:5–11. In kenosis, God limits his activity in creation in order that creatures have freedom, avoiding a tyrannical God. It appears in the Greek as κενόω, *kenoo*, which is translated as "emptied" in Phil 2:7,[3] and many theologians have accepted God as kenotically self-limiting his actions in creation. This approach works well in explaining why God does not act in some instances without limiting his omnipotence. God simply chooses to not exercise omnipotence in order to permit freedom in creation. The kenosis approach works well as it includes God in creation, divine immanence, but without

---

2. Catechesis is the process of introducing new converts to Christian faith to the teachings and practices of Christian faith.

3. Bauer, *Greek-English Lexicon*, 429.

holding God responsible for moral and natural evil,[4] something the New Atheists enjoy attacking.[5]

Chapter 4 explores the Christology of Polkinghorne which he mentions the first time in *The Way the World Is* (1983).[6] Christology weaves continuously in his work as he discusses the work of God through Jesus which leads to eschatological hope. The chapter also includes discussion of Moltmann's *The Crucified God* (1993) which significantly impacted Polkinghorne.[7] Polkinghorne exhibits his reasoned approach to the examination of the various accounts to argue successfully for the character and mission of Jesus.

Chapter 5 discusses eschatology, important for the theme of eschatological hope. It separates the apocalypticism of John Nelson Darby, Hal Lindsay, and Tim LaHaye from the eschatology of Polkinghorne.[8] I also discuss Hill's *In God's Time* (2002) for his careful differentiation of the apocalyptic and eschatology.[9] Eschatology in the work of Moltmann, Polkinghorne, and Wright grounds their arguments in Christian hope.

In making eschatology central in his work, Polkinghorne provides evangelism in Christian faith as centrally good news and not as bad news. And it is good news. His move has particular importance in the United States where evangelism is often associated with apocalypticism.

Chapter 6 discusses the announcement of the kingdom of God (heaven) which Jesus announces in the beginning of his ministry. The kingdom broke strongly with both Jewish and secular expectations. In the kingdom, the poor become rich, and the strong and powerful weak. Jesus' work will not finish until he has fully established the kingdom on earth. Evangelism keeps the message of the kingdom at the center; otherwise, it risks failing the evangelistic message, and Jesus becomes just another man who lived and died an ignoble death.

In chapter 7, Polkinghorne examines the evidence for the resurrection following his method of bottom-up and critical realism and concludes

---

4. Moral evil refers to incidents where humans intentionally inflict emotional and/or psychological pain on other humans. Natural evil refers to incidents where natural disasters such as hurricanes, volcanos, and earthquakes inflict emotional and/or psychological pain on humans.

5. New atheists include people like Richard Dawkins, Daniel Dennett, Sam Harris, and Christopher Hitchens Haught, *New Atheism*, ix–xiii.

6. Polkinghorne, *Way the World Is*.

7. Moltmann, *Crucified God*.

8. Apocalyptic refers to the literature that often describes the cataclysmic events when good eventually overcomes the evil of the time.

9. Eschatology refers to literature that describes the final events at the end of a particular period of time, usually the end of things as we know them on earth.

the resurrection occurred. Without the resurrection, Christian faith has no content. Like eschatology, the resurrection contributes to the weaving of the fabric for Christian hope. Polkinghorne presents a strongly and well-reasoned exposition of the evidence, both real and circumstantial, for the resurrection, and his work here greatly assists the message of evangelism.

Chapter 8 examines the foundation for Christian hope. It sees hope as a gift and distinguishes hope from secular optimism and wishful thinking. The chapter includes discussion of the anthropic principle which connects observed teleology in creation with its Creator. Christian hope emerges primarily in the resurrection as final destiny for the Christian life. Christian hope does not mean optimism or wishful thinking. It relies on the strong foundation of a loving, faithful, and trustworthy God.

I added discussion of meaning in chapter 9 to clarify that Christian faith includes far more than hope for human destiny. Otherwise, we miss the point that commitment to Jesus Christ transforms lives, the heart of the message of evangelism. Meaning in Christian faith provides purpose for living a life which makes a difference. Christian faith transforms individuals, families, and communities and in doing so becomes the source of intention and meaning for life. The chapter also discusses the nature of religion in the contemporary world in the light of the work of Harold Kushner.

Chapter 10, the centerpiece of this work, discusses the relevance of Christian hope. It begins with the acknowledgment that self-conscious human beings early questioned death and its reality. Secular hope anticipates a better life as seen in Ernst Bloch's *The Principle of Hope* (Bloch 1954, 1955, 1959) and does not examine human destiny beyond death.[10] The cross leads to Christian hope, and the principal sources in this work argue that faith begins in and has its roots in the cross consistent with Paul's remarks in Gal 2:20. Eschatological hope differs from the pessimistic view of science which projects the end of the world as we know it.

Polkinghorne develops thought regarding the soul as an "information-bearing pattern" that God will remember following death. He also advances propositions regarding classical theology including but not limited to omnipotence, omniscience, and temporality and supports much of his argument from free-will and free-process.

Chapter 11 elaborates on several additional themes in the work of Polkinghorne beginning with theodicy, moral and natural evil. Theodicy asks how a God of love avoids intervening in creation to eliminate suffering, an

---

10. Bloch, *Hope*, vols. 1, 2, 3.

objection also raised by New Atheism. Chapter 11 also discusses Polkinghorne's work for divine agency as well as his comments regarding the Trinity.[11]

Chapter 12 presents the conclusions of the work and answers the question of whether or not the work of Polkinghorne satisfies the concern expressed by Newbigin that the church respond to the impact of science on faith. In addition it includes my proposals for addition and amendment to the work of Polkinghorne.

The world has changed significantly over the last five centuries. Advances in knowledge, particularly in science, precipitated dissonance in some areas of the church's interpretation of Scripture. Polkinghorne's work stands out in its importance for evangelism.

---

11. Theodicy addresses the problem of evil in creation, moral and natural.

1

Evangelism in the Contemporary World

Introduction

NOTING THE IMPORTANCE OF the need for evangelism to reach people in contemporary times, Arthur R. Peacocke comments on Leslie Newbigin's *Foolishness to the Greeks* (1986): "No-one concerned with the future of the Christian, or indeed any other religion, can avoid facing up to the impact of science on faith. This encounter is identified by Newbigin as the crucial point at which the gospel is failing to have any impact on 'Western' men and women."[1] Generally, the church in some areas did not respond to scientific discovery when it conflicted with doctrine. In the worst scenarios, it stood resolutely intolerant of science as when it refuted Galileo Galilei's heliocentric view of the universe[2] and Charles Darwin's publication of the *Origin of Species* (1859). In doing so, the church missed the opportunity to examine the possibility that such discovery enriches the church's understanding of how God might act in creation. The work of Polkinghorne offers a credible singular response to the problem that Newbigin identifies and assists the evangelistic spread of the gospel message as well as catechesis.[3]

Evangelism has not only the crucial task to spread the message, but it also has the task to assure that those making a new or renewed commitment are linked into the church through discipleship and catechesis. At the forefront, evangelism not only announces the message of the kingdom, but evangelism spreads the message of expectancy and eschatological hope, both present and future, and invites everyone to meet the risen Lord.

Evangelism in too many instances presents the good news of the gospel in a negative framework, often rejects reason, and appears anti-intellectual. Rather than inviting people into the kingdom it threatens them with judgment which demeans those outside the church, and people treated in that

1. Peacocke, *Theology for a Scientific Age*, 1.
2. Machamer, "Galileo Galilei."
3. Catechesis includes complete instruction in the doctrines and practices of Christian faith.

fashion do not respond positively to the church. Moreover, commitment made in response to fear or intimidation does not come from the heart of the individual, and such commitment may not result in conversion. Response to the gospel from the heart results in conversion and a transformed life as Paul notes: "So if anyone is in Christ, there is a new creation: everything old has passed away; see, everything has become new!" (2 Cor 5:17).[4]

In addition, some evangelists oversimplify the message and present inadequate content. In doing so, the evangelist turns good news into bad news and provides no element of hope. The work of Polkinghorne offers the evangelist the positive framework of hope whereby an informed evangelist can invite those outside to the kingdom as does Jesus when he announces the kingdom in Matthew and says: "Repent, for the kingdom of heaven has come near" (Matt 4:17). Repent, μετανοέω, *metanoeo*, here calls one to turn from the world to the kingdom and away from one's past sins.

Unfortunately, misguided approaches lead people to make decisions for Christ that are not well-reasoned and do not emerge from a change of heart. Such decisions often do not stand the test of time, and the new Christian does not continue in the faith. Instead, evangelism presents the gospel, invites people to the kingdom, and grounds them in Christian faith through appropriate catechesis. In doing so, the evangelist does not need to back away from statement of Christian faith. Instead the evangelist can offer the eschatological hope for both present and future.

Protestantism in the 16th–20th Centuries

Rationalism of René Descartes and Empiricism of John Locke

The change in philosophy that began with René Descartes subtly impacted the church. Before the Enlightenment,[5] theologians such as Augustine (354–430) and Thomas Aquinas (1225–1274) wrestled with important theological questions. Now thought moved from theology in the church to philosophy and science in the culture, and science gained ever greater prominence. These changes set the stage for continued decline for the authority of the church and its questioned importance in Western culture and also resulted in disunity.

---

4. Unless otherwise noted, Scripture references are from the New Revised Standard Version (1989) of the Bible.

5. The Enlightenment was a period in eighteenth-century Europe when philosophy argued truth could only be obtained through reason (McKim, *Westminster*, 90).

Lack of unity across various segments of Christendom worsened the circumstances. Following the Reformation,[6] a variety of Protestant sects emerged with varying interpretation and emphasis. In England, the Anglicans lost control as clergy dissented, numerous sects emerged, and many new groups moved to the United States for religious freedom. Today, the United States contains a plethora of Christian groups, and one is hard put at times to know exactly for what the Christian religion stands. Change also began in science.

The circumstances of philosophical change, tremendous growth of science, and often Christian disunity fosters the rise of secularity in the culture. The church must repair disharmony and address concerns of the culture in order to retain any sense of relevance in the contemporary world and retain strong evangelism.[7] The church can address disharmony through the emphasis of its core doctrines, primarily of the need for salvation and restoration of relationship with God and community. These core doctrines—expressed in the creeds—should bind all Christians together, and their emphasis on the core doctrines can offset disunity over peripheral concerns.

Emergence of Science in the 16th–20th Centuries

The sixteenth through seventeenth centuries mark major change in the West with the heliocentric worldview of Nicolaus Copernicus and Galileo Galilei, Johannes Kepler's observational description of planetary motion, and Isaac Newton's publication of his *Principia* (1687).[8] Newton's deterministic worldview held until the early twentieth century and the work of Erwin Schrödinger and Werner Heisenberg in quantum physics.[9] Intermediately,

---

6. The Reformation marks the initial move to reform the Roman Catholic Church that begun October 31, 1517, when Martin Luther nailed his 95 thesis on the door of the castle church in Wittenberg (McKim, *Westminster*, 234).

7. Modern refers to the time initiated by the Cartesian rationalism of René Descartes where people adopted the scientific method approach to important questions. Postmodern rejects "objective truth, the powers of reason, and claims of universality" (McKim, *Westminster*, 214).

8. Nicolaus Copernicus (1473–1543) and Galileo Galilei (1554–1642) inaugurated the change from geocentric to heliocentric worldview (see Rabin, "Nicolaus Copernicus"; Machamer, "Galileo Galilei"). Johannes Kepler (1571–1630) discovered the laws of planetary motion in the data of Tycho Brahe (see Di Liscia, "Johannes Kepler"). Isaac Newton (1643–1727) published his *Principia* (1687) which lay the groundwork for classical physics (see Polkinghorne, *Quantum Theory*, 1–14).

9. Erwin Schrödinger (1887–1961) and Werner Heisenberg (1901–1976) developed the wave and matrix formulations respectively of quantum mechanics (Messiah, *Quantum*, 45–49).

Charles Darwin's *Origin of Species* (1859) set the stage to understand origination of life on earth.[10] In the early twentieth century, Albert Einstein proposed the theories of special and general relativity which completely upset the notion of time, and soon astronomers realized the universe was much older than anyone thought.[11] In the later twentieth century, astronomers, following Edwin Hubble's work, proposed an age for the universe of billions of years. This discovery conflicted with the 6,000 or so years for the age of creation from Bishop James Ussher's work.[12]

Change from the reformation to the present day confronts humanity with great benefit and with great challenge. Science in particular is slowly gaining increased acceptance and authority in society. Such change benefits humanity and challenges the church and evangelism. Nonetheless, existential benefits such as those provided by increased technology do not provide answers for ultimate concerns. Instead, eschatological hope responds to individual ultimate concern and should resonate in the evangelistic message.

Statement of the Problem

The changes in philosophical and scientific epistemology in the Western world resulted in a significant worldview shift. Before the Protestant Reformation and emergence of nationalism, the Roman Catholic Church held sway over the minds of people. People looked to their religion in times of difficulty and respected the authority of the Roman Catholic Church. Slowly new authority emerged, particularly in the Western world. Authority moved from the church to the government, locally and nationally.

In the twentieth century technology began to master the material world from nuclear energy to biomedicine and genetics. Some refer to this period as post-Christian and to Christianity as secular Christianity. Participation in organized religion declined in the Western world. It declined the greatest in Europe and Great Britain and to a lesser extent in the United States.

---

10. Charles Darwin's (1809–1882) *Origin of Species* (1859), description of the evolution and natural selection of biological organisms and species, accomplished in biology what Newton accomplished in physics.

11. Albert Einstein (1879–1955) resolved the problem of the speed of light in the theory of special relativity and later developed the theory of general relativity which also included gravity (Born, *Einstein's Theory*).

12. Edwin Hubble (1889–1953) discovered the expansion of the universe through the observation of redshift in light from distant galaxies (Palen, *Understanding Our Universe*, 356–81). Bishop James Ussher (1581–1656) through careful examination of biblical genealogy dated Gen 1:1 at 4004 BCE (Halvorson, "Cosmology").

In the latter part of the twentieth century, a group of scientists turned to theology. The move had its pivotal point with Ian G. Barbour's *Issues in Science and Religion* (1966) which quickly became the primary source for study in religion and science. Alfred N. Whitehead's earlier process theology influenced Barbour's thought which Whitehead espoused in his theology in *Science and the Modern World* (1967). Two additional scientist-theologians included Arthur R. Peacocke and John C. Polkinghorne. The work of these three scientist-theologians—Barbour, Peacocke, and Polkinghorne—established a foundation for response to questions in religion and science. This book addresses the work of Polkinghorne.

The important question for evangelism in the contemporary world is whether it responds to cultural expectancy. Does the evangelistic message persuade the hearer that accepting Jesus Christ will make a difference in life today and always? If it does not, the hearer will say "so what," and he or she will contend membership in the local church will not provide near the benefit, as for example, of membership in the local spa. Relevant evangelism tells the story of restoration and new creation available through commitment to Jesus Christ as Lord and Savior. It does not dwell on the evangelism of fear, that is, a message solely of hell and damnation. Jesus invites everyone to the kingdom and to the banquet table; we should do so with the expectancy he makes a difference today and for each generation to come.

In earlier times, most people looked to their religion for answers of meaning and purpose and turned to their faith for support when difficulty struck. Since then, the world through ever greater availability of more sophisticated tools of technology has eradicated many of the difficulties of earlier times. As a result, more people have turned from religion to science for answers, and the tremendous success of technology in all areas, particularly medicine, has made many less dependent on religion for support. Areas that affect everyday life from physics to medicine accord science the authority once relegated to the church, and this shift resulted in individuals consulting psychologists, scientists, and physicians when in trouble.

Scientist-theologians in the late twentieth century responded to important questions which arose in the religion and science dialogue.[13] The stature of scientist-theologians can assist evangelism in the contemporary world. In doing so, evangelism should not shy away from difficult questions or fall back on platitudes. Instead, evangelism should seek greater understanding of the questions and needs in the community and respond in

---

13. Such scientists included Ian G. Barbour, Arthur R. Peacocke, and John C. Polkinghorne.

community context. Such response requires an increasing fresh application of the Christian truth and teaching to the needs of the community.

Science in the contemporary world fails to provide answers to questions regarding meaning and purpose and cannot answer the important questions of why the world exists rather than nothing and why we see order in the world around us rather than disorder. Theologians cannot avoid response when a person asks why we need God today and argues that the sciences from medicine and psychiatry to biology and physics provide all one needs for a successful life. In evangelism, we look at such questions as hope and meaning which science does not address.[14]

There has been a tendency at times for the church to oppose emerging scientific thought as in the case of Galileo Galilei in the sixteenth through the seventeenth centuries and John T. Scopes in the twentieth century.[15] The two sides in the religion and science dialogue would do well to develop tolerance in place of defiance. Tolerance does at least two things. First, it accepts the individual. Second, it provides a caring, loving platform for discussion. Intolerance inevitably shuts down discussion and relationship. Scientist-theologians suggest the means for coming together, but the church must initiate discussion. Old models which are "dogmatic and manipulative" will not work as Abraham reminds us, for they are archaic and out of touch.[16] Too easily we fall back on out-of-date practices that do not relate to those in the community in which the evangelist shares the message. While the message is timeless, the

---

14. In this thesis, *hope* is belief and expectation a specific outcome will occur from strong trust and confidence in the faithfulness of the God of love, where God refers to the God of Christianity, Islam, and Judaism. Definition of *meaning* depends strongly on context. Context for meaning in this thesis includes meaning associated with transformed life through religion and individual purpose. A meaningful life is a life that makes a difference. Paul recalls: "So if anyone is in Christ, there is a new creation: everything old has passed away; see, everything has become new!" (2 Cor 5:17). Evangelism refers to knowledge and study of the mission of the church.

15. Galileo Galilei (1564–1642) promoted the Copernican view for a heliocentric view of the universe rather than a geocentric view which differed with Aristotle and the Roman Catholic Church. The Inquisition forced Galileo to retract and the Roman Catholic Church placed him under house arrest for the remainder of his life. The Roman Catholic Church forgave Galileo's crimes in 1992 (see Machamer, "Galileo Galilei"). John T. Scopes (1900–1970) taught evolution in a Dayton, Tennessee, high school, which violated Tennessee law. The court tried him with the result of guilty (Clouse, *Fundamentalist*, 265).

16. Archaic evangelistic approaches include examples such as "closed, plodding, propositional, simplistic, barren, static, dogmatic, superior, absolute, derivative, metaphysical, mechanical, traditional, imperialistic, manipulative, dishonest, and exclusivist." New models might include "vulnerable, creative, poetic, subtle, fertile, dynamic, insightful, humble, relative, original, intuitive, imaginative, new sensitive, loving, honest, and pluralist" (Abraham, *Logic*, 186–87).

application changes with the community's changing needs. New models such as "creative and honest" are required which take into account the concerns of the culture and not just the concerns of the church.

Examination of the model adopted by William J. Donovan in *Christianity Rediscovered* (1987) can spark the possibility for generation of new ideas. Donovan, a Roman Catholic priest, went to the Masai in Kenya and told them he wanted to talk about God. In doing so, he related to the Masai in their cultural context comparing their culture to that of the early church, and eventually, the Masai wrote their creed in cultural context. Donovan's approach seriously considered the concerns of culture. He did so by accepting Masai practices and went further to explain the similarity of Masai culture to church social and political culture, and his approach opened the door for dialogue with the Masai. Evangelism today should do no less and needs to address the concerns of the culture which have changed dramatically in recent years. To do so, evangelism needs to examine the questions that come from the culture. It must examine not only the questions posed by the intellect but also the questions of ultimate concern. Effective evangelism looks at what goes on in the community and identifies the community's concerns and needs.

Dale Carnegie, in *How to Win Friends and Influence People* (1936), argued for the importance to identify with the other in order to win their confidence. Jesus identified with those he met, from Zacchaeus to the woman at the well in Samaria, and in doing so, gained their confidence. The church can listen to critical questions from the culture, identify with the questions, and answer the questions with new, informed answers. Such questions include concern with whether or not Christianity makes a difference as opposed to other sources in culture such as medicine and psychology, why a loving God did not create a world absent evil, and why religion sometimes erupts in terrorism.

I suspect that evangelism when it fails does so because the audience fails to see the relevance of the message in the current time. A message solely in the context of the New Testament culture will not work. Jesus responded to where the people were and to their needs as we can see in John 4 with the woman of Samaria and in John 8 with the woman caught in adultery. Those of the New Testament had concerns regarding evil, disease, and foreign domination. These concerns do not resonate in the current Western world and turn people away from the message. The evil of today emerges in split families from high divorce rates. Disease of today emerges in the pressures of society. Finally, foreign domination emerges in the stresses of the workplace.

Religion

Huston Smith comments that throughout history humans looked beyond themselves to grasp deep questions of meaning, and religion emerged in the culture. Smith notes: religion in its broadest sense defines a "way of life woven around a people's ultimate concerns," while in its narrowest sense, it is "a concern to align humanity with the transcendental ground of its existence."[17] Smith's broad definition includes all religion from Confucianism to Christianity. However, the narrower definition fits Christianity for the discussion of eschatological hope. Therefore, the narrower definition guides examination of Polkinghorne's work for evangelism with his discussion of hope.

From what I can gather, humanity's ultimate concerns in the Western world might include the demise of the family and the struggle to keep up. In the third world, ultimate concern is far more existential with the need for proper nutrition and medical attention. It is difficult to see the relevance of the church if it cannot address those concerns.

Many suffer today in different ways. One suffers in a broken home. Another suffers in unemployment. Somewhere, someone suffers when unable to find proper nutrition and medical care. While the church does not solve these problems, it offers one who stands alongside through the good and the bad as he stood alongside Jesus in the terror of the crucifixion. Jesus suffered the humiliation of the cross and God empowered him back to life as God can empower those who suffer today. Jesus never said life was a bed of roses. He said: "And I will ask the Father, and he will give you another Advocate, to be with you forever" (John 14:16). Evangelistically, we need to strongly proclaim that God stands alongside the Christian in all that he/she does, through both good and challenging times. Those without Jesus lack that strong support.

Stephen Happel says, "*Religion* is faith expressed in particular first-level languages (the scriptures, popular piety, or devotion) and must be distinguished from, but not divided from, *theology*, a reflection upon those expressions (a linguistic version of *fides quaerens intellectum*)."[18] We are talking about religion as the deep practice of the presence of God in the everyday and religion in alignment with the world's suffering. Religion does not escape the everyday and the suffering of the world, or it ceases as religion, and faith will always be localized, either individually or communally. Happel's comments suggest that appropriate evangelism speaks pastorally of the good news Jesus ushers in for a new paradigm of eschatological hope.

---

17. Smith, *Religions*, 183.
18. Happel, "Divine," 177–203 (italics original).

Adolf Gründman asks why there is something rather than nothing.[19] Science cannot answer Gründman. Today, science can only theorize regarding the mechanisms which brought the universe into being and how it evolved to the present state. Religion explores the metaphysical questions of who, what, and why to align with the ground of one's existence. Evangelistically, we examine the ultimate concerns of the community and relate the gospel to those concerns.

Successful evangelism responds to humanity's "deep quest to align with the transcendental ground of its existence"[20] and does so through contextual identification with its audience. Its message proclaims that Jesus provides eschatological hope for human destiny both in and beyond this life. In doing so, it does not avoid questions that have emerged from the contemporary world to challenge its message. Polkinghorne's work assists that task.

Historical Evangelism

Introduction

David J. Bosch says the church continues in a world that has seen numerous paradigm shifts as Bosch discussed in "Primitive Christianity,"[21] and George Hunter's "Apostolic Congregation" suggests one such paradigm shift.[22] The European churches sit widely empty. I went to Sunday worship at Westminster Abbey in 2002, and the congregants barely filled the choir loft.[23] The United Methodist Church in the United States has been in decline for years and shows no sign of reversal.[24] Examination of the reasons for such decline exceeds the thrust of this work; however, that does not deny the need for the church to look for the reasons that membership declines in some groups and increases in others.

The timeless message of evangelism that God has made himself present in Jesus Christ never changes. The messenger, the method, and context change from the time of the patriarchs through the apostolic period to the current day. Prophets rose in Israel to deliver God's message that Israel had strayed, and upon repentance God would restore Israel to greater,

---

19. Wisdo, "Michael Ruse," 643.
20. Smith, *Religions*, 183.
21. Bosch, *Transforming Mission*, 181–238.
22. Hunter, *Church*, 28.
23. Callum G. Brown comments on the decline of the British church in *Death of Christian Britain*.
24. Retrieved March 3, 2015 from http://www.umc.org/gcfa/data-services-statistics.

everlasting covenant (Ezek 16:60). Jesus begins his ministry in Mark 1:15 calling for repentance, announcing the coming reign of God, and calling on everyone to believe in the good news, stating his coming would free the captives and oppressed and bring healing to the blind. The Greek, ἐγγίζω, *eggizo*, in the Markan passage has the sense the kingdom made itself felt in the first century.[25] An expectancy evolved that the presence of Jesus made a difference, and people flocked to him by the thousands. The expectancy shows up in John 1:14, "And the Word became flesh and lived among us, and we have seen his glory, the glory as of a father's only son, full of grace and truth," and again in John 11:21, 32 when Jesus goes to Bethany following the death of Lazarus. In the first instance, John in looking back reflects on the presence of the divine in Jesus. In the second instance, Martha and Mary say Jesus' presence made a difference. Evangelism needs to recover expectancy and the presence of God as Advocate and Comforter who empowers the Christian in the current world to work through everyday struggles.

In the latter part of John (chs. 14–16), Jesus began to pray regarding the παράκλητος, *parakletos*, translated Comforter in the KJV.[26] The Greek παράκλητος, *parakletos*, means to summon or call to one's side.[27] The New Revised Standard Version translates παράκλητος, *parakletos*, as Advocate. In the second beatitude, the παράκλητος, *parakletos*, translated as comfort, has the sense that Christians can call God alongside at any time, and this thought proclaims a powerful message for evangelism. Everyone faces times when prosperity will not carry the day. They need to prepare for that day and can do so in relationship with God through Jesus Christ who is central to evangelism. Communal Christian worship and practice prepares the Christian to face challenge and supports the Christian in difficulty—this is the evangelistic message.

Evangelism proceeds in partnership with Jesus Christ to disciple and instruct all Christians in his teachings and communicates the gospel best when it uses contextual language to which people outside Christian faith can relate and understand. Continually throughout his ministry Jesus used language of the people. He spoke in parables and metaphor to illustrate his point and did not use lofty language no one understood. The evangelist today can do so as well. The plain and understandable character of Billy Graham's words, to which thousands responded, provides an example, and Graham's message did not lack appeal for the intellectual.

---

25. Bauer, *Greek-English Lexicon*, 212.
26. The KJV is the King James Version (1611/1769) of the Bible.
27. Bauer, *Greek-English Lexicon*, 623.

A plain evangelistic approach does not ignore the intellectual. Its message uses easily understood language that does not ignore the intellectual aspects for the individual. It must make certain claims and support these—e.g., the reign of God in Jesus Christ. It must support other claims such as the work of the Holy Spirit and baptism.[28] Further, the church cannot ignore the rule of life—i.e., to love God with one's whole being and one's neighbor as oneself.[29] In other words, the church does not back down for the sake of mission. It does not water down the gospel. When the church does so, secular Christianity emerges, losing the message that the presence of Jesus Christ makes a relevant difference.

Relevant evangelism has always worked from Jesus' identification with those in his time, to Donovan with the Masai in Kenya,[30] and to the Pentecostals in South America.[31] The challenge for evangelism appears the greatest in the developed world where extreme forms of poverty and illiteracy have practically vanished. Here, many do not see the need for religion in their lives. As Abraham points out, evangelism needs to find a freshness to reach out to the developed world. Polkinghorne's work contributes to freshness, answers some of the questions from the developed world, and answers the deep questions of meaning and finality.

Evangelism as Radical Reorientation and Promise

Bosch proposed an extensive definition of evangelism:

> We may, then, summarize evangelism as that dimension and activity of the church's mission which by word and deed and in the light of particular conditions and in a particular context, offers every person and community, everywhere, a valid opportunity to be directly challenged to a radical reorientation of their lives, a reorientation which involves such things as deliverance from slavery to the world and its powers; embracing Christ as Savior and Lord; becoming a living member of his community, the church; being enlisted into his service of reconciliation, peace, and justice on earth; and being committed to God's purpose of placing all things under the rule of Christ.[32]

---

28. Abraham, *Logic*, 140–63.
29. Ibid., 117–39.
30. Donavan, *Christianity*.
31. Martin, *Pentecostalism*.
32. Bosch, *Transforming Mission*, 420.

Bosch used "radical reorientation," a term often ignored today, to signal the need for more than intellectual assent. It involves, as Bonhoeffer points out, dying for Christ.[33] Radical reorientation leads to discipleship which means far more than mere membership. Discipleship binds one's entire core of being to God. Otherwise, we do not resonate with 2 Cor 5:17 becoming the lukewarm Christian of Rev 3:16, the Laodicean. God wants no part of the lukewarm Christian. In short, radical reorientation redirects the path of one's life to that of the kingdom.

While Bosch uses "radical reorientation," Walter Brueggemann refers to "promise." Brueggemann introduces the key word *promise*, a biblical term and one that works well in the contemporary world. *Promise* begins in the Old Testament with Abraham and becomes the heart of Old Testament faith, and *promise* easily lends itself to Brueggemann's narrative. The female outsider from a dysfunctional family hears the story as *possibility*, a tired businessman hears *departure*, and the permanent member of the underclass as *entitlement*. The three individuals, previously open only to despair, open their vision to transformation in the common remembrance of *promise* in biblical narrative.[34] New Testament promise concerns what God did in Jesus Christ, and Polkinghorne's work resonates with promise when he continually talks of God as faithful and trustworthy. Evangelism offers promise which leads to practical application. Evangelistic promise argues that the presence of God in one's life empowers one for a better life both today and forever.

Brueggemann offers the practical aspect of "doing the text." In doing the text, the evangelist announces the soteriological circumstances in today's context, the *promise* of what God has done in Jesus Christ, and calls for commitment to Jesus Christ and the Christian faith.[35] The evangelist does the text in cultural language, and Billy Graham provides one model for doing the text in cultural context.

Then, we can summarize Brueggemann and Bosch. Brueggemann invites the new Christian to the promises of Christian faith, and Bosch invites the new Christian to new direction.

---

33. Bonhoeffer, *Cost of Discipleship*.

34. Brueggemann, *Biblical Perspectives*, 48–70 (italics original).

35. Ibid., 14 (italics original). Soteriology refers to salvation through Jesus Christ. It includes the state of humankind separate from God and God's means to restore relationship.

Discipleship

Discipleship represents an important aspect for successful evangelism. Undoubtedly, the success of Methodism in England came from the societies and classes organized by Wesley. Jesus said make disciples (Matt 28:19). Frazier Memorial Methodist Church, Montgomery, Alabama, in its small group ministry, illustrates one contemporary example of the Wesleyan model where over 83 percent of its 7,500 members participate in lay ministry through small groups from care for the sick to reaching the unchurched.[36] The corollary benefit for small group ministry means that resources are in place with laity commitment for channeling new members to discipleship. Frazier Memorial Methodist's small group ministry reflects the biblical practice of gathering, and it serves evangelism. Small groups enable members of a large diverse congregation to find their niche—and minister to members—members in turn minister in group activities.[37] Small group ministry radically reorients the church and its congregants, and small groups support the affirmation of spiritual experience, day-to-day struggles, and the proper catechesis of the individual. Without such support, the individual may not remain committed. Individuals, particularly in families with small children, have large claims for their time, and it becomes easy to set aside church for little league. Demands for two career families exacerbate the situation even more.

The power of small group ministry binds one to the congregation through the fellowship's discipleship, and evangelism without discipleship fails to integrate the new Christians into the church. Methodism grew through Wesley's discipling of new Christians into societies and classes, and Frazier Memorial Methodist's success resulted from discipling in small groups. Abraham in *Logic of Evangelism* (1989) argues for the necessity of catechesis which small group ministry accomplishes. However, small group ministry provides more than catechesis. In small group ministry, individuals bond to other Christians, which lessens the chance of their falling away from the local church. The Wesleyan movement grew rapidly through its societies and bands which supported the early Methodists as they grew in Christian faith.

Announcing the Reign of God

Evangelism has its foundation in announcing the kingdom of God, and Mortimer Arias states people experienced the kingdom in Jesus' proclamation. Jesus did not announce the kingdom as something in the future. For

---

36. Hunter, *Church*, 119–47.
37. Ibid., 81–117.

Jesus, the kingdom represented realized eschatology. The kingdom included unconditional forgiveness, total liberation, and new life. Finally, the kingdom meant restoration to community as in the instance when Jesus healed a leper (Mark 1:40–45). People experience through evangelism God's gift of grace.[38] "The kingdom of God was not, as the term 'kingdom' might suggest, the old order of a patriarchal despot, but the new order of love."[39] Matthew provides insight into the kingdom when Jesus says: "Repent, for the kingdom of heaven has come near" (Matt 4:17). Following his declaration, he discusses what the kingdom means in the next three chapters of Matthew. In John 14 and the following chapters, Jesus, as God Incarnate, expresses ultimate concern for us. He assured the disciples around him that he cared and would not forget. For us, his words assure us that we too will dwell with him forever in special places.

William J. Abraham adds regarding the relationship of evangelism and the kingdom of God:

> Whatever evangelism may be, it is at least intimately related to the gospel of the reign of God that was inaugurated in the life, death, and resurrection of Jesus of Nazareth. Any vision of evangelism that ignores the kingdom of God, or relegates it to a position of secondary importance, or fails to wrestle thoroughly with its content is destined at the outset to fail.[40]

Announcing the kingdom connects Polkinghorne's argument for eschatological hope with the evangelistic message. Announcement of the kingdom invites everyone to commit to the kingdom of God from which follows human destiny of eschatological hope. Evangelism cannot ignore the kingdom of God and retain evangelistic integrity. The kingdom stands at the core for the mission of Jesus both now and future as Jesus continues to establish it. The evangelistic task relates the kingdom to today's concerns as did Jesus in the New Testament period.

Conclusion

The New Testament record clearly records mission as one of reconciling the lost to new relationship with God. The Matthean commission (Matt 28:18–20) sends the church to disciple all nations. The church, its members, and its evangelists have primary mission to save and disciple souls. Proclamation is how

---

38. Arias, *Announcing the Reign of God*, 13–26.
39. Ibid., 17.
40. Abraham, *Logic*, 17–39.

the NRSV–NT often translates the Greek κηρύσσω, *kerusso*, which means to proclaim, herald, preach, publish, and announce.[41] Often, the church and its theologians focus on the proclamation, forgetting the mission.

Abraham makes the important point regarding the evangelism of future generations descended from their parents who were Christians:

> Moreover, by taking Christian initiation seriously, my proposal puts the evangelization of each generation on the same footing with those on the distant mission field without ignoring the peculiar position of those who are brought up in a Christian home or in Christian social environment. We need to acknowledge resolutely God has no grandchildren. Each generation must find its own way into the kingdom. To be sure, each new generation can adopt this or that civil religion, or it can settle for a nominal relation to its national faith that is satisfied with Christianity as a splendid system of rites adapted to cope with the vicissitudes of birth, marriage, and death. To confuse these with entry into the kingdom of God is ludicrous and self-serving. Yet elements of folk religion are not to be despised. They represent brittle aspects of Christian initiation that have been cut off from their natural home, and given the right handling they can be repaired and renewed in a process of evangelism that sees initiation as central to its goal and execution.[42]

Abraham makes the critical observation that God has no grandchildren. Unfortunately, the church at times overlooks that point, and succeeding generations often fail to remain in the church. Not only must each new generation find its way into the kingdom, but each new generation also requires catechesis. Further, each new generation requires binding to the local church which small group ministry provides. Otherwise, the secular world invites new generations to leave the local church.

As Abraham points out, initiation must lead to catechesis. Ignoring catechesis of each generation leads to ignoring the unanswered questions that emerge, and the church loses touch with its congregants. At the very least, this lack of resolve leads to lukewarm congregants and in the extreme to lost members. The work of scientist-theologians provides input for catechesis, and the addition of their work can mitigate members leaving the church when important questions are not answered. Evangelistically we need to provide answers through catechesis in the very beginning that will

---

41. Bauer, *Greek-English Lexicon*, 432.
42. Abraham, *Logic*, 114.

strengthen faith and prepare the community of the church in its positive and well-reasoned response to its detractors such as the new atheists.

Abraham quotes John Shelby Spong, who urges evangelism move away from regional and provincial thinking in the modern/postmodern paradigm:

> Evangelism is an intriguing word. It captures in its nuances the battle that is being waged between those whose minds are basically premodern in their thought form and those whose minds are postmodern. To look at this word helps us to examine the emerging new consciousness that will finally deliver us from regional and provincial thinking, which is a necessary transition before we can embrace the frontiers of the world where tribalism is now dying. If one cannot move out of a local and provincial mindset, the wider questions will never be raised.[43]

Clearly, these comments resonate with the religion and science dialogue. The church must avoid quick dismissal of emerging thought seemingly dissonant with traditional religious doctrine. Otherwise, the church risks irrelevance in the contemporary world. Instead, the church can examine the potential for emerging thought to add richness to catechesis and religious teaching. Rather than dismissing the Copernican suggestion of a heliocentric universe, the church could have seen that this suggestion pointed to a God far greater than imagined earlier. In similar fashion Darwinism suggests that God is continually active in the world which makes an important point for inclusion in catechesis.

Abraham continues to argue for catechesis and incorporation of new Christians into the full body of the local church:

> Finally, if the modern situation is as bleak as many postulate, initiation in all its fullness is as crucial as I have described it above. There will be no advance against the acids of modernity if Christians simply proclaim the good news of the kingdom, or invite people to a personal decision, and leave it at that. To proceed in this fashion is both unworkable and cruel. It is unworkable because it does not equip the Christian to lay hold of the significance of the coming of the new age of God. It is cruel because it offers people light and hope in the midst of darkness

---

43. Ibid., 186. Abraham takes a broad view of premodern, postmodern, and modernity. He views premodern as the classical view of evangelism steeped in the early views of the church which relied on stereotypical presentations of the gospel message. In the modern period, or more precisely the postmodern period, the secular culture relegates religion to a position of less importance, and the rationalism of the scientific mind has taken front stage. For evangelism to succeed in the modern period, it must seek fresh approaches congruent to the modern mind, particularly in the West.

and despair and then leaves them to continue their journey in the wastelands of superficial religion, greed, and idolatry. Extensive catechesis or instruction, incorporation into the body of Christ, the handing over of basic spiritual disciplines, participation in the works of the Holy Spirit—all these are minimum equipment to enable the convert to stand up to the ravages of the world. One suspects that Christianity has lost ground in the West precisely because it has neglected these matters for so long. It cannot hope to regain it if these continue to be neglected or if they are treated haphazardly in the work of evangelism. So an analysis of modernity reinforces the approach we have taken to evangelism on independent grounds.[44]

In other words, the mission of the church is not to just seek converts. The mission of the church is to make disciples. The ministry of Jesus made disciples as people responded to the message and sought a new life of hope and realized his presence made a difference. They gathered regularly and supported each other in worship as we see in Acts 2:42. Such faith and relationship sustained the early Christians even in the face of severe persecution. Those outside commented on how much they loved each other, love that drew others to the church. We need to recover that experience and can do so in local church small group ministry.

The evangelistic message persuades that the presence of Jesus Christ makes a difference in the life of everyone. It appeals to the heart of the individual and does not demean the intellectual. Successful evangelism requires follow-through in discipling as in the example of the small group ministry of Frazier Memorial Methodist Church and in the eighteenth-century Wesleyan movement. Finally, small group ministry supports the catechesis Abraham argues for and binds the new member to the local church.

---

44. Ibid., 207.

2

Enquiry in Religion and Science

Introduction

IN ORDER FOR POLKINGHORNE'S work to commend itself to evangelism, the thesis of this work, the contemporary world should view it as credible. Otherwise, people will discard it and the evangelistic message as well. Enquiry in religion and science discusses the foundation for epistemology, foundations for discovery such as critical realism, and application to religion and science.[1] Enquiry in religion and science requires a careful, methodical approach. Religion and science examine the world, metaphysically and materially, respectively. This chapter discusses the aspects for evangelism in Polkinghorne's approach to religion and science. Polkinghorne identified in his earliest work the importance of critical realism and bottom-up approaches in his examination of the evidence in religion and science.[2] In his early work, he avoids the top-down approach to discovery but later acknowledges it to a limited extent. His concern seems that he feels a top-down approach to truth can result in gaps in knowledge.[3] The difficulty occurs in that emergence of complexity requires top-down examination as complex objects like the human eye do not reduce to summation of its parts. In the instance of the eye, its complex structure has a causality that does not appear in the bottom-up examination of its properties. However, some scholars approach questions in religion and science top-down and as process.

Alfred N. Whitehead Whitehead's process theology influenced the twentieth-century dialogue between religion and science[4] whereas Polkinghorne addresses creation as *creatio continua*.[5] Process thought easily

---

1. Realism refers to the scientific process having the nature of discovery and does not represent human generation. Critical refers to the combination of experience and interpretation in the process.
2. Polkinghorne, *Way the World*.
3. Polkinghorne "Metaphysics of Divine Action," 151–53.
4. Barbour, *Issues*.
5. *Continua* means continual.

explains Darwinian evolution which also accounts for God's continuing activity in creation and easily assists the scientist-theologian contribution to the epistemology of religion and science. Nonetheless, problems emerge with process theology which contends God changes and the understanding of God changes over time along with the changing of the world. The ascription of immutability, God as unchanging, to God creates a problem for process theology which *creatio continua* avoids.

This chapter discusses epistemology, how we know what we know. Epistemology has been and will continue to be a subject for dissonance between religion and science. Therefore, it cannot be avoided in this work. So this chapter covers the important topics for the basis of Polkinghorne's approach including critical realism and bottom-up examination of the evidence for enquiry in religion and science.

John Polkinghorne—Physicist and Theologian

Polkinghorne published extensively in particle physics, and with Eden et al. presented a carefully reasoned discussion for the S-matrix[6] in particle physics which addressed strong interactions.[7] He made his personal contribution in physics with S-matrix theory on singularities, scattering amplitudes, and deep inelastic scattering and did most of his work with the Department of Applied Mathematics and Theoretical Physics (DAMTP) at Cambridge. He published extensively in physics; his well-received *Quantum World* (1984) in quantum physics continues in print.

The quantum mechanics description of reality collapses in the measurement, and all we know about the system is no longer available.[8] The

---

6. Eden at al., *Analytic*, 1–38.

7. Polkinghorne published *The Particle Play* (1979), his first book about particle physics, during his last two years at Cambridge when he was professor of mathematics and studying for ordination to the Anglican priesthood. He published *Models of High Energy Processes* (1980), a teaching text covering the details for models in high energy processes (Polkinghorne, *Models of High Energy Processes*, xi–xii). He published his second book on particle physics in 1989, *The Rochester Roundabout*. At Cambridge, he coauthored a number of papers with one of his first graduate students, Peter Landschoff. Polkinghorne's *Quantum World* (1984) was the best-selling of his books, selling well into six figures and continues in print. He followed later with *Quantum Theory: A Very Short Introduction* (2002). He wrote *Beyond Science* (1996) (Polkinghorne, *Physicist to Priest*, 63–71).

8. Quantum mechanics begins in 1923–1927. Two representations emerge, wave mechanics and matrix mechanics. Wave mechanics emerges with Erwin Schrödinger, and Werner Heisenberg's matrix mechanics modified Schrödinger's wave mechanics. The Schrödinger and Heisenberg pictures are equivalent and only differ mathematically in the approach (Messiah, *Quantum*, 45–49). The Heisenberg equation is the

approach, espoused by the logical positivists, considers the experience of the observer paramount. We interpret reality in terms of the experience of the observer who takes the measurement and interprets the results. Perhaps Feynman provides the best insight here. Polkinghorne noted: "As Feynman has said, we are asked to believe that the historian who makes a statement about Napoleon simply means that there are books in libraries which make assertions similar to his own. There is no past; there are only sources."[9] In a sense, quantum mechanics encounters a similar task. We examine the results understanding they come from sources which no longer exist as they did before the measurement. The Copenhagen school has the best answer which focused on the instruments of measurement rather than the observer,[10] and Bohr very cautiously avoided making any ontological statement about "what is."[11] Yet, the position of the Copenhagen school does not eliminate the problem of the observer as the instrument is also an observer.

Polkinghorne when he refers to Feynman's comment accepts the realist approach that reality exists independent of the observer. Through experimental probing, the physicist examines the world of electrons and quarks and submits himself to the way things are. In quantum mechanics, the physicist talks about the wave function for the object rather than the object itself, and it contains all the information the physicist possesses regarding the object. Polkinghorne continues with the discussion of potentiality.

Polkinghorne states that accordingly we see electrons as carrying potential. These notions can do little more than offer a way of understanding reality.[12] Polkinghorne steers a narrow course here. While not rejecting the positivist, he moves toward his critical realism position which is discussed in more detail later in this book. Heisenberg along with Niels Bohr was associated with the Copenhagen School which held the wave function represented the probability of a reality.[13]

---

following: $i\hbar \frac{dH_A}{dt} = [A_H, H_H] + i\hbar \frac{\partial A_H}{\partial t}$ where A_H is the observable and $[A_H, H_H]$ is the commutator of A_H and H_H (Messiah, *Quantum*, 316). The Schrödinger picture relies on calculus solely and the Heisenberg on vectors. Both contain eigenstates, eigenvectors, and eigenvalues. The Schrödinger picture develops from the equation for the wave function $i\hbar \frac{\partial \Psi(t)}{\partial t} = H\Psi(t)$ where H and $\Psi(t)$ represent the Hamiltonian and wave function, respectively. Quantum mechanics develops probabilities for occurrence of certain events. In that sense, it does not represent an actual measurement, hence the problem with the observer and the wave function.

9. Polkinghorne, *Quantum World* (1989), 78.
10. The Copenhagen School followed the matrix mechanics of Werner Heisenberg.
11. Polkinghorne, *Quantum World* (1989), 78–79.
12. Ibid., 79–82.
13. Russell, introduction to *Quantum Mechanics*, i–xxvi.

Polkinghorne comments that particle physicists such as he were well-prepared to accept unseen realities provided sufficient evidence for proof existed for them.[14] The Standard Model contained the associated math of the quark, clever means to explain observations from cosmic rays and from accelerator experiments.[15] It has held up because it has continually agreed with experiment. Further the acceptance of unseen reality in physics for a particle physicist makes it easier for Polkinghorne to accept unseen reality in religion. In particle physics, physicists manipulate and measure the object. Unfortunately, that does not work in religion. The closest the religious person comes occurs in his or her religious experience. Even there, the risk always exists that what one calls religious experience may be another kind of experience entirely, a problem that does not occur in science's examination of the natural laws.

Polkinghorne argues the source of the natural laws that govern creation come from God, and development of quantum mechanics assists our understanding of the working of these laws with the implication that God guarantees the Schrödinger equation. "Until creation occurs, we have no natural laws or reality to observe. Until we have natural laws and reality, we have no content for the wave function. Until we have the wave function, we have no possibility for its collapse."[16] God did not guarantee the Schrödinger equation. God guarantees the fundamental laws of physics which permitted the development of the world as we know it. Physicists use quantum mechanics to examine the products from these laws, and quantum is a model and not reality. Even there, some fundamental constants emerge from the math. The cosmological constant provides a good example.[17] While acknowledging God as the ground and support of all that is in a fourteen billion-year-old creation, it seems a stretch to extend that to quantum mechanics.[18]

---

14. Polkinghorne, *Physicist to Priest*, 63–71.

15. No one has ever seen a quark. Therefore, it has unseen reality.

16. Polkinghorne, *Quantum World* (1989), 67.

17. Originally, Einstein altered the field equations with the addition of the cosmological constant in order to provide static solutions for the equations. Practical discussions of the big bang often ignore the temporality question, particularly the differences between proper times (Barrow and Tipler, *Anthropic*, 373–457). An important principle concerns the size of the cosmological constant to which physicists assign a value of 10^{-120}. The cosmological constant refers to a type of energy called "dark energy." In the early universe, physicists believe an undiscovered highly symmetric Grand Unified Force broke down into the unsymmetric forces observed today such as the gravitational, electrostatic, magnetic, strong nuclear, and weak nuclear (Polkinghorne, "Inbuilt," 247–50).

18. Current scholars assign an age for the universe of 13.7 billion years (Palen, *Understanding Our Universe*, 365).

Polkinghorne says creation began in a very simple state fourteen billion years ago. The world developed from the laws of nature through the process of evolution accompanied by many "contingent" features (chance) in a "particular" environment (necessity). The physical rules of the universe had to possess a particular form for biological life to develop as we know it (the anthropic principle).[19] The anthropic principle offers one possible explanation of the origin of life on earth. The anthropic principle in its several modes attempts to explain the origin of life from an anthropocentric view. In other words, we project human understanding on the meaning behind the creation of the world in which we live.

Polkinghorne throughout his work discusses the fact that the origin of life emerges from the laws of physics acting over extended time periods. *Homo sapiens* did not appear until billions of years following the beginning of creation, and the emergence of life required at least ten billion or so years of stellar evolution for the fusion of the larger molecules in hydrocarbons.[20] Development to carbon required an energetic process called nucleogenesis, the evolution of nucleons to new atomic nuclei, first suggested by Fred Hoyle (1915–2001) even though he did not know what the process might be. A beautifully scoped process formed the elements in the atomic chain. This process represents the primary fine tuning we observe in the universe today. Gravitational and electromagnetic forces govern the stellar formation and evolution astronomers observe.[21] Fine tuning refers to the necessity that the laws of physics and the accompanying physical constants be such that the universe evolves to support life. It is also sometimes called the anthropic principle. Slight differences in the constants would not have permitted life to evolve as we know it.[22]

Polkinghorne points out that were the universe not the way it is, we humans would not be here discussing it, the weak anthropic principle. Polkinghorne proposes the moderate anthropic principle which says: "the contingent fruitfulness of the universe" is "a fact of interest calling for explanation." That is, the finely tuned laws are not sufficiently clear as to require

---

19. Polkinghorne, "Inbuilt," 246. The anthropic principle in its various forms argues laws and constants of physics had to be what we observe for intelligent life to evolve. The slightest change in the physical constants underpinning physical laws would eliminate the possibility of intelligent life as we know it.

20. Our solar system formed ca. 4.6 billion years ago, ca. 9.1 billion years following the origin of the universe. Therefore, I infer that hydrocarbons were available, as evidenced from earth, ca. 9.1 billion years following the origin of the universe and possibly sooner.

21. Polkinghorne, "Inbuilt," 247–50.

22. Ibid.

no further explanation.[23] Unseen reality occurs in the time before the Planck time of general relativity when an energetic event resulted in creation. The Genesis account better fits a later time with the emergence of earth.[24]

At most, one can make the claim that the observed order and regularity have a source somehow and somewhere we associate with God. We do not describe God as a mechanic, nor do we describe God as the supreme intellectual either. God as Creator created the novel and ingenious world we explore.[25] Polkinghorne offers a rebuttal to intelligent design, an example of the carryover of his thought in physics to theology.[26]

Polkinghorne had considerable success in physics which he carried on to theology. The recognition he received throughout his life supports the acceptance of his later work for the commendation of Christian faith. Consequently, Polkinghorne's accepted authority in science carries over to his accepted authority in theology.

Polkinghorne tells us immediately he is a bottom-up thinker.[27] Key points in his work which I discuss include:

- bottom-up approach to the evidence,
- Christology,
- continuity and discontinuity,
- critical realism,
- free-will and free-process defense,
- hope,
- kenosis,
- kingdom of God,
- psychosomatic human person,
- resurrection,
- soul as pattern,
- temporality and atemporality,
- transformation of the body following death, and
- a world that creates itself.

---

23. Ibid., 250–55.
24. Planck time is 10^{-43} seconds after the beginning of creation.
25. Polkinghorne, "Inbuilt," 251–54.
26. The design argument assigns the human attribute of design to God positing God as an engineer, a position out of touch with the classical understanding of God and seriously detracts from God as omnipotent.
27. Bottom-up refers to the scientist's beginning with the object of investigation and moving to conclusion.

All these themes relate strongly to his exposition of eschatological hope. We will see also that he suggests revision of classical thought in several areas. For example, he argues the free-will defense fails in some sense for humans did not emerge until billions of years after creation of the universe.[28] This claim leads to his argument for a world that creates itself.

Polkinghorne emphasizes throughout his work that God made a world that creates itself.[29] In his theological writing on religion and science, Polkinghorne notes he addressed his work to "believers and honest enquirers rather than simply professional scholars."[30] Science addresses objective reality open to interrogation whereas religion examines whether meaning and purpose exist in what is happening. He critically distinguishes between

---

28. First free-will gives humankind sovereignty in creation without the interference of God. The free-will defense argues moral evil as a by-product of human free-will.

29. See, e.g., Polkinghorne, *God of Hope*, 114–16.

30. Polkinghorne wrote his first book in religion and science *The Way the World Is* (1983) followed by *One World: The Interaction of Science and Theology* (1986), *Science and Creation: The Search for Understanding* (1988), and *Science and Providence: God's Interaction with the World* (1989). These last three books made up a trilogy of Polkinghorne's first exploration of religion and science. He went on to a tighter cycle with the publication of *Reason and Reality: The Relationship between Science and Religion* (1991) where he presents critical realism in greater detail. In the Gifford Lectures, published in 1994, he sought to approach theology bottom-up in the same manner as in science. The Gifford Lectures appeared under two titles, *Science and Christian Belief* (1994) in Britain and *The Faith of a Physicist* (1994) in North America. He followed with *Quarks, Chaos, and Christianity* (1994). He wrote *Serious Talk: Science and Religion in Dialogue* (1995) and *Searching for Truth: A Scientist Looks at the Bible* (1997) [1996]. He analyzed the work of the three scientist-theologians in *Scientist as Theologians: A Comparison of the Writings of Ian Barbour, Arthur Peacocke, and John Polkinghorne* (1996). He published *Beyond Science: The Wider Human Context* (1996). Yale University published his lectures there in *Belief in God in an Age of Science* (1998). He also wrote *Science and Theology: An Introduction* (1998) as a textbook for university courses in science and religion, and it was a more academic version of *Quarks, Chaos, and Christianity* (1994). He wrote *Faith, Science, and Understanding* (2000). Most of his books had a single unifying theme. He published *The End of the World and the Ends of God: Science and Theology on Eschatology* (2000) which he and Michael Welker edited, and later, he wrote *The God of Hope and the End of the World* (2002). In 2003, Polkinghorne wrote a book for Advent and Christmas following the pattern of his book on Lent, *Living with Hope: A Scientist Looks at Advent, Christmas, and Epiphany* (2003). He wrote *Faith in the Living God—A Dialogue* (2001) with Welker. He published *The Work of Love: Creation as Kenosis* (2001) after a meeting at Queens' College supported by the Templeton Foundation. His recent writings seek to provide greater trinitarian insight. Two of his recent books, *Science and the Trinity: The Christian Encounter with Reality* (2004) and *Exploring Reality: The Intertwining of Science and Religion* (2005), adopt a trinitarian approach. Polkinghorne published two pamphlets, *Traffic in Truth: Exchanges between Science and Theology* (2000) and *The Archbishop's School of Christianity and Science* (2003) (Polkinghorne, *Physicist to Priest*, 131–56).

"epistemology, what can be known, and ontology, what is the case,"[31] and continually, Polkinghorne relies on his experience in physics as he examines theological questions.

Polkinghorne approaches the questions in Christianity drawing on the analogies of science with which he has the greatest familiarity. The complexity of the world of science renders a subtlety about the world not always obvious, and he argues we should be surprised if that were not also the case with Christianity. He prefers a "fragmentary grasp" of reality rather than a neat construction derived from well-formed over-simplification. Often in science, the discovery of a new paradigm provides considerable insight into the object investigated. Further examination and explanation only comes from tedious pursuit. He suggests the examination of the Christ event has the same outcome. Consequently, he sticks to broad insights rather than miniscule detail. When he pursues the Christian description of the way the world is, he relates it to other prevailing worldviews.[32] The subtlety in Christianity emerges in kenosis, theodicy, Jesus as both human and divine, the resurrection, apocalypticism, and eschatology. The gospels relate Jesus' activity while on earth, and the early church examined who Jesus was theologically. In doing so, it also of necessity examined its understanding of God. Throughout the history of the church, Christians have continued the search for greater understanding of God, a process which I applaud and accept my part. Imaginative theology unmasks the subtlety of the unseen reality, and this unmasking has importance for provision of answers to important questions in the contemporary world. Yet, many questions cannot be answered.

Polkinghorne points out much about the Christian faith cannot be verified. Scientists rely on evidence in their search for truth, and that approach works in the discussion of Christianity as well. Scientists have a different way of looking at the world than do others as they ask "what and where" regarding the evidence. Science has the advantage that it works with things it can examine and manipulate. Polkinghorne must go beyond simple comments that religion brings comfort as religion can only adequately do so as long as its statements contain truth. Therefore, the primary task remains first to demonstrate the truth of Christianity from which follow statements regarding comfort.[33] However, I can infer that much cannot be verified in the same way the physicist infers the state of the system before the measurement from the measurement itself. In science, peer review assists the shaping of the process. Similarly, Scripture, reason, tradition, and experience

---

31. Polkinghorne, *Physicist to Priest*, 131–56.
32. Polkinghorne, *Way the World*, ix–xii.
33. Ibid., 2–3.

shape theological understanding in the church. In Christianity, I infer truth from examination of the sources, interpretation, tradition, and experience, all of which Polkinghorne used in his examination of theological themes.

Important theological themes emerge in Polkinghorne. First is the christological foundation for his faith. Second, he sees in the doctrine of the Trinity the richness and complexity of divine revelation. Third, referring to Augustine, he sees the relational aspect of the Trinity and the analogy of the Trinity of love. The gospels, particularly John, along with the Pauline corpus projected a strong christological picture. Yet, within these texts references emerge continually regarding the relationship of Jesus and God. Theologically, we seek to understand that relationship which begins to emerge in the creedal development of the early church. Interestingly, such a point provides an opportunity to move toward the creeds and worship where we acknowledge belief in the Trinity.

In addition to the important theological themes mentioned above, broader themes emerge from his views as a physicist examining religion and science. The world is ordered, intelligible, and a source of beauty. A theistic view of God sees God as the source of order, intelligibility, and beauty. In beauty, we experience his joy in creation, and in moral law, we experience his divine will and purpose.[34] Beauty slips through the scientist's net. Art and music move us without saying how and why. Art out of cultural and time context may remain elusive.[35] The laws of physics assure the order seen in the universe. Life forms evolve with the intellectual capacity to develop mathematics and tools for observation and the ability to interpret the findings. A scientific worldview emerges from the understanding that the laws of physics support creation.

From his reflections in theology, Polkinghorne discusses five points for a scientific worldview. We should look at the present rather than past or future which leads to five points for the scientific worldview. In the first, the world is intelligible,[36] and the example and success of the Standard Model theory causes one to feel they come to greater understanding and penetration of reality.[37] Nonetheless, a preferable statement would say that humans evolve with the intelligence for examination of the world, as the material world does not possess the character of intelligence. Humans do. There are

---

34. Ibid., 20–22.

35. Ibid.

36. Ibid., 9–10.

37. Polkinghorne, *Way the World*, 10. The Standard Model explains subnuclear interactions from the modeling of the quark.

no arguments for either the existence or the nonexistence of God which leads to the second point regarding chance and necessity.[38]

The second of five points includes chance and necessity as noted in Jacques Monod's *Chance and Necessity* (1972).[39] Without the possibility of contingent chance, the world would not develop as it has. These observations of chance and necessity do not lead to a design argument; they do lead to the possibility of the ultimate.[40] Contingent chance refers to Charles Darwin's idea of natural selection. Emergence of a new species required mutation, suitable environment for survival, and reproduction to continue the species. The third point addresses the importance of the universe's structure to permit the emergence of life, the anthropic principle.[41] Emergence of life required fine tuning of the constants associated with the physical laws underpinning the universe.[42] Fine tuning leads to the source for all that exists and permits the enormity of the universe around us which leads to the fourth point for the size of the universe. While chance and necessity adequately explain evolutionary process, we cannot conclude that only that process could lead to evolution as we know it. Further, the constants which we associated with the fine tuning come from the mathematical models. Different models might develop a fully different set of constants. Therefore, we cannot say that the constants are universal characteristics.

In the fourth point, Polkinghorne argues that the enormity of the universe also makes a statement. He suggests that perhaps the universe needs to be as large as it is for life to develop on at least one planet.[43] In the fifth and final point, Polkinghorne argues that evolution from the big bang through complex molecules to life and the world as we know it points to something behind creation, the Transcendent Power we call God.[44]

Polkinghorne says a proper worldview must take into account the Transcendent Power we call God. Until modern times, most of the world accepted

---

38. Ibid., 10.

39. Jacques Monod argued in *Chance and Necessity* (1972) biological change occurred by chance and necessity which referred to the circumstances be such as required for survival and reproduction.

40. Polkinghorne, *Way the World*, 11–12.

41. Ibid., 12.

42. Recent research calls into question the stability of the fine-tuning to which Polkinghorne refers. Astronomers conclude they have discovered the fine structure constant may not be constant throughout the observed universe. While this discovery does not detract from the marvelous fact the observed structures of physics permit the emergence of life, it does suggest we should not pin our arguments to the reliability of theories from physics ("Ye Cannae Change the Laws of Physics," *Economist*, Aug 31, 2010).

43. Polkinghorne, *Way the World*, 13–14.

44. Ibid., 15–16.

a theistic worldview. A religious dimension exists which must be taken seriously, as must the religious sense of the Transcendent Power we call God. Ultimate power in the universe comes from God, and the experiences of St. Francis and St. Augustine provide evidence for God in the world.[45] Both religion and science strive for a complete and holistic worldview which must account for the immaterial as well as the material. The new atheists fail in not accounting for the immaterial and in not looking for explanation.[46] Religion and science should work together. Religion can do so through pursuing the bottom-up, critical-realistic approach Polkinghorne advocates and which he pursues in examining the texts for Jesus Christ. However, the problem in theology comes in the point that revelation is top-down and not bottom-up. We can only know God as he reveals himself to us. Yet, developing greater understanding of the world may perhaps open windows to the character and nature of God, important for a religion-science worldview.

Polkinghorne says the coming of Jesus Christ raises concerns regarding the historical accuracy of the events related to Jesus.[47] The New Testament provides the historical record and has strong attestation as represented by the many and various texts from ancient times, far more than exist for other major texts from either the current period or antiquity. Examination reveals small differences among the texts, either from scribal variations or otherwise. However, these variations do not detract from the authenticity of the texts. They simply indicate editorial gloss. Jesus as far as we know did not write anything, and we depend on these texts for our record. In addition, the texts do not have recorded dates, and we examine their context for clues as to the date for their origination. Analogically, in observational science as in astronomy for example, scientists draw conclusions from their observations, and we do the same with the New Testament record. The lack of precision in the gospels at times does not mean the events never occurred. Often when several people observe an event or an object, they give differing descriptions of the event or object. The differences occur when people look for different aspects and/or remember the event or thing differently, and possibly the gospels suffered similar difficulties. In the case of the gospels, the writers had different intentions for their presentation. For example, Mark in his text emphasized the servanthood aspect of Jesus whereas John emphasized the

---

45. Ibid., 27–30. St. Francis of Assisi took the vow of poverty and founded the Roman Catholic Franciscan Order (Robinson, 1909). St. Augustine committed his life to Christ in Milano following reading the life of the monk St. Anthony (Augustine, *Confessions*, 152–54).

46. New atheists include people like Richard Dawkins, Daniel Dennett, Sam Harris, and Christopher Hitchens (Haught, *New Atheism*, ix–xiii.).

47. Polkinghorne, *Way the World*, 33.

fact Jesus was the Son of God, and the differences in approach for the gospel writers does not discredit their accuracy.

Polkinghorne remarks the primary concern is first not the conclusions we make from the texts but the accuracy of the texts themselves. Close examination of the Synoptic Gospels indicates a great deal of common material, and the existence of material in one gospel omitted in another suggests the presence of earlier literary material used in the formation of the Synoptics.[48] Accuracy for the texts concerns several things. In the first instance, it concerns the accuracy of the teachings of Jesus. There does not seem to be difficulty there. Second, it concerns the relationship of Jesus with Hebrew prophecy, again a concern for biblical scholars but not the religion and science dialogue. The sharpest and the most important points come from Jesus' conception, his miracles, and his resurrection. In the first instance, the means of conception does not impact his identity as both human and divine. Jesus as both human and divine remains greatly mysterious as does the nature and character of God, and the disciples held him close in heart and mind in the gospels. The miracles of Jesus established him as prophet and as sent from God, and Nicodemus said: "Rabbi, we know that you are a teacher who has come from God; for no one can do these signs that you do apart from the presence of God" (John 3:2). And without the resurrection, we would not have eschatological hope for our eventual presence with God for eternity.

Polkinghorne points to *sitz em liben*, the situation in life, to effectively argue the stories emerge in the gospels for the fact they were distinctly memorable at the time and later in the community. These recollections recall the significance for life of the individuals in the time of Christ, and the stories represent the person of Jesus and not the imprint of the community on Jesus.[49] Views differ across Christendom as how to handle the texts from the literal views of fundamentalism to the mythological views of Rudolf Bultmann.[50] The Christian Bible contains a library of books from a variety of authors over an extensive time period, and lack of unity of description does not mean the event never occurred. In the instance of the gospels, the different descriptions provide a richer view as we see in the Gospel of John's different approach.

Polkinghorne concludes with the Gospel of John and espouses a Christian worldview that accepts members of other religious faiths as fellow travelers. He says Christian claims about Jesus answer the deep questions, particularly of pain and suffering and point to a God involved with

---

48. Ibid., 37–48.
49. Ibid., 38–42.
50. Ibid., 88–90.

creation.⁵¹ Polkinghorne moves later to examine pain and suffering in eschatological hope.

Polkinghorne explored the importance of Christian hope in *The God of Hope and the End of the World* (2002) and in *Living with Hope* (2003). I examined his work in these two books and its importance for evangelism and his theology which I discuss later in this work.

This brief discussion of some of Polkinghorne's important work in physics and theology addresses the thesis of how one would interpret and commend the Christian faith in the contemporary world. Polkinghorne exhibits grasp of Scripture and doctrine. In addition, he explains his thought in an easily understood manner. We will examine in later chapters his basis for argument and the important subjects he argues in support of Christian eschatological hope.

Epistemology

Critical realism stands out as absolutely central in Polkinghorne's work for it supports the interpretation and commendation of Christian faith in the contemporary world. Polkinghorne continually argues for his critical realist approach from physics for his approach to truth as in *One World* (1987) and says critical realism becomes one means to guide the approach to the acquisition of knowledge.⁵² Cartesian and Enlightenment approaches to knowledge failed, as has been noted by Robert E. Ulaniwicz.⁵³ The world

---

51. Ibid., 109–11.
52. Polkinghorne, *One World*, 17–21.
53. "The Enlightenment worldview consisted of five axioms that were formulated by consensus in the wake of Isaac Newton's *Principia* (1687) around the turn of the nineteenth century. David Depew and Bruce Weber (1995) conveniently enumerated the basic assumptions:

1. Newtonian systems are causally closed. That is, only mechanical or material causes are legitimate, and they always co-occur. Other forms of action are proscribed, especially any reference to Aristotle's "final," or top-down, causality.

2. Newtonian systems are atomistic. They are strongly decomposable into stable least units, which can be built up and taken apart again.

3. Newtonian systems are reversible. Laws governing behavior work the same in both temporal directions. This is a consequence of the symmetry of time in all Newtonian laws.

4. Newtonian systems are deterministic. Given precise initial conditions, the future (and past) states of a system can, in principle, be specified with arbitrary precision.

5. Physical laws are universal. They apply everywhere, at all times and all scales"

(Ulanowicz, "Pessimism to Hope," 941–42).

as contingent historically showed the ability for intellectual discovery as strongly evidenced in science's success. New discovery and expansion of knowledge, critical realism, happen in science and not continuous change; the world that science investigates does not change. Instead, science reveals the nature of the world as continual change physically, chemically, and biologically. However, historical critical realism does not appear so simple in theology. The primary distinction between theology and science rests in their respective experiences.[54] Science has succeeded in the examination of the material world and the discovery of new applications for the benefit of humankind. The success of science argues strongly for its critical realistic methods, methods which also work in theology.

Polkinghorne states critical realism describes an approach to epistemology. Theologians have sometimes received criticism in substituting god as an explanation for lack of knowledge. Scholars refer to this move in theology as "god of the gaps," and Polkinghorne points out that theology no longer promotes proper recourse to gaps in knowledge.[55] "God of the gaps" secured epistemology in the past when theologians lacked explanation, but such a move risks associating incorrect characterization for God. In incorrect characterization, we tend to project anthropocentric characterizations on God. God far exceeds such characterizations, and those characterizations demean God and bring him down. Not only did it have the risk of improperly characterizing God, but it closed off the search for truth.

Stephen J. Gould notes that in epistemology the question arises regarding whether or not religion and science can pursue truth together. Gould suggests they cannot and argues they occupy different magisteria which he referred to as "non-overlapping magisteria (NOMA)."[56] Paul Tillich agrees when he says science examines different regions; therefore, science can only conflict with science, and religion can only conflict with religion. Further, religion examines historical truth and goes no further. Science on the other hand declares what has occurred and what may occur in the future. Philosophical truth proposes the path to truth and defines philosophical categories. Philosophical truth explains truth of being, and faith truth of ultimate

---

54. Polkinghorne, *Scientists as Theologians*, 16–18.

55. Polkinghorne, *Traffic*, 29–41.

56. Gould introduced the principle of NOMA, non-overlapping magisteria, which argues religion and science examine different realms, and they do not overlap (Gould, *Rock*, 1–10). McGrath and McGrath say NOMA is too tight and prefer POMA. McGrath notes POMA, or partially overlapping magisteria, offers the possibility of effective interchange between religion and science for the mutual benefit of both. Francis Collins points out that the principles of faith complement the principles of science, and nature has many legitimate interpretations that permit atheism, deism, and theism (McGrath and McGrath, *Dawkins*, 33–51).

concern. None of these other paths (scientific truth, historical truth, psychological truth, or philosophical truth) can verify or not verify the truth of faith.[57] Science only discovers material truth and does not answer questions of meaning or why the universe exists rather than nothing. Science does not pursue these questions as they do not provide insight into the way the material world is put together. Questions of meaning and purpose rightly belong in philosophy and questions regarding God in theology.

Polkinghorne comments continually regarding the authority of Scripture and the creeds for his work. Scripture, tradition, reason, and experience provide guidance and authority in this work. God provides revelation through Scripture to humankind. Individuals received the revelation and could have possibly erred in its transmission. Therefore, inerrancy cannot be claimed for the texts; however, the texts which were written long after the events they record provide all that salvation requires for one to come into full relationship with God.[58] Errancy in Scripture does not denigrate the texts; errancy requires scholars exercise greater care in the exegesis and interpretation of the texts.

Many of the texts were recorded long after the events to which they refer. In the Old Testament, generation to generation relayed the stories orally before Israel recorded its sacred scrolls. The oldest New Testament texts occur in the Pauline corpus written years following the time of Jesus. Finally, the texts are always subject to interpretation and theological bias when examined for their contribution to epistemology. Today, theologians continue to expand our understanding of the doctrines promulgated by the sacred texts.

Both religion and science look for truth. Experience gives the evidence for religion and the material world for science, and both approach the subject systematically. To some extent religion is theory-laden as is science. We often comment in science on the problems associated with theory-laden interpretation of experimental results. The problems exist in religion as well when the interpreter approaches the texts with presuppositions. Religion has a greater difficulty than science in unpacking long-held doctrine. And religion should take great care when it attempts to unpack long-held doctrine. Science has little to do with how we conduct our daily lives whereas doctrine guides us in our daily life with God and with others.

---

57. Tillich, *Dynamics*, 74–98.

58. Biblical inerrancy holds all biblical Scripture is inspired and completely accurate in every detail. It is part of Fundamentalist core doctrine. Other aspects include divine dictation.

Critical Realism

Polkinghorne describes critical realism as the primary approach to truth, and Andreas Losch in "On the Origins of Critical Realism" provides a strong description of critical realism.[59]

> "Critical realism" has been the dominant epistemology in the (Anglo-Saxon) science theology debate for several decades. One can expect this to be a result of the impact of Ian G. Barbour's influential *Issues in Science and Religion* (1966), where he advocated this concept. However, it is interestingly very difficult to track the sources Barbour used when advocating his understanding of "critical realism." Given the importance of the concept for the contemporary dialogue between science and theology, it appears worthwhile to elucidate its historical origins.[60]

Critical realism has formed the basis of thought in the religion and science dialogue and has also formed the cornerstone in Polkinghorne's examination of eschatological hope and that suggests further investigation of its source and use before Polkinghorne.

Losch explains the use of critical realism term preceded Barbour whose work preceded that of Polkinghorne.

> The first use of the term "critical realism" (as "Kritischer Realismus") seems to be German, as the newer meaning of the expression "realism" that it presupposes. In German philosophy, it designates those positions which take account of Kant's critical epistemology but deny that the subjectivity of our experience makes it impossible to acquire valid knowledge of the external world as it is in itself.[61]

Losch makes the important point that critical realism possibly originated in German philosophy and not in science as Polkinghorne's work might imply.[62] Nonetheless, its origination outside science does not detract

---

59. Losch, "Origins."
60. Ibid., 85.
61. Ibid., 86.
62. "In a narrower sense, 'Kritischer Realismus' signifies an opinion presented by C. Stumpf, O. Külpe, E. Becher and A. Messer. . . . Külpe believes, that only in eighteenth century's English philosophy (critical) realism as philosophical mainstream has been questioned, and he believes that at his time it still remains—besides phenomenalism—the ruling opinion. . . . Külpe refers as one source of his ideas to his teacher Wilhelm Wundt, who wrote as early as 1896 on 'naïve and critical realism'" (Losch, "Origins," 86–87). For greater exposition of critical realism, refer to Losch, "Origins." Losch also explores American use of critical realism which differs from the German. This work

from its use in science or in Polkinghorne's development of eschatological hope. Polkinghorne does not comment on its origin for his use which might have been Bernard Lonergan as Losch notes.

> Polkinghorne was also influenced by Bernard Lonergan, who employed the term "critical realism" sometimes as well (cf. his unpublished lectures "Critical realism and the integration of the sciences," Six Lectures at University College, Dublin, 1961). However, Polkinghorne does not refer to Lonergan in *One World* (1986), but only later in *Reason and Reality* (1991), Polkinghorne expanded his awareness of Lonergan to the former's *Method in Theology* (1972) where Lonergan used the term "critical realist:" The naïve realist knows the world mediated by meaning but thinks he knows it by looking. The empiricist restricts objective knowledge to sense experience; for him, understanding and conceiving, judging and believing are merely subjective activities. The idealist insists that human knowing always includes understanding as well as sense; but he retains the empiricist's notion of reality, and so he thinks of the world mediated by meaning as not real but ideal. Only the critical realist can acknowledge the facts of human knowing and pronounce the world mediated by meaning to be the real world; and he can do so only inasmuch as he shows that the process of experiencing, understanding, and judging is a process of self-transcendence. Bernard Lonergan, *Method in Theology* (New York: Seabury, 1972), 238s.[63]

Critical realism guided Lonergan and Polkinghorne in their epistemology and approach to the discovery of reality, a common ground between religion and science for dialogue and approach to epistemology. Critical realism provides the framework in science for the discovery of truth and offers the same to theology.

Polkinghorne clarifies his position on critical realism:

> In both science and theology, I believe that we can affirm a stance of critical realism-called "critical" because the method of enquiry is subtle, with a delicate intertwining of experience and interpretation, and called "realism" because the investigation has the character of a process of discovery, rather than that of human construction.[64]

---

did not permit further discussion of critical realism, and its inclusion in this footnote serves the purpose of providing a possible date for its origin in German philosophy.

63. Losch, "Origins," 103.
64. Polkinghorne, *One World*, x.

Polkinghorne notes the subtlety of the process of discovery with the interweaving of experience and interpretation, critical realism, a definition he refines later when he describes critical realism as:

> Critical realism is a philosophical position based on the actual experience of the scientific community, rather than on a claimed abstract necessity things had to be this way. This basis in experience is why it is the position adopted, consciously or unconsciously, by the overwhelming majority of working scientists, despite the criticisms leveled at it by some of their philosophical colleagues.[65]

In his later comment, Polkinghorne has given a more complete statement in favor of critical realism. However, as Losch has pointed out, critical realism originated in philosophy and not science, let alone physics. That point does not mean scientists did not use it before the late nineteenth century. They simply did not refer to the scientific approach as critical realism. Critical realism guides the method and search for epistemology which still requires a particular vantage point in the examination of the material world.

Polkinghorne claims that in the grounding of knowledge in interpreted experience of reality we follow the adage that "Epistemology models Ontology" and thus consider such interpretations as reliable. Realism assumes *experience* precedes *theorizing*; our interpretation of reality proceeds from its intelligibility (emphasis Polkinghorne's). Intelligibility necessarily requires adoption of a particular interpretive view, and critical realism requires a particular lens for its application. Moreover the view the observer chooses must be capable of revision as experience warrants.[66] Epistemology modeling ontology refers to explaining what we observe through the use of models. Particle physics explains nuclear behavior through the Standard Model, and theology models God as loving Father. In neither case do we claim the absolute for the model. To do so in the case of God would imply that God has all the physical attributes of a male *Homo sapien*. Circularity comes from the theory-laden character of the view chosen by the observer. Theory tells the observer where to look and how to interpret the measurement; when the expected result differs from theory, insight into new physics becomes possible. Realism leads to the discovery of new physics. Polkinghorne describes the weakness in applying critical realism to science as coming from the phrase the "intertwining of experience and interpretation." Experience in this instance refers to experimental examination of the evidence in science, fact-laden and theory-laden. Experimental evidence in science continually changes whereas the historic evidence in religion does not. Therefore, religion cannot apply

---

65. Polkinghorne, *Beyond Science*, 16–18.
66. Polkinghorne, *Scientists as Theologians*, 14–16.

the phrase the "intertwining of experience and interpretation." Nonetheless, Polkinghorne's later definition does open up that possibility for theology.[67] Also in this instance, we see how Polkinghorne's thought matures. Finally, as noted, critical realism originally occurred as philosophical epistemology and has full application to theology understood as analogous to science. Critical realism encourages theologians to critically examine the reality of revelation and not to fall back on blind acceptance.

Over time, Polkinghorne continued to expand on the meaning of critical realism in analogy with science. Science's goal strives for theory, precise and elegant, and science claims verisimilitude, not absolute truth.[68] Critical realism provides the middle road between intellectual certainty and doubt, between logical guarantees and solipsistic individualism or social determinism. The term critical recognizes the problem for motivated belief rid of intellectual precariousness, and realism recognizes that nonetheless we can obtain verisimilitudinous reality.[69] Religion differs from science in that it claims absolute truth which has fomented conflict with science as in the instances of Galileo Galilei and Charles Darwin. Generally, the church has protected core doctrine in its creeds, and the more conservative groups claim absolute truths for its inspired texts. The church would do well to continue its practice of examining the relation between religion and science as it did in the examination of its core doctrine in the early period through the Council of Chalcedon in 451 CE. The problem occurs in the fact that the church considers its positions absolute whereas science does not claim absolute truth and accepts the advancement of knowledge through scientific process. Still, critical realism does not lack some problems.

Polkinghorne suggests that problems exist in the critically realistic approach. First, critical realism recognizes science can only accomplish verisimilitude, that is semblance of reality, at any particular point. Second, everyday experience may not be satisfactory when we move into areas distant from human experience as in the quantum world where experience in the larger world does not have analogy. Third, critical realism acknowledges the role of judgment in the scientific enterprise where experiments are fact-laden as well as theory-laden. The power of theory exists in its ability to continually probe experiment, and when theories hold over extended time and experiment, they demonstrate fruitfulness. Finally, the value of science comes in its continued tightening of the understanding of reality through critical

---

67. Polkinghorne, *Beyond Science*, 16–18.

68. Verisimilitude in this instance means science only depicts reality similar to the actual and not the actual.

69. Polkinghorne, *Faith, Science & Understanding*, 32–34.

realism.[70] Polkinghorne acknowledges that science can only represent reality, that certain experiences lack sufficient analogy for successful explanation, and that judgment can cloud the conclusions. Yet science has achieved an ever greater grasp for its picture of the material world. Judgment always presents difficulty as the process of discovery in both religion and science starts with presuppositions which scientists refer to as theory laden.

In conclusion, Polkinghorne's critical realist approach works well to commend his work to evangelism and can be expected to receive acceptance in the philosophical and science communities. An examination of the relevant evidence favors realism because it involves discovery and favors its critical character because it involves experience and interpretation. The observer examines the evidence to discover its character and from the experience of the examination interprets the observations, understanding that the conclusions explain the observation that then are not absolute. Critical realism describes the process and its outcomes, and bottom-up and top-down accounts of causality or discovery tell the observer where to begin the process as explained in the next two sections.

Bottom-Up Discovery

From the very beginning Polkinghorne insists that he begins with the evidence or the phenomena requiring explanation. Whereas critical realism explains the guide to acceptance of truth, bottom-up describes one way in which scholars approach the examination of the evidence, metaphysically or materially. Bottom-up thinkers begin with phenomena which require explanation, and scientists pursue a similar approach which begins in the basement of thought.[71] A bottom-up approach works up from examination of the evidence to conclusions.[72] Physics begins bottom-up in the exploration of material reality and moves from the simple to the more complex. Unfortunately a complex system does not completely reveal the physics of its inner working parts. When physicists talk about the structure of matter, they discuss nuclear, atomic, and molecular structure but not complex biological organisms.[73] A bottom-up approach fails to explain emergent behavior in complex biological systems, as say, in the human eye. In the human eye as in other complex organisms, the whole influences the parts, and the synergism of the parts far exceeds that predicted by the combination of the parts.

70. Polkinghorne and Oord, *Polkinghorne Reader*, 22–24.
71. Polkinghorne, *Way the World*, vii–viii.
72. Ibid.
73. Polkinghorne, *Reason and Reality*, 39–40.

A critical realist bottom-up thinker begins with examination of the experience in religion and/or the evidence in science for examination. He or she follows with the subtle combination of experience/evidence to discover and interpret the experience/evidence. Undoubtedly, experience as subjective creates the possibility for wrong conclusions. Therefore, the theologian falls back on the benefit of his/her association with the community. Sometimes, it will take time for new thought to gain acceptance as was the case with both the theory of relativity and quantum mechanics in physics.

Top-down Discovery

As noted above a bottom-up approach fails to account for emergent behavior in complex systems. Polkinghorne explains that a top-down approach to truth begins with the whole and then generalizes to the influence of the whole on the parts, whereas a bottom-up approach begins with the parts and argues top-down causality will result in gaps and in the existence of indetermination.[74] Top-down causality requires some careful reworking scientifically; science's description of a world open to becoming also describes a world science cannot predict.[75] Generally, scientists identify an effect with a cause, but in top-down causality, the effect is apparent but the cause is not.[76] Polkinghorne again shows how his thought matures from 2000 to 2009 when he begins to lean toward inclusion of both bottom-up and top-down in discovery. From time to time, he notes that recent discovery in chaotic systems might eventually provide the means for discovery in complex systems, and that physical dissipative systems exhibit chaotic behavior in certain circumstances. I would like to see Polkinghorne explore top-down not only for its value in understanding complex systems but also for its value in understanding the relationship of the divine through top-down revelation.

Physical dissipative systems with intrinsic unpredictabilities have the metaphysical capability for openness as well as supposing in this instance that there is top-down influence. Such patterns could be identified as information.[77] Polkinghorne refers to top-down causality as the instantiation of

---

74. Polkinghorne, "Metaphysics of Divine Action," 151–56.

75. Polkinghorne, *Theology in the Context of Science*, 114–16. Openness refers to emergence of new properties when systems increase in complexity.

76. Ibid.

77. A dissipative system is one that operates away from equilibrium where it can exchange energy and matter with the environment. Such systems can exhibit chaotic behavior. A pendulum swinging in a viscous medium represents a dissipative system where energy transfers to the environment.

"active information."[78] The energy dissipation in physically dissipative systems eliminates determinism, and chaotic response often results. He deploys his view at times for top-down influence of energy in explaining divine agency.

Process Thought

Arthur R. Peacocke has argued that stellar and biological evolution concern a process which calls for theologians to look at creation as process.[79] The processes can be characterized as *emergence*. The picture as a whole appears as a continual unchanging process, and evolution supports the thought of an immanent God (emphasis Peacocke's).[80] Evolution proceeds naturally and does not require outside intervention. Instead the creative power of chance and law prevail;[81] each stage of evolution becomes the platform for new emergence; consequently, this limitation represents contingency with the succeeding level contingent on the preceding. Biological evolution presents specific trends,[82] and the propensity for natural selection appears built into the process seen as a network of features that are more likely than others to lead to complexity than one such feature alone.[83] Process theology works extremely well as we see in Peacocke's explanations. Importantly, it qualifies God's presence in creation, immanence, and love for creation, and one might expect a biologist who examines the evolutionary biological world of process to lean toward process. Process theology, while it has its own limitations, does not eliminate the critical realist, bottom-up, or top-down methods. Interestingly, we approach complex questions from our individual framework, bottom-up in physics and top-down in biology. In that sense, the approach to biology for a physicist and to physics for a biologist is theory-laden. Applying Gould's NOMA argues one cannot cross from physics to biology or vice versa. A similar problem occurs in going from physics to theology as the latter relies on top-down revelation.

Process theology, however, also has its shortfalls as Craig A. Boyd and Aaron D. Cobb explain:

> Process theologians, in their emphasis upon divine love, characterize God as one who, while sympathetic to human travails,

---

78. Polkinghorne, *Meaning in Mathematics*, 46–48.
79. Peacocke, "Cost," 21–22.
80. Ibid., 22–24.
81. Ibid., 24–26.
82. Ibid., 26–28.
83. Ibid., 28–30.

cannot act unilaterally to bring about changes in the created order. The God of Process theology acts only by persuasion. On the other hand, classical theologians, in their emphasis upon divine power, describe God as one who acts through secondary causes but maintains a controlling power over the world as distant and "invulnerable" potentate. Polkinghorne briefly dismisses the Process view as placing unreasonable limitations on divine action and focuses his full attention on the classical model and its grounding in the causality distinction.[84]

Boyd and Cobb make the important point that process theology argues that God acts persuasively in creation. This observation seems to me more in keeping with kenosis which I discuss in chapter 3. What I see here can be explained in analogy of a precious stone with multiple facets. Different viewers see varying aspects of the object which does not discount one view in favor of another as in the instance for the duality of light in physics.

So physics can come to the aid here. Physics has not discovered an all-inclusive explanation for physics as for example in the duality of light as sometimes a particle and sometimes a wave.[85] Physicists continue to look for an all-inclusive explanation. Theologians should do no less and not simply discard one position because of a shortfall.

In conclusion, because Polkinghorne does not pursue process theology, this work only mentions process theology in passing for its significance in the religion and science dialogue. In doing so, I suggest that this dialogue should include it as well as both bottom-up and top-down approaches. Many conclude creation appears as process, and Whitehead promoted this approach in his process theology. Process theology had the benefit that it could account for observations in areas such as evolution and that it could remove God as a causal factor in moral and natural evil. In doing so, evangelism has the possibility to increase the credibility of its commendation of Christian faith in the modern world, the thesis of this work.

Although different disciplines examine the world, both materially and nonmaterially, through differing lens, greater insight can be gained from a coming together of the various disciplines for a more profound worldview.

---

84. Boyd and Cobb, "Causality," 393.

85. Physicists explain interference phenomena of light when light acts as a wave. They explain phenomena such as the photoelectric effect and absorption/emission spectra when light acts as a particle.

Enquiry in Science

Polkinghorne takes up the debate about the Cartesian dualistic view of mind and body. He argues that a sole material account of reality results in gaps. At the very least, an account of reality must hold metaphysical and material together for a complete view of reality as when the physicist speaks of complementarity in the discussion of the phenomenon of light coexisting as particle and wave.[86] Our direct experience has a mental character. It argues material bodies represent mental constructs from sense data. That is, we describe the material from our contact with it through our senses. Science does so as well in its successful description of reality.

Polkinghorne further comments regarding the success of science:

> The natural convincing explanation of the success of science is it is gaining a tightening grasp of an actual reality. The true goal of scientific endeavor is understanding structure of the physical world, an understanding which is never complete but ever capable of further improvement. The terms of that understanding are dictated by the way things are.[87]

Polkinghorne reminds us that the project of science is never complete but continues to develop within the relevant scientific discipline.

Cartesianism fails to explain the connection between mental and physical events, as say, how the thought to raise the hammer connects with the act of raising the hammer.[88] The world must be far more than rational. A purely rational approach does not suffice, hence the necessity to consider physical and metaphysical together in the search for truth. However, it remains a challenge to combine the material and metaphysical, and I do not see how that can be resolved within physics. When the physicist enters the laboratory, he or she has eyes only for the material. When he or she asks what it means, meaning has material context only. True, the scientist exercises metaphysical in terms of judgment but judgment addresses only the material result.

Polkinghorne argues that judgment does, however, connect the material and the metaphysical, as we can infer from his deployment of Michael Polanyi's proposals on judgment in science. Evaluation of theory as well as analysis of experiment involves personal judgment according to Polanyi,

---

86. Polkinghorne, *One World*, 1–3. Complementarity represents the mutual indwelling of characteristics which the theologian refers to as *perichorēsis*. The complementarity principle asserts wave and particle descriptions for matter or light complement each other (Polkinghorne, *Science and Creation*, 70).

87. Ibid., 71.

88. Ibid., 69–71.

and the connection of theory and experiment results in a certain amount of circularity.[89] Polkinghorne explains the critical realist nature for connection of theory and experiment as follows:

> The account . . . is a realist position because it claims the attainment of increasingly verisimilitudinous knowledge of the nature of the physical world. It is a critical position because knowledge is not directly obtained by looking at what is going on, but it requires a subtle and creative interaction between interpretation and experiment. This acknowledgement of somewhat oblique discernment gives science a degree of kinship with other forms of human enquiry. Science is not perceived as dealing with clear and indubitable facts, while other disciplines have to be content with cloudy opinions. On the contrary, all human knowledge is personal knowledge, though science's power to manipulate the object of its investigation and to put it to the experimental test gives it a technique of confirmation not available in other realms of experience, such as personal encounter, where the integrity of the other demands a greater degree of restrained respect.[90]

Polkinghorne goes on to reemphasize the subtle but important connection between interpretation and experiment. Analogously in religion, the subtlety appears in the interpretation of religious experience. And in both religion and science the process of discovery requires judgment. In both instances, the parties begin with initial theories in the case of science and initial presuppositions in the case of religion.

Of necessity, query begins with a theory of some sort. In doing so, the inquirer extends experience. As an example, one might theorize this way: If it looks like a duck, walks like a duck, quacks like a duck, it must be a duck. But this could result in an easy falsification, for in this instance, circularity might identify more than one object, the real and the falsified, as a duck. Should the falsified have additional properties, the investigator instead of asking why his theory was falsified might make an erroneous revision to theory. Here, discovery of new information would have failed.

---

89. Circularity refers to the theory-laden nature for the interpretation of experimental data. In particle physics, elaborate computer programs dependent on theory in the Standard Model assist the experimenter in examination of data from collider trials. That identifies the examination as theory-laden. Seemingly, theory tells the physicist what he or she will see in the trial, and one asks whether he or she discovered new physics. One theory-laden experiment stands out as an example that clearly worked unmarred by theory. Einstein's 1915 general theory of relativity predicted light bent in a gravitational field. Arthur Eddington confirmed in the 1919 eclipse of the sun that light from a star behind it bent so that it could be seen on earth (Polkinghorne, *Way the World*, 19).

90. Polkinghorne, *Beyond Science*, 16–18.

Both religious studies and scientific investigation examine the why of the unexpected. In religion, the investigator will look deeply, say, into the resurrection. The analogy of the duck cautions both the theologian and the scientist to question preconceptions of theory-laden observation. The discovery of quantum physics in the early twentieth century meant Newtonian determinism no longer applied in some instances.

Polkinghorne points out that Newtonian determinism collapsed. Mechanistic and organismic approaches replaced it in the twentieth century with the emergence of quantum theory that revealed a lack of predictability on the microscopic level, indeterminism. Causality became cloudy in certain instances requiring judgment as to whether or not determinism or indeterminism was present.[91] In quantum mechanics, probability replaced determinism, and classical metaphysical methods required revision. Polkinghorne says regarding classical metaphysics:

> The classical metaphysical options were materialism, idealism, and dualism, and none seems satisfactory. Materialism implausibly devalues the mental. Idealism implausibly devalues the physical. Dualism has never succeeded in satisfactorily integrating the disjoint realms of mind and matter, and it faces the problem of how to account for the apparent continuity of evolutionary history, in which a world which was once a hot quark soup (apparently purely material) has turned into the home of human beings.[92]

The strong point comes in that a totally materialistic picture completely leaves out the mental. While Polkinghorne does not say so here, it leaves out the Aristotelian and Thomistic idea of the human soul. Polkinghorne discounts some aspects of classical metaphysics for its shortfalls.

In conclusion, this section has explained the shortfalls in scientific enquiry and knowledge which encourage the drive to discovery. Science, unlike religion, does not deal in absolutes. Scientific discovery is limited by the extent of current technology. For example, the energy available in the large collider facilities limits the extent to which physicists can probe nuclear matter. Next we examine religious enquiry for its contribution to the search for truth that stands paramount in the commendation of Polkinghorne's work for evangelism.

---

91. Polkinghorne, *Encountering Scripture*, 8–10.
92. Polkinghorne, "Metaphysics of Divine Action," 154.

Enquiry in Religion

Polkinghorne moves to extend critical realism to theology when he says:

> Even so brief a survey shows that there is material on which critical realist theologians can base their study, though its assessment will need much greater subtlety and discrimination than are required in the analogous task faced by the scientist. The cultural and social factors have much greater influence on religion than on science. Formation within a particular community insures this influence. Natural theology which looks outside the community, as does science, can open up cultural limitations.[93]

While science suffers the limits of the available tools and resources for further exploration, religion suffers the limits of the culture as in the instance of Galileo and Darwin.

Critical realism in theology faces considerably more, according to Polkinghorne, resistance from the culture than it does in science.[94] To some degree, this position reflects the culture's inadequate grasp of the scientific endeavor. Unfortunately, culture does not have a greater grasp of the metaphysical implications either. In too many instances, superstition and blind submission to authority guide the culture. In both religion and science, the discoveries are often beyond the comprehensibility of the average person. Then the average person tends to hold on to that with which he/she is most comfortable. The task before both the theologian and the scientist is in the need to present sufficient discussion in support of new thought and to explain it in an easily understood manner.

Polkinghorne says theologians see the central religious question as quest for truth, and that the best way to discover truth theologically comes through motivated belief and not blind submission to authority. The bottom-up thinker proceeds from experience to understanding.[95] Unfortunately, experience in some instances lacks the credibility associated with examination of the material world. The material world has consistency across the universe whereas experience can vary significantly from individual to individual. Because of this, Polkinghorne often refers to art and music.[96] In both of these fields, the experience does not have consistency from person to person. Those who value Renaissance art may not grasp Impressionism. Similarly, one may not be as moved by a popular country and western song as by an operatic

---

93. Polkinghorne, *Belief in God*, 121.
94. Ibid., 120–22.
95. Polkinghorne, *End of the World*, 28–30.
96. Polkinghorne, *Way the World*, 20–22.

aria. At the very least, theological reflection has greater hurdles for achieving a view of reality than matches what goes on in science. The discovery of truth in religion is more difficult in its examination of the unseen.

Polkinghorne continues to examine theology's pursuit of truth and acknowledges that both theology and science encounter *unseen realities* from the invisible reality of God to quarks and gluons in physics. Physicists believe in quarks and gluons because they make sense of unseen physical reality. Similarly, theologians believe in the Triune God because such belief clarifies spiritual experience (emphasis Polkinghorne and Welker's).[97] In this instance, Polkinghorne introduces a point to bridge the religion and science dialogue. Both examine unseen realities and thus have the potential to agree on the approach. Theology and physics both examine the evidence critically realistically, as the texts of both disciplines show. Therefore, the theologian can explain the faith of the religious person as analogy with the confidence of the physicist who has never seen a quark. Both rely on pointers, religious experience in the instance of the religious person and measurement in the instance of the physicist.

In the case of religion, particularly Christianity, theologians go to the New Testament texts. Scripture plays the role of evidence, an important aspect for bottom-up thinking. In a bottom-up approach, we consider what we can properly say regarding such things as the life, death, and the resurrection of Jesus.[98] In this instance, Polkinghorne does not account for the top-down nature of the texts which represent the top-down revelation of God. In other words, revelation has greater complexity. However, I agree that the bottom-up approach works better with the acknowledgement of the complexity and the top-down divine action of God. Further, Polkinghorne extends his position through natural theology where he refers to creation as God's footprint which points back to God. The Bible contains the important record of religious experience and truth. In the New Testament, we see God choosing to become known through Jesus and how the story affected the imagination of early Christians. People wrote the Bible; it was divinely inspired rather than divinely dictated. Interpretation requires we separate truth from the cultural practices of the day, and that we make judgments regarding truth as we read Scripture. We judge the texts through interpretation and in turn the texts judge us. A bottom-up thinker starts with the phenomena. The world contains many surprises which lead us to believe God also exceeds our expectations.[99] The Bible then provides evidence for discovery as the material world provides the

---

97. Welker, "Romantic Love," 134–36.
98. Polkinghorne, *Science and the Trinity*, 38–40.
99. Polkinghorne, *Searching*, 10–17.

evidence for scientific discovery. As science has expanded its understanding of the material world, theology has expanded its understanding of God, and both can continue to do so. And in doing so, they have the opportunity to ask how the merging of scientific and theological thought can offer a deeper and more profound worldview.

In conclusion, it would seem more than one method of enquiry works in religion. Certainly, sanctification is process. That suggests knowledge of the divine might process as well. Revelation is top-down as well as divine agency, and the examination of the experience of the divine is bottom-up. The common aspect for all three includes the critical realist method.

Conclusion

This chapter covered a range of thought to ground Polkinghorne's work as available to evangelism. First, it established his approach as a bottom-up thinker who looked at reality in a critical realistic manner which the scientific community he addresses would find acceptable. Polkinghorne sees the starting point for examination as bottom-up in both religion and science.

I suggested that greater congruity would develop when scholars seek to develop thought that includes both bottom-up and top-down approaches. Polkinghorne will talk later of divine agency as energy input, a top-down approach. An exclusively bottom-up approach does not accommodate divine agency, and a bottom-up approach must also accommodate top-down. Shortfalls like these should not completely be allowed to discredit an approach. Instead, shortfalls call for further examination and modification.

Neither should one discard process theology which appears more congruent with God immanent in creation and with *creatio continua* as advocated by Polkinghorne. At this point, it seems to me panentheism, which Polkinghorne rejects, might open a possibility.[100] In examining the presence of God in the world, we too often view the world as solid when in fact it is not. The nuclear and electronic matter occupy an infinitesimal volume of the atom, and the atom is predominantly empty space.

---

100. Polkinghorne, *Faith, Science & Understanding*, 92–94. "Panentheism" is a term coined by K. C. F. Krause (1781–1832) for the view that God is in all things. This view also sees the world and God as mutually dependent for their fulfillment. It differs from "pantheism," God as all and all as God (McKim, *Westminster*, 199).

3

Kenosis

Introduction

POLKINGHORNE USES KENOTIC THOUGHT throughout his development of theology.[1] It works well for evangelism as it answers some of the objections to Christianity such as why a loving God permits moral and natural evil. Further, it explains how God provides freedom for humans to act freely in creation without the interference of God, and how God creates a world that makes itself. Seeing God as acting kenotically in creation lends itself to a compelling interpretation of the Christian faith for the contemporary culture, the thesis of this work.

Keith Ward states that God in relation to creatures assumes a divine reality other than it would be did he not relate to creatures. In this manner, he can participate in and know the sufferings of his creatures. Such thought leads to the idea that creation itself, the cosmos and all that exists within it, becomes a kenotic act.[2] Ward's reference to God's creation as a kenotic act argues that God gave up control of creation once he set the creative process in place. Following his initial act of creation, God kenotically chooses where to become involved or not involved in creation. When he does so, he limits himself so as to not overwhelm creation or his creatures as in the example of Moses and the burning bush (Exod 3:2).

---

1. Kenoticism refers to God's limiting himself in creation in order that creatures have freedom, avoiding a tyrannical God. It is derived from the Greek κενοω, *kenoo*, and is usually translated as emptied in Phil 2:7. "Let the same mind be in you that was in Christ Jesus, who, though he was in the form of God, did not regard equality with God as something to be exploited, but emptied himself, taking the form of a slave, being born in human likeness. And being found in human form, he humbled himself and became obedient to the point of death—even death on a cross. Therefore God also highly exalted him and gave him the name that is above every name, so that at the name of Jesus every knee should bend, in heaven and on earth and under the earth, and every tongue should confess that Jesus Christ is Lord, to the glory of God the Father" (Phil 2:5–11).

2. Ward, "Cosmos," 156–58.

Kenosis in Polkinghorne

Polkinghorne makes the strongest point for kenosis when he acknowledges God's kenotic act in the crucifixion. God could have intervened and prevented it. Instead, as Polkinghorne says, God limits himself, kenosis, in creation and does not intervene, for example, in the crucifixion.[3] God had no necessity to create the world. However, once he did, it became intrinsically necessary to him, and he became involved in its fate. The presence of evil represents the precariousness of God's position. First, God kenotically permitted free-will for humankind which meant moral evil would take place in creation. Second, creation that continued to evolve after God's initial act meant free-process with the result that natural evil would take place.[4] The cross represents the sacrifice of Jesus as well as the kenotic emptying of God in both creation and the incarnation.[5] Actually, God would have seen the kenotic necessity before creation. He would have omnisciently known all the possible outcomes and would have of necessity decided for his self-limiting in certain instances to permit free-will and free-process. Yet God did not choose to divorce himself from the consequences of his kenotic act and intervened from time to time in creation, even when the circumstances made his position difficult, as in the instance of the crucifixion, and the cross sends a strong message of the willingness of God to face humiliation for the sake of humankind's redemption. Despite the precariousness, God kenotically permitted human freedom as Polkinghorne notes.

In the kenotic view of nature, God allows creatures to have their part in bringing about the future as cocreators with God, and kenosis permits human freedom in creation.[6] However, by insisting on this kenotic view of nature, that God allows creatures to have their part in bringing about the future overlooks the smallness of the creature relative to the cosmos. The universe extends 13.7 billion light years from our earth, a distance of $\sim 8 \times 10^{22}$ miles.[7] Humankind has not the means to cover these distances and cannot in any fashion impact what goes on in our sun or any star or galaxy in the universe. When one considers the enormity here, one is reminded of the marvelous point that God cares for an individual on such a small scale.

---

3. Polkinghorne, *One World*, 34–36.

4. Polkinghorne, *Science and Creation*, 62–64. Free-process allows creation to evolve without the interference of God. The free-process defense argues natural evil as a by-product of creation free-process.

5. Barbour, "God's Power," 8–10.

6. Polkinghorne, *Faith, Science & Understanding*, 126–27.

7. Palen, *Understanding Our Universe*, 365. Light travels in space at 186,000 miles per second. One light year contains $\sim$ 31,557,600 seconds (computation mine).

The psalmist says it best: "What are human beings that you are mindful of them, mortals that you care for them?" (Ps 8:4). Humankind as cocreators in the continuing act of creation in the world supports an evolutionary view of creation.

The process that is evolution, continued creation, fits nicely into Polkinghorne's introduction of the idea of *creatio continua* which he sees as consistent with evolution. In the nineteenth century, Charles Darwin disclosed continual changing of species; in the twentieth, physicists disclosed the continual changing of the cosmos; and today, we live on a second-generation planet.[8] What emerges here is a world that creates itself, a related kenotic thought. These views differ significantly from those of classical theology which emphasized *creatio ex nihilo* and transcendence and did not view them as conflicting.[9] *Creatio ex nihilo* has morphed into *creatio continua*, and *creatio continua*, creation that makes itself, clearly fits kenosis where God self-limited to allow creation to make itself.[10] Before Darwin's discovery of evolution, science did not realize the biological and material world changed and accepted *creatio ex nihilo*, the world set in place and unchanging from its beginning. After Darwin, biologists identified the evolution of species from the archaeological evidence, and in the twentieth century, astronomers discovered stellar evolution, acknowledging evolution for the entire cosmos. Creation that makes itself does not require God to limit himself entirely. God put in place the natural laws and knew omnisciently in advance how they would function to bring about the universe as we know it today, a world which makes itself.

As Polkinghorne remarks, the world makes itself, and such a world contains the transience necessary for new life. The old dies so the new can emerge. Old life-forms die to make way for new ones. In this progression, chance mutations occur which create new life-forms, and evolution becomes creative process. The kenotic act of the Creator resulted in the world around us, and kenotic self-limiting permits the fruitfulness of a world which creates itself.[11] Life as we know it required ten billion years of stellar evolution for carbon, one of the building blocks of cellular biology, to emerge.[12] Our solar system with earth formed in that time, and life slowly began to evolve.

---

8. New stars form from dust and gas in the universe. When a star explodes, it spews dust and gas into the surrounding universe. New stars form from the residual dust and gas. The sun formed from the dust and gas of another star and its surrounding planets; hence, the earth is a second-generation planet.

9. *Creatio ex nihilo* means out of nothing.

10. Polkinghorne, "Kenotic Creation," 94–96.

11. Polkinghorne, *God of Hope*, 114–16.

12. Polkinghorne, "Inbuilt," 247–50.

In kenosis, God has allowed for the continual emergence of the new in creation. Emergence of ever greater complexity moves from stellar to biological evolution as God kenotically allowed for the development of human life.

Polkinghorne says God in kenotic love turns to humans to free them from those forces which constrict—confusion, lostness, and sin—and permits humans space for freedom. Kenotic love means passionate interest in others, and as in 1 John, humans through love become "children of God," and God's kenotic love draws us to him in a variety of ways.[13] Kenotically, God let us go, knowing those who loved him would return to him. Polkinghorne's kenosis moves away from the classical view of God as omnipotent without demeaning him. Craig A. Boyd and Aaron D. Cobb comment:

> Emphasis on divine power seems to lie behind Classical Theology's picture of a God who, through primary causality, is in total control and whose invulnerability is such that there is no reciprocal effect of creatures upon the divine nature, of the kind that a truly loving relationship would seem to imply. The scheme, as articulated by its principal exponents such as Aquinas, is intellectually impressive, but it is open to question whether its picture of the divine nature is not so remote and insulated from creation as to put in question the fundamental Christian conviction that "God is love."[14]

Undoubtedly, the Thomistic model has problems.[15] We should try to solve those problems without scaling down the characteristics of God. In addition, the kenotic model of now seeing God as not a possible cause of evil places responsibility for moral evil on humankind through free-will.

Polkinghorne continues to build on his position of kenosis when he notes that humans sharing in creation with free-will also has significance for theodicy—humans can no longer hold God responsible for all that happens. When God provided humans free-will, he limited his control for how humans might act which meant the possibility for moral evil. Second, God's creating a world that creates itself meant a world where the process of its continuing to evolve had the potential to cause natural evil from natural disasters such as earthquakes and from genetic changes leading to disease. Free-will and free-process eliminated God's exerting divine power within creation, and the classic confrontation between claims of divine power and

---

13. Welker, "Romantic Love," 134–36.

14. Boyd and Cobb, "Causality," 394.

15. "St. Thomas Aquinas maintained that God created all things through 'primary causality,' but also gifted the created order with its own causal powers or what he calls 'secondary causality'" (ibid., 391).

love fails in the face of God's kenotic acts.[16] The kenotic Creator who limits his involvement in creation cannot overrule creatures and must interact in continuing creation.[17] Kenosis does not deny God as love, as it requires greater love to let something go. God gave humankind free-will to choose or not to choose eternal relationship with him which did not eliminate God's acting from time to time in creation, and God's self-limiting raises the question for what God wills.

The recognition that God cares for us and does not will evil, moral or otherwise, for humans makes a strong argument in support of this work; free-will and free-process result in evil, not God. Polkinghorne says all that occurs involves God's providence but not all that occurs happens according to God's will. God does not will evil; evil results from free-will and free-process. Divine kenosis affords such qualification, but kenosis of eternity accepts that God knows events temporally. Such acceptance of the temporal also involves kenosis.[18] The temporality assertion here steps outside classical theology which held God outside time, atemporal. Polkinghorne argues for the necessity of God as temporal in order to interact with creation continually. Otherwise, we have the God of deism, removed from creation. This broader understanding of God requires simultaneous temporality and atemporality. In some instances, God interacts in creation which requires his temporal nature, and when he does not interact in creation, his atemporal characteristic dominates. Classical theology held the view that God had knowledge of all events—past, present, and future, and Polkinghorne does not agree.

Polkinghorne moves to his position that God limited his omniscience in creation which means even God does not know future events before they happen, and kenosis of causality includes God's allowing divine providence to act as a cause along with other causes. The incarnation is such a self-limitation of God and shows God's willingness to act with creatures. As God allows creatures freedom, there must be a mixing of providential and creaturely causalities.[19] God acted causally with Mary in the incarnation. A problem emerges with Polkinghorne's thought and with prophecy, as for example in Isa 61 and in Luke 4:17. Jesus had foreknowledge of the future in various statements he makes to the disciples as in various Old Testament circumstances. For example, after David had Uriah the Hittite put

---

16. Polkinghorne explains the process of an evolving world as free-process (Polkinghorne, *Science and Providence*, 66–68). Free-process refers to the free evolution of the cosmos and of biological entities to ever greater complexity. It means God does not interact in the process.

17. Polkinghorne, "Kenotic Creation," 96–98.

18. Ibid., 102–4.

19. Ibid., 104–8.

in the battle where he would face certain death, Nathan appeared. Nathan explained the future consequences for David from his having Uriah killed by the enemy in battle (2 Sam 12:1–14). Nathan would not have known the future consequences had God not omnisciently revealed them to Nathan which required he omnisciently know them. It does not seem necessary to connect kenosis as extensively as Polkinghorne does. Phil 2:7 referred to Jesus emptying himself in the incarnation, and in doing so, he as divine limited his power in creation which did not imply God did so beyond the incarnation. However, observing the way the world works as in the case of moral and natural evil, one can conclude God has limited his continued interaction with creation and does interact from time to time in the case of miracles and continually with creatures through the Holy Spirit. Polkinghorne has developed an explanation of kenosis which assists understanding when God acts and does not act, his points for kenosis.

Polkinghorne makes several strong points for kenosis beginning with the comment that theologians understand an evolutionary world as one allowed by its Creator to make itself. Such understanding markedly differs with Augustine and Aquinas who sought to preserve divine power though the action of primary causality for God and secondary for his creatures. Polkinghorne's first point contends God must be separate from creation for redemption. Theology goes beyond and encourages the immanence of God which requires *creatio continua* in contrast to *creatio ex nihilo*.[20] Creation allowed to make itself has kenotic character with creatures as "created co-creators" in the words of Philip Hefner.[21] Second, the sharing of power has important implications for theodicy, as an evolutionary world inevitably has periods of disruption on both a natural and a creature scale. Third, continuing creation means God's providential guiding power is part of evolutionary history putting kenotic creation and divine power at the opposite sides of the same coin.[22] These views of creation go too far. No one knows how creation originated so we can only speculate. Such speculation projects human thought on the divine and on divine activity. Not knowing the origination details does not preclude making the observation of *creatio continua*. *Creatio continua* notes the universe continues to evolve with the implication that God willed it so. Redemption requires God as separate in the same way understanding the carpenter works on the wood from the outside. God's sharing of power in self-limiting himself in creation results in the possibility for moral and natural evil, and evidence does not exist that God continues to

---

20. Polkinghorne and Oord, *Polkinghorne Reader*, 72–73.
21. Ibid., 73.
22. Ibid., 73–74.

guide creation. Instead, the stronger argument contends he put everything in place in the beginning with natural law which determined how the world would evolve to ever greater complexity, an important point for causality.

Boyd and Cobb discuss the results for Polkinghorne's causality: "According to Polkinghorne, the causality distinction leads to three unpleasant results. First, it undermines the analogy between divine and human action."[23] Boyd and Cobb make the second point: "Second, since God's power undergirds all human activity, given that some human activity is evil (and manifestly so), then God is ultimately responsible for this evil."[24] But God does not of necessity exercise primary causality beyond origination of the laws and constants of physics that govern the universe. Instead God exercises primary causality in response to his creatures as revealed in the sacred texts. Creatures exercise secondary causality, and one will never discern the mode of God's activity, only the result. Physicists wrestle with that problem all the time with the equation of state for an ideal gas. A mole of gas contains 6.02×10^{23} molecules, far too many to observe as the gas changes from one state to another. Physicists do not observe how the gas molecules change (mode), only the result.

Boyd and Cobb point out that Polkinghorne's third observation makes the point: "Third, Polkinghorne maintains that the causality distinction makes scientific discovery and development irrelevant to theology."[25] Polkinghorne's third point refers to God's intervention in creation as in the resurrection for example. It does not refer to God's initial creative act and does not impact the relevance of scientific discovery and development to theology. Polkinghorne talks here of how God acts in creation and not how the material world works.

Polkinghorne explains that Thomists view the divine causality distinctly different from human causality. First, he answers association of primary causality with the divine eliminates any connection with creature causality. Second, God becomes a part of every event by allowing it to happen. Third, the separation of primary causality from secondary causality permits its continuing activity regardless of the discoveries of science.[26] Primary causality works with qualification. First, primary causality results in the creation of the physical laws that govern creation and its evolution. Second, primary causality results in the event referred to as the beginning of space-time which represents our understanding of God's initiating creation

---

23. Boyd and Cobb, "Causality," 394–95.
24. Ibid., 395.
25. Ibid.
26. Polkinghorne and Oord, *Polkinghorne Reader*, 74–76.

into being. Stephen Hawking's proposal for creation of space-time in the beginning avoids the problem of the singularity.[27] Third, primary causality concerns instances when God intervenes in creation. The most significant events were the rescue of Israel from Egypt and the incarnation. Miracles also are primary. Polkinghorne sidesteps God's involvement when he says God continues involvement in his allowing events to occur. God set everything properly in motion and knew omnisciently how natural law would guide the emerging creation.

Boyd and Cobb continue by discussing the implications of Polkinghorne's kenosis for cosmology:

> Polkinghorne appeals to the idea of "kenosis" as a model for explaining God's relationship to the cosmos. The term comes from Paul's Letter to the Philippians when he speaks of Christ "emptying" himself of divine privilege and taking the form of a servant. Kenosis therefore is a model for understanding how the sovereign Creator of the universe can allow for experiment and play in the process of creation. By divine self-limitation or "self-emptying" God allows for genuine novelty and development in the created order. As Polkinghorne uses the term, it refers to four different—but related—kinds of kenosis:
>
> 1. Kenosis of omnipotence;
> 2. Kenosis of simple eternity;
> 3. Kenosis of omniscience;
> 4. Kenosis of causal status.[28]

Boyd and Cobb categorize Polkinghorne's points as his model for kenosis and not regarding omnipotence. With regard to the kenosis of omnipotence, Polkinghorne notes that general providence is never thwarted, but that individual evil acts are permitted since God chooses not to dominate creation with divine power but allows created beings to act in ways that may or may not be in accordance with God's desires. It is therefore possible for creatures to act against God's wishes, and evil is a consequence of "omnipotent kenosis."[29] God's kenotic limitation of omnipotence does not mean he lacks omnipotence. It says he chooses not to exercise it, that is

---

27. Alister McGrath points out that Stephen Hawking proposes the origination of space-time rather than the big bang which avoids the problem of the singularity in general relativity (McGrath, "Tweaking," 18).

28. Boyd and Cobb, "Causality," 396.

29. Ibid., 396.

tyrannically overrule creation, a position which moves away from classical theology, particularly timelessness.

Boyd and Cobb comment with regard to classical theology:

> In a departure from much of the classical Augustinian and Boethian understandings of timelessness, Polkinghorne asserts the kenosis of simple eternity. Instead of viewing God as "knowing all things in one act of knowing," he defends the view that God can know things in their successive states. Polkinghorne writes, "We may suppose that God knows things as they really are and so, if time is real and events are successive, surely God will know them temporally in their succession, and not merely that they are successive." It is important to note, however, that Polkinghorne insists that God does not thereby cease to be timeless. Rather, "there has been 'added' (so to speak) a temporal pole of divinity that corresponds to the Creator's true engagement with created time." Polkinghorne posits the addition of this "temporal pole of divinity" to make sense of the fact that God must be able to be responsive to the real changes in the nature of the world (i.e., the change from the state of the universe immediately following the big bang to the state of the universe inhabited by sinful human beings). Although God is unchanging in God's character, God must have the flexibility to change in some respects to be related to the unfolding creation God brought into existence out of nothing.[30]

Then, according to Polkinghorne, God can only know time in progressive states which limits omniscience as seen in classical theology. Polkinghorne does not need to make this move to preserve free-will and free-process. In this instance, one risks imposing the human view on the divine in omniscience and limits omniscience to past and present.

Boyd and Cobb remark with respect to natural law in Polkinghorne's position:

> Since Polkinghorne's view of the world includes the interplay of natural laws, creaturely freedom, and divine action, omniscience must be limited to the past and the present. Again, this view contrasts with much of classical theism's emphasis upon God's "absolute knowledge" of past, present, and future. But Polkinghorne is quick to point out that this is a self-limiting omniscience. It is imposed by God, not by some external agency or factor.[31]

30. Ibid., 396.
31. Ibid., 397.

While one may claim God self-limits his omniscience, that does not prove he does so. Limited omniscience means God could not have known the universe would evolve, a position that does not make sense in light of observed purpose in the evolutionary world and its associated causal nexus.

Boyd and Cobb point out with respect to causal nexus:

> And finally, with regard to the kenosis of causal status, Polkinghorne claims that "the Creator's kenotic love includes allowing divine special providence to act as a cause among causes." As evidence for this claim, he appeals to the Incarnation as the paradigmatic example of God's kenotic love in action by becoming a cause among causes. What the Incarnation shows is not that God relinquishes all control of the universe but that God allows others to act and respects the autonomy of those actions.[32]

Causal nexus works with classical theology which assigned primary cause to God and secondary to humans and how God involves himself in creation, which pantheists and panentheists reject.

Polkinghorne objects to panenetheism when he says God cannot be considered as infinite if he is limited by creation outside himself. Here panentheism runs the risk of replacing the unsatisfactory position of the absolute power of God with the absolute comprehensiveness of God.[33] However, God can have both absolute power and comprehensiveness without kenotically choosing to exercise either.

It seems difficult to avoid theodicy as Polkinghorne notes when he brings up panentheism. Panentheism presents the problem that the more closely one identifies God with creation the greater the difficulty for his exclusion from moral and natural evil.[34] Creation is God's, and disassociation of God from creation does not work. By analogy, a parent can be with a child when the child misbehaves and not have direct responsibility for the child's behavior, only indirect responsibility. God has presence throughout creation, and eliminating his involvement presents a problem. Otherwise, it says God's witness has limited witness in creation such that some creatures may not have resource to God. Still, Polkinghorne does allow God as temporal so that there can be interaction with creation.

Polkinghorne moves to his strong argument regarding temporality and atemporality:

---

32. Ibid.
33. Polkinghorne, *Faith, Science & Understanding*, 92–94.
34. Polkinghorne, *Science and the Trinity*, 96.

> If the physical universe is one of true becoming, with the future not yet formed and existing, and if God knows that world in its temporality, then that seems to me to imply that God cannot yet know the future. This is no imperfection in the divine nature, for the future is not yet there to be known. Involved in the act of creation, in the letting-be of the truly other, is not only a kenosis of divine power but also a kenosis of divine knowledge. Omniscience is self-limited by God in the creation of an open world of becoming.[35]

This position challenges classical views of omniscience. Polkinghorne's argument regarding time says that God in order to be temporal kenotically limits himself with respect to time. These arguments are treating God with characteristics in creation such as being temporal. Further, treating God as temporal puts him in a particular place at an instant in time, risking the doctrine of omnipresence; however, the doctrine of immanence has the same challenge. The temporal aspect occurs on the human side. In order for humans to experience God, they do so temporally which does not necessarily require God as any more than immanent, and Polkinghorne does not prove the necessity for that limitation. Further, examination of God as both immanent and transcendent can clarify this position. Once the move is made to temporal kenoticism, there is no limit as how far one can go. For example, God had to know temporally what would occur when he made creation. Otherwise, there was no assurance the world would evolve as he intended. It also presents a problem for prophecy for the times when Jesus spoke of the future. The argument for a temporal aspect to God does not work. Temporal only applies to process which limits temporality to creation, and Gould's point of NOMA works here. There are certain aspects of the divine and human which do not overlap, and Polkinghorne handles these conflicts through his concept of polarity for God.

God's temporal pole represents another aspect of divine kenosis. Classical theists insist on God's current knowledge as knowledge of all time. God knows now all that can be known. He can see how creation develops and not the future, and such a view of divine omniscience fits Hebrew prophecy. God's warning that Egypt would not rescue Jerusalem from the Babylonians in Jer 37:3–16 did not imply God saw the eventual burning of the temple. Recent reflection sees God's relationship as including suffering with creation which indicates God's openness to mutability.[36] Consequently, we take

---

35. Polkinghorne, *Belief in God*, 72–74.

36. McKim explains mutability as: "A shared sense of responsibility and care for others in a relationship of equality. It is pointed to by feminist theologians as a more genuinely Christian and authentic way of relating to persons than the relationships

seriously God's engagement with time.[37] Classical theology developed over centuries with very careful thought on the part of the theologians of the church. We need to exercise care in discarding classical thought and check how it impacts systematic theology. For God to want humans to emerge in creation, he had to know that the laws and constants of physics would lead to life on earth. While some make the claim that divine kenoticism means God cannot assure the emergence of life, I do not accept that position for the express reason that it goes against the order and purpose we observe in an evolutionary world. Otherwise, he could not assure emergence of life. Therefore, I cannot dismiss omniscience. Also, we do not know what time looks like from the viewpoint of God and err when we superimpose human thought on time for the divine.

Polkinghorne acknowledges that classical theology thought of God's relationship to time as atemporal. However, God must relate temporally to the way things are in order to actively participate. Temporality implies God's engagement, consistent with the scriptural account. In this instance God knows all that is available temporally for him to know. In other words, he cannot know the future for it has not developed. He does so kenotically through limiting himself in creation. One of the difficulties in time is we know time only after it occurs and fades into the past. Polkinghorne quotes Augustine, who says in the *Confessions*, "We cannot rightly say what time is, except by reason of its impending state of not-being." The point that we know time only after it occurs and fades into the past has the problem of "now."[38] I agree God cannot be solely atemporal. He has both an atemporal and a temporal character which the instances of theophany in the Old Testament, the incarnation, the coming of the Holy Spirit at Pentecost, and Paul's experience on the way to Damascus (Acts 9:3–6) make clear. He limits his activity in the world so as not to interfere. Undoubtedly, he knows natural and moral events will occur. Kenotically, he does not interfere. On the other hand, God must set aside kenoticism in order to respond to the prayers of his people. Kenoticism has some issues Polkinghorne does not address.

In addition to the time question there is the question as to whether God can participate in creation and continue to omnisciently know all past, present, and future events.

Kenosis has great appeal for Polkinghorne to eliminate God as either tyrannical or as uninvolved spectator. For Polkinghorne, the theological problem comes in seeing the world as a world of becoming and not as

---

based on authority and power that are prevalent" (McKim, *Westminster*, 189).

37. Polkinghorne, *Science and the Trinity*, 108–10.
38. Polkinghorne, *Exploring Reality*, 118–20.

already formed. Such a view means God does not know the future. But God knows all that can be known which according to Polkinghorne means God limits his omniscience. God, then, must also know a sense of time in order to interact in creation. Polkinghorne concludes God limited his knowledge of the future in order to create a world of becoming. This position means that God kenotically limited his knowledge of future events as well as his self in creation. Polkinghorne concludes from these points that theology challenges our everyday assumptions. Given that science often surprises, we might expect theology to surprise even more.[39] Still, we cannot allow reduction of God to the level of human. The church early on saw human language alone could not contain Christ. Here Polkinghorne moves away from classical theology which asserted God's complete omniscience. I do not see the necessity in Polkinghorne's argument for the limitation of omniscience. His point implies when taken to the extreme that God had no clue how creation would develop which does not make sense of the observed purposeful emergence of complexity in biological systems. In this instance, theology expands in kenosis to accommodate today's understanding in science. It accommodates evolution as well as Albert Einstein's space-time in relativity; however, God can know the future and not interact. Polkinghorne's position here limits God and concludes God limits his knowledge of the future. That position seems unlikely and inconsistent with God's foreknowledge of how creation would begin and evolve, and it risks demeaning God to the level of human. After all, even the incarnation preserved the divine. Finally, Polkinghorne's argument for a world that makes itself does not require that God kenotically give up omniscience. Kenoticism does qualify God's activity, but it does not limit his ability to know the outcomes, and his omniscience does not have the limits Polkinghorne suggests. The contemporary world has greater understanding of how the world works than did those in medieval and earlier periods when much of classical theology took shape.

Ian G. Barbour asserts that the medieval view of omnipotent, omniscient, and unchanging does not have acceptance today for five reasons: "(1) the integrity of nature in science and in theology; (2) the problem of evil and suffering; (3) the reality of human freedom; (4) the Christian understanding of the cross; and (5) feminist critiques of patriarchal models of God."[40] These objections have encouraged many theologians to speak of God's creation as kenosis, voluntary self-limitation.[41] The lack of acceptance in the contemporary world does not rule out the classical view of God. Instead, the emergence

---

39. Polkinghorne, *Serious Talk*, 54–56.
40. Barbour, "God's Power," 1.
41. Ibid.

of contradiction leads to requalification of omnipotent, omniscient, and unchanging. Unchanging does not require the requalification. What does require requalification is whether or not God suffers. In the first instance, God chose a creation in relationship which kenotically meant free-will. Regarding human suffering, the world that makes itself makes strong advances technically which benefit human welfare for better living and health. God omnipotently created the world and self-limited his omnipotence in creation. We conclude he did so from the observation that the world evolves to ever greater complexity on its own with nothing in the driver's seat, and that conclusion does not mean God no longer involves himself in creation as spectator or otherwise and self-limits his omnipotence.

Like Polkinghorne, Jürgen Moltmann also argues for God's limiting his omnipotence. The thought of God's self-limiting of omnipotence can be extended to other areas as well. God does not have knowledge of everything before it happens because he has not willed to do so. Instead, he waits for the response of humans. Orthodox theology says God's love, not his power, means what we see as almighty in 1 Cor 13:4, 7, and God waits patiently.[42] Moltmann makes the best argument here for the self-limiting of God. Unfortunately, his position implies limits to God. As soon as theologians limit God, he no longer remains ultimate, much less omnipotent. God's lack of willing a thing does not prove he does not know he will at some time will it, nor does it prove that he does not know the outcome, should he will it to come to pass in the future. Here the atemporal nature of God takes over. Then the event remains atemporal until he actually wills it. For example, I know I will leave Huntsville at 9:30 a.m. for an 11:30 a.m. doctor's appointment next Thursday. I will "will" that event next Thursday. However, since I am not omniscient, I do not know exactly the time I will leave nor exactly the time I will arrive. However, God does not have those limitations.

Polkinghorne's use of kenosis provides a good model for explanation of God's relationship with creation. It works well systematically with theodicy, free-will, free-process, and *creatio continua*. We observe that God does not appear to overtly control activity in creation, and we can infer he has limited his activity, kenosis, in creation, and that God does not have responsibility for moral and natural evil. Further, he chooses to not intervene and allows humans to handle it through free-will. In addition, he allows the world to evolve as it has through free-process and does not choose to intervene when natural disasters occur.

None of these claims mean that God is not involved. Rather, he involves himself as fellow sufferer, a point of assurance for all Christians, and

---

42. Moltmann, "God's Kenosis," 144–50.

we rely on the example of the crucifixion for support. Nor do these points prevent God's choosing in some instances to intervene as we saw in the exodus and in the incarnation.

Limiting omniscience provides such an instance. God can omnisciently know the future and choose kenotically to not intervene, consistent with what we observe. Limited omniscience, on the other hand, does not fit the observed purpose in creation for a world that has evolved to greater complexity. It does not make sense that God had to decide to limit his knowledge in creation to permit *creatio continua* or limit it in stages. In conclusion, there does not appear to be any evidence that God self-limits omniscience.

Conclusion

Polkinghorne's moves fall into the same trap as theologians who ushered in a "god of the gaps" when they failed to discover explanations for questions of science. Most theologians today would not pursue such a route.

On the other hand, it can easily be argued from the observation that God does not appear actively creating, he limits himself in creation. And since theologians have adopted kenosis to cover his self-limitation, that position does not present a problem. The next step addresses kenosisology, and it must systematically work with all areas of Christian theology. In that manner, theologians can more adequately address some of the apparent difficulties with current kenotic thought.

Polkinghorne has systematically developed his views on kenosis, limited omniscience, and temporality from the vantage point of looking at God from the human perspective outside God's eternal realm. Barbour similarly argued for kenosis to accommodate common understanding for nature in religion and science, evil and suffering, free-will, the Christian understanding of the cross, and feminist critiques of the patriarchal models of God.[43]

Undoubtedly, kenosis adds richness and depth to our understanding of God's involvement in creation and with humankind.

---

43. Barbour, "God's Power," 1.

4

Christology

Introduction

EVANGELISM DEPENDS ON A proper understanding of Jesus, the subject of Christology. Very simply, without Jesus Christ, we do not have Christian faith which makes an important claim for the thesis of this work. Interpretation and commendation of Christian faith in the contemporary world depends critically on Christology. Examination of Christology answers the question regarding the significance for Polkinghorne for the interpretation and commendation of Christian faith in the modern world. Polkinghorne's first book, *The Way the World Is* (1994), and even more so *From Physicist to Priest* (2007), indicate his strong christological focus. Craig C. Hill in *In God's Time* (2002) gives an excellent introduction to Jesus and at the same time identifies some of the questions regarding the gospel depiction. Many scholars, particularly since the nineteenth century, have devoted considerable research to discover the "historical Jesus," and the gospels provide the portrait we follow in our examination. Several writers wrote the gospels, relying on differing sources and addressing differing concerns in the community. The dates associated with the gospels vary and most reliably place their composition in the late first century, several decades after the ascension of Jesus. Such a delay in composition as well as the changing view of Jesus after the resurrection makes it difficult to argue for their thorough historical accuracy. Nonetheless, this conclusion does not infer the writers did not get Jesus right. Rather, they most likely got him right, but emphasized differing areas for him personally, his actions, and his overall ministry. For example, Mark argues for the Markan secrecy of Jesus as Messiah, and John has Jesus declaring it almost immediately to an unnamed woman in Samaria. I doubt

CHRISTOLOGY

either author got it wrong, but perhaps Mark overemphasized some of the statements attributed to Jesus.[1] The writers of the gospels emphasized different aspects for Jesus. Matthew emphasized his Jewishness, Mark, Jesus as Servant, Luke, Jesus as man, and John, Jesus as the Son of God. In addition, they spoke about his mission in different ways and in some instances followed different chronologies. Raymond Brown notes Mark, the earliest gospel, was written 60–75 CE.[2] While Mark followed the Q source, it likely lacked precise detail.[3] Further, the gospel writers did not appear intent on writing a historical account as would have been the case in the contemporary world. From oral traditions and other sources, they recorded the message of Jesus as well as the controversy surrounding his life.

As Walter Brueggemann reminds us, controversy surrounded Jesus from his birth. Jesus functioned as a prophet, criticized the royal consciousness, and dismantled the dominant culture. Controversy develops immediately following Jesus' birth and in the last gasp of ruling power as Herod slaughters the innocents under two years of age. Following his baptism and the temptation by Satan, Jesus immediately announces the coming of the new kingdom in Mark. He breaks with the accepted practices in Judaism for forgiveness, keeping the Sabbath, sharing fellowship at meals, healings and exorcism, women, taxes and debt, and in the prophecy regarding destruction of the temple. Culture treats Jesus as it always treats its prophets—as the cause of the coming destruction rather than the one who proclaims the circumstances and declares the ultimate outcome.[4] Controversy surrounded Jesus everywhere he went. He did not follow the accepted practices of Judaism in his day in, for example, his healing people on the Sabbath, a day when Jews did not work, and his practices, particularly overturning the money changers' tables in the temple, aroused the ire of the political leaders among the Jews.

As noted in the preceding paragraph, Brueggemann discussed Jesus' conflict with the political order of the day. Later, when he began his ministry, he upset the social order of the day. Jesus in his compassion toward the marginalized further criticizes the culture, and compassion stands out as the theme of both the Good Samaritan and the Prodigal Son parables. Jesus' stories combine internalization of the pain in the culture and the transformation that results when Jesus comes in contact with individuals, and

---

1. Hill, *In God's Time*, 130–42.
2. Brown, *Introduction*, 127.
3. The Q source was an undiscovered textual source New Testament scholars believe existed before Mark, and from which, Mark took much of his material.
4. Brueggemann, *Prophetic*, 81–99.

compassion moves Jesus at Lazarus' tomb.[5] As he compassionately grieves for the current pathos people face, Jesus condemns the circumstances while at the same time holding out new hope for a different future.[6] Ultimately, Jesus' passion criticizes the establishment in each progressive scene. He criticizes in suffering, in total submission, and in demonstration of a different system of values. Such contradiction forms a major theme throughout the Bible, illustrating God's concern for equity in society. Both Moses and Jesus contradicted the establishment, offering a new reality.[7] Jesus criticized the accepted order in society in his words and in his actions. He stands up for the woman caught in adultery—unheard of at the time—shares meals with tax collectors, consorts with a former prostitute, and tells the story of the Good Samaritan to challenge the contemporary view for what it meant to be a neighbor. Even today, his actions would appear revolutionary and would likely cause conflict and have as deep an impact on people as it did then.

We see when Polkinghorne examines the Johannine texts that Jesus had a more profound character than merely upsetting the political and social order. The prologue of John talks about the union of the eternal with the temporal. John sees the Incarnate one as the true union of the divine with humanity and through the *logos* associates the passage with Greek thought. For the Greek, it represented the ordering principle of the cosmos, a point physicists would feel very comfortable with, and John's gospel brings together divine order and process.[8] God must have a temporal aspect in order to appear in the incarnation. He has already disclosed his temporal character in the Old Testament though his various appearances to the patriarchs throughout Genesis and to Moses in Exodus. In the Old Testament appearances we catch a glimmer of God as stern and at times vindictive. In the incarnation, we see him as loving, trustworthy, and faithful.

Polkinghorne continues to examine Jesus and moves to Paul's Col 1:15–20 text, adding it for the cosmic significance it claims for Jesus and finding the last verse particularly significant in that Jesus reconciles "all things" and not just people.[9] These passages contribute to Polkinghorne's kenotic examination

---

5. Ibid.
6. Ibid.
7. Ibid.
8. Polkinghorne, *Encountering Scripture*, 95–98.
9. Ibid., 98–102. Col 1:15–20: "He is the image of the invisible God, the firstborn of all creation; for in him all things in heaven and on earth were created, things visible and invisible, whether thrones or dominions or rulers or powers—all things have been created through him and for him. He himself is before all things, and in him all things hold together. He is the head of the body, the church; he is the beginning, the firstborn from the dead, so that he might come to have first place in everything. For in him all the

of eschatology to be discussed in chapters 8 and 10 of this work. John, 1 John, and Paul at several points paint a deep christological picture for Jesus which would have appealed to the Greek mind of the day. John begins with the *logos*, very Platonic in thought. Certainly, these passages would have assisted the early church in its development of doctrine for Jesus Christ.

Daniel L. Migliore and Bernhard Lohse examine the development of Christology in the early church. The early church devoted much attention to the doctrine of Jesus Christ, which reflects its significance for the church and the individual Christian. Incarnation meant God became human flesh and dwelled among us, and our salvation depends on the incarnation. Otherwise, Jesus as only a human being could not save us from sin. Second, the incarnation requires Jesus be simultaneously divine and human, both God and man. Third, Jesus must be on the same level as God and not some lesser deity, as a lesser deity could not save us.[10] Migliore gives a succinct assessment for the impact of Jesus: "Christian faith sees no less than God in the transforming, suffering, and victorious love at work in Jesus' ministry."[11] Lohse comments on the 451 CE Chalcedonian creed: "The Chalcedonian creed witnesses to the faith of Christianity. It does so in a way that is simple and yet unsurpassably clear and striking by asserting Jesus is one person and at the same time God and man."[12] The Council of Chalcedon expanded on the work of the earlier Council of Nicaea to address Jesus' nature and relationship with respect to God. While the New Testament relates much about Jesus and who he was, it

---

fullness of God was pleased to dwell, and through him God was pleased to reconcile to himself all things, whether on earth or in heaven, by making peace through the blood of his cross."

10. Migliore, *Faith*, 149.

11. Ibid., 149.

12. Lohse, *Short History*, 94. Chalcedonian Creed: "In agreement, therefore, with the holy fathers, we all unanimously teach that we should confess that our Lord Jesus Christ is one and the same Son, the same perfect in Godhead and the same perfect in manhood, truly God and truly man, the same of a rational soul and body, consubstantial with the Father in Godhead, and the same consubstantial with us in manhood, like us in all things except sin; begotten from the Father before the ages, as regards His Godhead, and in the last days, the same, because of us men and because of our salvation begotten from the Virgin Mary, the *Theotokos*, as regards His manhood; one and the same Christ, Son, Lord, only—begotten, made known in two natures, without confusion, without change, without division, without separation. The difference of the natures being by no means removed because of the union, but the property of each nature preserved and coalescing in one *prosopon* and one *hypostasis*—not parted or divided into two *prosopa*, but one and the same Son, only—begotten divine Word, the Lord Jesus Christ, as the prophets of old Jesus Christ Himself have taught us about Him and the creed of our fathers has handed down" (ibid., 92).

did not always explain some of the subtlety. The church did that later with the early fathers who interpreted the creedal material.

In conclusion, Jesus appears on the scene and immediately threatens the leaders of the time, causing Herod to have the infants under the age of two murdered. One might have thought Herod's actions would have settled things, but they did not. Even at the age of twelve in the temple, Jesus demonstrated there was something different. And the early church explained it further in the early councils through Chalcedon.

Jürgen Moltmann—*The Crucified God*—Influential for Polkinghorne

While Jesus has importance for the examination of the work of Polkinghorne for commendation of Christian faith in the modern world, the crucifixion and resurrection have central importance for Jesus' work to redeem creation and restore humankind to right relationship with God. Polkinghorne read Jürgen Moltmann's *The Crucified God* (1993) as he entered seminary, and it has central importance for his work, which is the reason we examine Moltmann's central thought first. Moltmann reminds us that all statements regarding God, creation, sin, and death center in the cross. We cannot have theology of the incarnation without theology of the cross. When we describe Jesus as the image of God, we also describe God as like Jesus—crucified, helpless, and rejected. God cannot be greater than he is in his humiliation and helplessness. God cannot be more divine than in the humanity of Jesus. The new Christology then must take into account the doctrine of *kenoticism*. In the cross the knowledge of God emerges in being killed in order to bring new life. Whereas indirect knowledge of God can come from his works, direct knowledge only comes in the cross.[13] Jesus' life, particularly in John, moves toward the crucifixion. In the latter part of John beginning with the fourteenth chapter, Jesus begins to prepare his disciples for the events to come. When he prays in Golgotha, he shows he knows what lies ahead but moves resolutely to the cross. John sets these events before Pilate in the Day of Preparation (John 19:14) whereas the other gospels set the time as Passover (Mark 14:12). While I do not believe John got the events wrong, I believe he did not get the dates right. When I reflect on John's description of Jesus' path along the Kidron valley with his disciples, I cannot imagine the thoughts in Jesus' mind as he knew crucifixion was around the corner. As he and the disciples walked through the valley, they could not help but note that the stream flowed with the blood of the many lambs sacrificed for Passover. I cherish these times and the poi-

13. Moltmann, *Crucified God*, 200–22.

gnancy I suspect Jesus felt as he approached his condemnation, crucifixion, and resurrection. How could I not love such a one? He never condemns those who pursue him as he walks this final path, knowing that he will make the ultimate sacrifice for those who condemn him to an ignoble death. Such grace and power call one to Jesus the Christ, the message of evangelism.

The theology of the cross has less emphasis in Protestantism than in Martin Luther's *theologia cruces*. Douglas John Hall explains the theology of the cross thus:

> The theology of the cross declares: *God* is with you—Emmanuel. *God* is alongside you in your suffering. *God* is in the darkest place of your dark night. You do not have to look for God in the sky, beyond the stars, in infinite light, in glory unimaginable. God is incarnate. That means: God has been *crucified*. To become flesh, to become one of us, means that God was born. However, it means that *God* died and failed, as well. It means that God has been crucified; and, therefore, that the way of the cross (which is, in any case, our way) needs no longer to be regarded as producing only negative results. There may, after all, be a kind of expectancy that is not extinguished but that actually grows through the experience of negation.[14]

Moltmann comments on the implications of such theology remarking that the cross tests everything which can be called Christian.[15] As Paul says when one identifies with the crucified Christ, the world dies to him (Gal 6:14). Dietrich Bonhoeffer in *The Cost of Discipleship* (1973) said it plainly that when Jesus calls one, he calls one to come and die, die to the world to live for Jesus. To know Jesus is to say as Paul says: "For through the law I died to the law, so that I might live to God. I have been crucified with Christ; and it is no longer I who live, but it is Christ who lives in me. And the life I now live in the flesh I live by faith in the Son of God, who loved me and gave himself for me" (Gal 2:19–20). Just as Jesus' last moments resonate in my heart, so do Paul's. Paul accepted his call and never wavered, writing the beautiful letter to Philippi while a prisoner of the Roman Empire and facing his martyrdom. Even at the last, the words of Paul impacted Agrippa when Agrippa said to Paul: "Are you so quickly persuading me to become a Christian?" (Acts 26:28). And the events with Jesus and with Paul persuade and draw me to deeper faith. And we see Paul had a high Christology as Moltmann noted. From his comments regarding the cross, Moltmann turns to epistemology:

---

14. Hall, *Lighten*, 151.
15. Moltmann, *Crucified God*, 7–31.

> Christian theology very early adopted the epistemological principle of the Platonic school and introduced the principle of analogy into its doctrine of the knowledge of God. Either the invisible God is known in the analogies to him in the order of creation or in acts of history which point to him, or else he is known in his self-revelation, or only in the Holy Spirit of God.[16]

However, Moltmann says that the principle of analogy has the difficulty of being one-sided. Moltmann argues that to be correct analogical knowledge must be supplemented by dialectic. Friedrich Wilhelm Joseph Schelling said every being can be revealed in its opposite. This means God is revealed in his opposite, godlessness and abandonment. Then, in the epistemological principle of the dialectic, God is revealed in the cross. The unrighteous not the righteous recognized Jesus. In summary, theology of the cross starts with contradictions.[17] The horrific evil of the cross revealed God. It did not reveal him as vengeful; it revealed him as the suffering God who stood alongside Jesus. The world sees that moment as Jesus' worst moment whereas we see him in his opposite, conquering evil that we might live, and we do not consider the cross of no import. Too easily, we discard the picture of the cross and lose the memory of the tremendous God who paid for my relationship with him. I cannot take the cross lightly nor my relationship with God.

Moltmann reminds us to not take the cross lightly. The cross signifies suffering and rejection, and those who take on the cross take on suffering and rejection. Paul reminds us in Rom 6:4 and Gal 6:14 that the one who takes up the cross becomes crucified to the world, and the world becomes crucified to him or her. World in these passages refers to the laws of sin and death's power, and Paul understood Jesus speaks in the "word of the cross."[18] Again, we turn from the world and what it would call great to take up the cross in our daily lives. We do not do so in the trivial way when someone says "I have my cross to bear." The turmoil that I face from time to time seem pale in the light of what God has done for me. I rejoice that I can call him to my side each and every moment. We take it on acknowledging the cost for relationship with God, and in doing so we share his suffering.

Moltmann issues serious challenges to classical theology's concepts of God's not suffering and of God's omnipotence. In the first instance, Moltmann states:

> But even apart from this extreme position, which [Fyodor] Dostoevsky worked through again and again in *The Demons*, a God

16. Ibid., 26.
17. Ibid., 26–31.
18. Ibid., 55–81.

who cannot suffer is poorer than any man. For a God who is incapable of suffering is a being who cannot be involved. Suffering and injustice do not affect him. And because he is so completely insensitive, he cannot be affected or shaken by anything. He cannot weep, for he has not tears. But the one who cannot suffer cannot love either. So he is also a loveless being. Aristotle's God cannot love; he can only be loved by all non-divine beings by virtue of his perfection and beauty, and in this way draw them to him. The "unmoved Mover" is a "loveless Beloved."[19]

Moltmann's eschatology of hope requires a God who suffers. The classical doctrine of impassibility of God argues God does not suffer or experience pain. Undoubtedly, God does not experience pain and suffering in the manner humans do, and how he does so must remain a mystery. God can experience suffering and pain and still not change. We argue God is love, a human emotion also. We argue God is faithful, a human characteristic also. It does not seem at all unreasonable that God experiences pain and suffering on some level. Moreover, Moltmann points out the problem in classical theology concerning omnipotence: "Finally, a God who is only omnipotent is in himself an incomplete being, for he cannot experience helplessness and powerlessness. Omnipotence can indeed be longed for and worshipped by helpless men, but omnipotence is never loved; it is only feared."[20] Moltmann continues:

> He is, if one is prepared to put it in inadequate imagery, transcendent as Father, immanent as Son and opens up the future of history as the Spirit. If we understand God in this way, we can understand our own history, the history of suffering and the history of hope, in the history of God. Beyond theistic submissiveness and atheistic protest this is the history of life, because it is the history of love. . . . "From first to last, and not merely in the epilogue, Christianity is eschatology, is hope, is forward looking and forward moving, and therefore also revolutionizing and transforming the present." God is no longer understood as the "God above us" or "in the depths of being," but as the "God before us," going before us in history as the God of hope.[21]

Eschatology transforms us and the world, providing hope in the future from the experience of the past. The cross speaks to me of the love that God has for me, a love that transforms me into ever deeper faith. The word eschatology does not adequately convey what God has done for me. Only

19. Ibid., 222.
20. Ibid., 223.
21. Ibid., 256.

the cross conveys that message. Moltmann goes further to remind us of the depth of our relationship with God.

Moltmann notes Christians are absorbed into God and all that he is. We cannot separate ourselves from those who suffer, even from those who suffered in places like Auschwitz. We rise up, then, like Paul and know what it means to say we share crucifixion with Jesus. The Christian cannot escape the cross.[22] It is in the cross that we realize our most profound relationship with God. Moltmann rightly challenges classical theology's concept of God. A God who cannot suffer cannot express empathy with the world, and no one is drawn to one who does not show concern. When we become absorbed in the crucifixion, we immerse ourselves in God and move toward our resurrection. I can see how Moltmann must have affected Polkinghorne deeply. Moltmann affects me deeply as well.

Moltmann moves from the crucifixion to the resurrection of Jesus Christ and argues that the crucifixion provides the foundation for Christian hope. Hope without remembering can be no more than illusion, and remembering without hope can be no more than resignation.[23] There is nothing lovable about the cross. Yet only the crucified Christ can provide the freedom to change the world because in doing so the world no longer fears death. The theology of the cross begins with Paul and jumps forward to Luther. Theology of the cross represents the opposite side of the theology of hope. It steps back. Theology of hope begins with the resurrection, while theology of the cross steps back to the crucifixion.[24] Moltmann does not hesitate in advocacy for a complete and not a partial Christology. Christian faith must not choose some parts of Jesus and discard the others. Moltmann says seeing Jesus' death solely in the resurrection leads to a Christ-myth where his death is simply an important fact and no more. When his death is examined only in terms of the life he lived, it has no greater significance than the life of other prophets. Only the relationship of the crucifixion and the resurrection establish Christian faith.[25] Christian faith looks forward from the cross to the future in the resurrection. Moltmann does not glorify the cross; he points to it for what it is. Without the crucifixion, we lose the rich significance of the resurrection and risk setting aside the event as no more than myth which fails to see the future in the cross. The cross becomes more than hope for me. It becomes promise, the promise that I see in God from the suzerain covenant with Moses to the promise of grace which Paul reminds us of when he says: "For by grace you

---

22. Ibid., 278.
23. Ibid., ix.
24. Ibid., 1–6.
25. Ibid., 112–59.

have been saved through faith, and this is not your own doing; it is the gift of God" (Eph 2:8). How can I not love such a God who requires nothing of me but my acceptance of his call.

Moltmann continues by connecting the cross and future when he says:

> Correspondingly, the creed of early Christian faith that "Jesus was raised *from* the dead" expresses a certainty about the future of the Jesus who was killed and by his death was condemned to the past. The Christian resurrection hope is kindled by the appearances of Jesus; as a result it first casts its light backwards on to the Jesus who died on the cross. Only from him and through him does the resurrection hope then extend to the living and the dead. "For to this end has Christ died and come alive again, that he might be Lord of both dead and living" (Rom. 14.9).[26]

The good news is that Jesus reigns for both the dead and the living. God has raised him, and in his resurrection, we share resurrection with him. Wonderfully, the music of Easter celebrates the resurrection. The church heaves a sigh of relief and moves fast away from the crucifixion. We want no more of that and cannot embrace its horror. We hurry for Pentecost is just around the corner, and we have lost the content for faith. The content for faith occurs in God's showing up and suffering with humankind. Jesus was crucified, buried, and raised with a new body but not a restored life.

Moltmann clarifies that the resurrection did not mean that Jesus simply gained a restored life. Resurrection eliminates any thought of mere resuscitation which would have simply meant the revival of the previous body of Jesus. Further, it would also have meant his return to life which meant death. Had Jesus merely experienced resuscitation, he would at some later point as merely mortal have experienced death, that is Jesus as human would have died and not have been marked by resurrection. Instead, resurrection from the dead refers to a new life and does not refer to life after death as in some religions. In the end, the new creation begins with the resurrection of the dead.[27] Resurrection cannot mean that Jesus experienced restoration to new life, as that would have also implied lack of divinity. Even more importantly, it would have denied any possibility for resurrection for the Christian. In fact, it would have denied everything he promised as in John 14, when he explained he went to his Father to prepare our place. For Moltmann, resurrection meant eschatological hope for human destiny.

---

26. Ibid., 162–63.
27. Ibid., 164–74.

To summarize Moltmann, it seems appropriate to remind ourselves he suffered as prisoner of war in World War II Germany.[28] I doubt that anyone who went through those times in the camps takes suffering lightly. Further, they would not take lightly oppressive regimes such as the Third Reich or the one which caused the crucifixion and would have understood the helplessness of the innocent. Moltmann's call to the crucifixion calls the world to not take things lightly or for granted. To avoid doing so, the church must return to the crucifixion and not merely celebrate the resurrection.

My faith resonates with the words of Moltmann. It reminds me of St. John of the Cross and his drawing of the crucified Christ. I have for many years kept Salvador Dali's replica print. It faces me now as I write these words and draws me deeply into God. I cannot turn away.

Christology in Polkinghorne

Polkinghorne approaches Jesus bottom-up. We can know Jesus through his words and deeds, through the reports from his contemporaries who knew him firsthand, and from the unrest among the Jewish authorities that confirms the authenticity of Jesus' deeds.[29] Earlier ages would have accepted the deeds of Jesus as strong evidence for him and his origination. The gospel writers present the story in a simple way with no expanded explanation. Some instances of the story could have been coincidences as in the stilling of the storm. The contemporary world which sees the regularity of the cosmos would dismiss these deeds as fairy tale and invention.[30] The world in the first years following his crucifixion did not, and the early Christians were far more accepting of Jesus' story as literal than the contemporary world might be. Polkinghorne will argue much more strongly from the evidence of the witnesses to Jesus in his development of the case for the resurrection in chapter 7.

Polkinghorne introduces Jesus' announcement of the kingdom when Jesus appears in the first chapter of Mark (Mark 1:14–15).[31] Israel always recognizes the reign of God and his rule as a hidden one. In keeping with this, Jesus showed reticence to acknowledge his role.[32] The phrase "Son of Man" in Greek and English, although mysterious, had significance in Ara-

---

28. Viviano, "Eschatology," 82–83.
29. Polkinghorne, *Way the World*, 52–54.
30. Ibid., 54.
31. Mark 1:14–15: "Now after John was arrested, Jesus came to Galilee, proclaiming the good news of God, and saying, 'The time is fulfilled, and the kingdom of God has come near; repent, and believe in the good news.'"
32. Polkinghorne, *Way the World*, 56–58.

maic and Hebrew, for example, and occurred more than eighty times in the gospels such as Matt 8:20; Mark 10:33; Luke 18:8; and John 13:31 as possible reference to Dan 7:13-14. Jesus quotes Daniel in his trial before the high priest, Mark 14:62.[33] Jesus uses the phrase in two ways, first in reference to himself and second in reference to the one who will appear at the "denouement" of all things in Mark 8:38.[34] Jesus uses "Son of Man" eschatologically in reference to his appearance at the dramatic climax for all things. When Jesus quoted Daniel to the high priest in his trial before the Sanhedrin, the high priest understood what Jesus meant, and Jesus' comment caused the high priest to tear his clothes, emblematic that Jesus had blasphemed according to the high priest; however, Jesus as divine did not blaspheme and will go on to draw all creation to himself, and the "Son of Man" phrase stands out for its eschatological importance.

Hill carefully expands on the "Son of Man" phrase and notes that Jesus used it consistently leading to considerable later debate regarding its meaning. In these statements, Jesus refers to his ministry, his coming rejection and death, and his role in coming judgment reminiscent of Dan 7:13-14.[35] Paul corroborates Jesus' use of the term in 1 Thess 4:15-18 which uses the word of the Lord, also found in Matt 24:30-31. In using the term "Son of Man," Jesus as well as the gospel writers assert the eschatological nature of Jesus' mission, going beyond the office of a mere prophet. Support comes from Jesus' anticipation of impending events such as his own death which he memorializes in the Last Supper, and later tradition, as noted in 1 Cor 11:20-34, supported Jesus' awareness of his impending death. Jesus also believed he would receive vindication beyond the crucifixion (Mark 14:60-64). The sign "The King of the Jews" placed atop the cross appears to confirm that others recognized his potential fulfillment of the messianic expectations that he truly was the "Son of Man."[36] His crucifixion supports this view as well. Hill concludes this section as follows: "The early church was an eschatologically oriented community because of, not in spite of Jesus."[37]

33. Mark 14:61-63: "But he was silent and did not answer. Again the high priest asked him, 'Are you the Messiah, the Son of the Blessed One?' Jesus said, 'I am'; and 'you will see the Son of Man seated at the right hand of the Power,' and 'coming with the clouds of heaven.' Then the high priest tore his clothes and said, 'Why do we still need witnesses?'"

34. Polkinghorne, *Way the World*, 58-60.

35. Dan 7:13-14: "As I watched in the night visions, I saw one like a human being coming with the clouds of heaven. And he came to the Ancient One and was presented before him. To him was given dominion and glory and kingship, that all peoples, nations, and languages should serve him. His dominion is an everlasting dominion that shall not pass away, and his kingship is one that shall never be destroyed."

36. Hill, *In God's Time*, 150-59.

37. Ibid., 159.

Jesus identifies himself as the Messiah three times in the gospels in Mark 8:27–33, Mark 14:62, and John 4:25–26.[38] While Jesus did not use the term Messiah, he did imply it in more than one instance, as, for example, in his statement following the reading of the scroll from Isaiah in Luke 4:21 and in his statement to the woman of Samaria in John 4:26. In other places, the gospels make it clear that Jesus understood his mission as messianic, particularly in the latter part of John. Still the early church struggled with the identity for Jesus as did Paul, despite the fact that he met Jesus on the road to Damascus, and that meeting was no vision.

Polkinghorne points out that when Paul refers to Jesus as Lord, he uses the term in its Greek form for YHWH in reference to Jesus as divine. In doing so, Paul does not turn the Christian movement into a Jesus cult but acknowledges the divinity of Jesus. Jews did not use the name of God directly, and the action of the early church to do so represented a major paradigmatic shift. Greek-speaking Jews of the third century substituted the Greek *kyrios* for YHWH in the Greek translation of the Hebrew Scripture.[39] The early Hebrews turned to the use of YHWH, הָוְהִי, *Yahweh*, which the NRSV usually translates as Lord.[40] When Paul uses it, Polkinghorne contends he appears to struggle with referring to Jesus as God. Yet, Paul in many passages such as Phil 2:11 refers to Jesus as Christ, Paul's acknowledgement that Jesus was indeed divine. Therefore, Paul's usage may actually reflect his understanding of Jesus as divine and his Jewish inclination to use the traditional YHWH. Jesus in his language shows he understood who he was and that he was God's Son. I am grateful that I do not possess Paul's seeming reticence today and can go to Jesus in prayer with the confidence that he knows and loves me.

Polkinghorne points to the mystery surrounding Jesus when he acknowledges that Jesus did not make the direct statement that he was the "Son of God." Those pictured in the gospels also struggled to come to grips with the identity of Jesus. The mystery of Jesus as both human and divine becomes the subject of discussion and debate in the early church. Wave/particle duality in physics guides our understanding of Jesus as human/divine. Yet there will always be an element of mystery.[41] It does not appear we will understood the dual nature of divine and human in Jesus. It denies to some extent the omnipresence of God, for if God is present locally, how can he be omnipresent throughout the world? Consequently, God must be simultaneously local and not local. As Polkinghorne has argued, he is temporal

---

38. Ibid., 150–59.
39. Polkinghorne, *Way the World*, 62–64.
40. Brown, *Hebrew and English Lexicon*, 217.
41. Polkinghorne, *Way the World*, 66–68.

and atemporal. As God must have a temporal pole in order to interact in creation, he must have a local pole as well. That argument makes it possible for the divine in Jesus, both local and temporal. Any other position would deny his ability to interact with creation and limit his significance.

The disciples did not appear to fully grasp Jesus' significance. John seems to grasp it when he says: "And the Word became flesh and lived among us, and we have seen his glory, the glory as of a father's only son, full of grace and truth" (John 1:14). Then we also have the statement at Jesus' baptism: "And just as he was coming up out of the water, he saw the heavens torn apart and the Spirit descending like a dove on him. And a voice came from heaven, 'You are my Son, the Beloved; with you I am well pleased'" (Mark 1:10–11). Following the baptism, Jesus goes into the desert for his later meeting with Satan who clearly recognizes the divinity of Jesus when he says: "The tempter came and said to him, 'If you are the 'Son of God,' command these stones to become loaves of bread'" (Matt 4:3). These references and the record from the Pauline corpus through the gospels clearly present Jesus as divine, the heart of the incarnation.

Undoubtedly, as Polkinghorne notes, mystery surrounds any attempt to resolve the foundational points of Christology and the incarnation. The church decided it had to simultaneously use both human and divine terms in speaking of Jesus.[42] The church realized the necessity for Jesus as simultaneously human and divine. It required Jesus as human for God could not have died. The church insisted on the divinity of Jesus. Otherwise Jesus' death would have no difference from other human deaths. Further, Jesus as only human could not provide our salvation which required God, a conclusion easily made from a bottom-up examination of the evidence.

Polkinghorne points out that three scientist-theologians—Barbour, Peacocke, and himself—approach Christology in similar fashion that is, discussion from below. Emphasis on incarnational Christology coheres with the life, death, and resurrection of Jesus along with the experience of the church with Jesus.[43] A corporate dimension exists as well as the personal. The New Testament writers spoke of the incorporation, *en Christo*, of the Christian with Jesus. The events of history ground faith in Jesus Christ, and the story of Jesus provides insight into God.[44] When Polkinghorne notes that the three scientist-theologians approach Christology from below, he means they examine the evidence and interpret it before reaching a conclusion. The evidence in this instance includes the experiences of Jesus and that

---

42. Polkinghorne, *Science and Christian Belief*, 134–36.
43. Polkinghorne, *Scientists as Theologians*, 70–72.
44. Polkinghorne, "Faith in Christ," 54.

of the church. Polkinghorne's bottom-up critical realist approach guides his epistemology. Similarly, I can say that my experience of God verifies without a doubt of his presence in me and in my life. I have experienced rich relationship many times through the years, and those experiences give me the evidence of his presence and care for me.

Polkinghorne refers to epistemology and ontology together. He says that bottom-up thought regarding Jesus moves from epistemology to ontology. Polkinghorne means when he notes epistemology models ontology that what one believes might possibly be the case. Early Christian writings provide evidence for Jesus, and their denial lacks weight. Jesus differs in a significant way from other religious leaders such as Buddha and Mohammed in that in midlife Jesus died an ignoble death, deserted by his followers. Clearly, something happened to continue his story. The New Testament writers point to the resurrection as that something. The validity of the resurrection rests in the appearance stories and the empty tomb.[45] When the Christian and the church experience God through the Holy Spirit, what one believes becomes one's experience and one's being, ontology. In this experience, the Christian has the assurance as do I of Rom 8:16, "It is that very Spirit bearing witness with our spirit that we are children of God."

Polkinghorne systematically examines the evidence for Jesus, and he notes the gospels do not appear to gather the full picture of who he was. While he questions Paul, it can equally well be argued that Paul did understand, that his Jewishness prevented his using the word "God" in his writing, and that he used YHWH, יְהוִֹה, *Yahweh*, instead. Clearly, Jesus understood who he was and the writers of the gospels must have understood that in order to retell the story.

I see in Jesus the personification of the divine in all that Jesus does and says. I thank God that he chose to appear in Jesus and that I can count of his presence with me for all time through the Holy Spirit. We have a marvelous story to tell, the heart of evangelism.

Conclusion

The Johannine gospel had an extremely profound character for Polkinghorne. He saw in it the union of the eternal with the temporal. Not only did John impact Polkinghorne, but the Christology of Paul in Colossians did so as well as did Moltmann's *The Crucified God* (1993).

Despair overtook Jesus' disciples following the crucifixion. Jesus, whom they deeply loved and who had made such a difference in a very short

---

45. Polkinghorne and Beale, *Questions of Truth*, 20–22.

time of only three years, died. The disciples arose that first Easter and went about business as usual while the women went to the tomb. Jon Meacham reminds us of what might have been their expectations:

> Yet there the disciples were on that first Easter, trying to make sense of a crucified king and an empty tomb. As they recalled the words of Jesus in his lifetime—words they had not understood at the time—early Christians started to work out a powerful new vision of human destiny. Those who believed in Jesus were to be saved, which did not mean a glorious eternity in an ethereal region. It meant, instead, a two-step process. First, when a believer died, his body was left behind and his soul went to a place of rest in preparation for the second phase: a bodily resurrection into "new heavens and a new earth"—not simply a heaven.[46]

Jesus the Crucified founds Christian faith. In the crucifixion, we see God suffering humiliation and abandonment by the world, willing to make such a sacrifice for his love of all creation. In the resurrection of Jesus who has received everything from God, eschatological hope arises for human destiny which had not existed previously. Then I can say with assurance that I reside with God through Jesus Christ today and look forward to the time when I will reside with him for all eternity. Hope is optimism that things will be better. Hope assures me that God is alongside now and through all eternity.

Jesus receives everything from God in creation and God includes Jesus in every aspect of creation from the beginning. In Jesus all things came into being (Col 1:16). He was life which was the light of all people and in whom all things consist and hold together. Jesus holds everything in creation together and restores humankind to perfect harmony in response from faith in him to God. He is head of the church, the firstborn from the dead; he has first place in everything, the one in whom the fullness of God dwells. He has reconciled all things to himself through the blood of the cross and as our Advocate reconciles us and presents us, blameless and irreproachable, to God. He precedes us as the firstborn from the dead, confirming the promise to us that we will also reside with him in eternity. In his life, we have the example for what it means to live in relationship with God.

Perhaps the greatest gift Jesus gave beyond the sacrifice of his life for salvation was his example to and encouragement of humankind in its relationships with each other along with the means to live without anxiety for tomorrow. He exhibits the love of God for all regardless of ethnicity, background, social status, political status, or wealth. Jesus demonstrates the inbreaking of his ministry in his relationships with the poor and oppressed, in

---

46. Meacham, "Heaven," 33.

his radical maleness, and in his loving and caring for others. All share equally the benefits of both creation and the reign of God in the kingdom. Moreover, God extends salvation through Jesus beyond Israel to the gentiles. His mission extends to all, the rich and privileged as well as the poor and marginalized. In his life, he extends salvation to all and reveals the God of love.

The primary stakes in the doctrine of Jesus Christ include revelation, salvation, and the sacraments. When we experience Jesus as well as God, we experience something in our lives larger than we are. It empowers as we recall Jesus' command: "Follow me" (Mark 1:17). Jesus as both divine and human helps us rethink who God is and redefines the human being in Christian anthropology.

Lohse notes that Jesus possessed both a soul and a body as well as two natures and two wills. Jesus existed in two natures and modes of being as both divine and human and together without separation, without ability to sin through the incarnated Logos, begotten of the essence of God, not created by God but conceived through the Holy Spirit, and born of the Virgin Mary. The presence of both the divine and the human in Jesus required existence of both the will of the divine and of the human as well as their natures. They shared equally in the full essence of God and of humanity. They were indistinct and yet not commingled. Were they distinct, Jesus would at times appear divine and at others human whereas he always appears as divine and human simultaneously.[47] God did not portion out the divine nature in Jesus. Instead, he shared that nature completely. God also did not limit the human side of Jesus who was fully divine and fully human. Jesus shared everything with God in the incarnation which meant the incarnation did not demean his nature or will. As our savior, he existed simultaneously as divine and human without separation of the divine from the human with both a soul and a body.

How can there be two natures? We can never fully understand that. However, we can relate to our human experience. We might think of a "close human relationship," e.g., a marriage marked in sharing intimately and knowing without discussion the other's thoughts and feelings. God's conception of Jesus through Mary and the Holy Spirit enabled the divine's becoming human, and Jesus' conception through the Holy Spirit clarifies the means of the incarnation. Explanation of the conception in Matt 1:23 tells us God is with us through Jesus Christ and the power of the Holy Spirit.

Jesus in his ministry opened new understanding of what it means to be human and to be his disciple, and his setting a new paradigm guides the church in relationship with God and others. God demonstrated power and governance over creation through the miracles of Jesus. Further the miracles of Jesus set him apart as a prophet and the long-awaited Messiah.

---

47. Lohse, *Short History*, 71–99.

5

Eschatology

Introduction

CHAPTER 5 DISCUSSES ESCHATOLOGY, a topic that is important for the thesis of how one would interpret and commend Christian faith in the contemporary world. Eschatology, the center of Polkinghorne's work, stands out for its importance and inclusion in the message of evangelism. As Polkinghorne so interprets eschatology, he notes that science introduces a pessimistic view for the future of the universe. Kathryn Tanner agrees,

> The scientific view that the world will end differs from the optimistic eschatological view. Christian eschatology has no more concern for how the world ends than Christian creation on how the world begins. Consequently, a reasonable theological position might turn questions of cosmology over to science. Following Old Testament, life often refers to fruitfulness and death to suffering, oppression, and isolation. Secondly the Old Testament identifies life with how one lives or dies, and specifically whether one lives or dies for God (others). Eternal life is now ours in the present as well as the future. Eternal life does not depend on the ultimate fate of the world. Eternal life places one in God and does not depend on the world. Eternal life is also identified with the kingdom of God.[1]

Christian eschatology has concern for human destiny, eternal life, not how the world began or will end. In terms of human destiny Christian eschatology says ultimate human destiny looks forward to resting in God always. Tanner reminds us to focus our attention on Jesus Christ and the future with God and not the sensational.

Robert John Russell elaborates on the view of science, explaining this view for the destiny of the universe.

---

1. Tanner, "Eschatology," 222–37.

There is growing evidence that the universe is marginally open (approximately flat) and destined to expand forever. Moreover, recent evidence indicates that its expansion rate is not slowing, as it would in the standard flat or open big bang models; instead it is actually speeding up. So the evidence for an open universe seems increasingly strong—although certainly not conclusive. In any case, the prognosis for biological life is grim:

- In 5 billion years, the sun will become a red giant, engulfing the orbits of Earth and Mars.
- In 40–50 billion years, star formation in our galaxy will have ended.
- In 10^{12} years, all massive stars will have become neutron stars or black holes.
- If *the universe is closed, then in 10^{12} years, the universe will have reached its maximum size and then will recollapse back to a singularity like the original hot big bang.*
- In 10^{31} years, protons and neutrons will decay into positrons, electrons, neutrinos, and photons.
- In 10^{34} years, dead planets, black dwarfs, and neutron stars will disappear their mass completely converted into energy, leaving only black holes, electron-positron plasma, and radiation. All carbon-based life forms will inevitably become extinct.
- *If the universe is open, it will continue to cool and expand forever. All of its early structure, from galaxies to living organisms to dust, will vanish forever without a trace.*[2]

Russell lays out the scientific worldview which on the surface appears grim. However, the cosmological times far exceed the time for *Homo sapiens* who appeared on earth two hundred thousand years ago.[3] The more important time occurs for the earth which current science predicts will only last another five billion years.[4] These points make it all the more important to gain a clear grasp of God's purpose in creation, the subject of eschatology. Eschatology addresses what the future holds for those in the present. Even apocalypticism does so as well. While I find it difficult to imagine that humankind itself has no future, I find that eschatology speaks of my future which is with God. Therefore, though humankind may disappear at some point, eschatological hope promises the future with God for those who have answered his call.

2. Russell, "Cosmology," 566.
3. Ayala, *Darwin's Gift*, 56–78.
4. Palen, *Understanding Our Universe*, 480.

John J. Collins says Friedrich Lücke introduced the term eschatology in 1832 in connection with the book of Revelation,[5] and David Bentley Hart presents detailed summary for the origins of apocalypticism, a species of eschatology.

> The first entirely eschatological faith of which we know is Zoroastrianism, established by the Persian prophet Zarathustra early in the sixth century BC (at least according to tradition).[6] The idea of a final judgment was so absolutely central to his creed that Zarathustra abandoned the ancient sacrificial cosmology of IndoIranian Aryan culture more or less completely—even demoting the *devas* (the gods of Persia and Bharata) to the status of devils—in order to proclaim in its place a cosmic history, with a beginning, middle, and end. Indeed, in the Zoroastrian vision of reality, the natural order is in no true sense a sacred reality at all, and hence it provides no proper model for religious practice or belief; it is at best ambiguous, a mixture of darkness and light, upon which both good and evil spiritual forces have worked. Nature as we know it is merely an episode within a greater story, the site of the spiritual struggle between good and evil. The true horizon of human and cosmic meaning lies beyond the closed circle of natural life and natural death, at the end of time; and the deepest truth of existence is to be found not through a perpetual ritual return to the circularity of organic nature, but through perseverance in the good and through anticipation of a divine future in which the cosmos and the self will be given their true forms. At the end of time, according to developed Zoroastrian thought, the world will be consumed in a great conflagration, the Wise Lord (Ahura Mazda) will pronounce his final verdict upon all things, the righteous will be raised to a new life in a perfected creation, and the wicked will be destroyed. Till then, the souls of the departed must cross the Bridge of Retribution, upon which the good will find easy passage to heaven and from which the evil will lunge into the darkness of hell. And, in its aboriginal

---

5. Collins, "Apocalyptic," 40–55.

6. "Eschatology as a term first appeared in 1677 in Abraham Calov's *Systema locorum theologicorum* (Sauter 1988: 499). Yet prior to the last century, in Barth's equally famous statement, Protestant theology had relegated eschatology to a perfectly harmless chapter at the conclusion of *Christian Dogmatics* (Barth 1933: 500). Its rediscovery came from biblical scholars such as Weiss and Schweitzer who looked again at the New Testament understanding of the Kingdom of God and saw the eschatological dimension of the gospel. Much debate then followed over the relationship of the present and future elements of the Kingdom and whether the New Testament speaks of a visible return of Jesus to inaugurate the definitive Kingdom (Schwöbel 2000: 217–241)" (Wilkinson, *Christian*, 2).

form, as well as in all its later, more dualistic forms (Mazdaism, Zurvanism, etc.), Zoroastrianism placed its emphasis upon the moral condition of the soul before God. Zoroastrian ideas, it is generally assumed, influenced the eschatological speculations of postexilic Judaism and, derivatively, those of Christianity and Islam (though an exact chronology of the emergence of certain ideas, such as resurrection, is difficult to establish).[7]

In summary, Zoroastrian apocalypticism poses the conflict between good and evil. The good God arises, and retribution for evil results. Easily, the connection between Zoroastrian apocalypticism and Judeo/Christian thought stands out. In Judeo/Christian thought, God vanquishes evil. Current thought prevalent in the culture often spills over into religion, and it seems plausible Zoroastrian thought raised questions in postexilic Judaism.[8] Zoroastrian apocalypticism more than likely influenced some Old and New Testament writers. It provided the means to discuss the current struggles in the culture in a veiled fashion. The early church fathers such as Augustine did not pick up the apocalyptic interpretations. While the apocalyptic texts may not apply in the current day, they are extremely important for their representation of a God who stands by Christians in the midst of great difficulty. That is the place of the apocalyptic in the modern world.

Brian Daley suggests Augustine adopted Tyconius' interpretation of Rev 20 as a figure of the current church. The Cappadocian Fathers followed Origen, including some of his approach to eschatology.[9] Basil of Caesarea referred to the biblical scenes of judgment and damnation whereas Gregory of Nazianzus posed a spiritualized understanding of judgment. Gregory of Nyssa expressed a restoration of humans to their original state. The fifth century features an unexplained foreboding of death and the end of the world.[10] We see here that the early church did not have a concrete position regarding apocalyptic eschatology; although, there did appear to be a foreboding of doom. Undoubtedly the fall of Rome in 410 CE influenced

---

7. Hart, "Death," 484–85.

8. Scholars date the apocalyptic sections of Daniel at ca. 165 BCE. This date follows the time when Antiochus IV erected the altar to Zeus in 167 BCE in the Jerusalem temple. Conservative scholars nonetheless strongly oppose any pseudonymous association for Daniel, despite the fact they accept it for 1 Enoch and 4 Ezra (Hill, *In God's Time*, 100–102).

9. Origen usually followed a straightforward reading of the biblical passages with a tendency to spiritualizing. He tended to consider the millennium passages in view of individual spiritual growth (Daley, "Eschatology," 97–98).

10. Ibid., 96–104. The Cappadocians included Basil, Gregory of Nazianzus, and Gregory of Nyssa.

the sense of doom in the fifth century CE.[11] Regarding the possibility of the apocalyptic for today, we need to ask how God speaks to us today when we face difficulty either individually or corporately. I believe that God speaks to us today through the sacred Judeo-Christian texts which represent him as always standing by from the suzerain covenant with Israel through the promise of eschatological hope in the resurrection.

Christopher Rowland suggests a different view.

> As Friedrich Engels rightly saw, the Book of Revelation offers an example of theology which is at the heart of earliest Christian conviction rather than being marginal to it. Millennial beliefs were still widely held from the second century onward, as is evident in the writings of Justin Martyr, Irenaeus, Hippolytus, Tertullian, and Lactantius. Augustine reinterpreted the millennium as the whole interval from the first advent to the last conflict, the "reign of the saints," namely, the church's. The hope for the messianic kingdom was for this earth. The expectation was for a time of great prosperity, in which people would enjoy long life, as is evident from the words which the early second-century writer Papias attributed to Jesus about a this-worldly hope for the future. He recalled a saying of Jesus in which he said the creation would return to and exceed the perfection of the original creation *(Adversus Haereses* v.33.3–34). This type of belief was the earliest phase of the Christian doctrine of hope in which an earthly kingdom of God was earnestly expected, echoing the Matthean version of the Lord's Prayer where there is an earnest longing for God's kingdom to "come on earth as in heaven." It is exactly this view set out in the final chapters of the Book of Revelation, where the New Jerusalem descends from heaven to a restored earth. A this-worldly promise in Rev 5:6–11 and 20:4–6 represents a markedly different kind of eschatology from the mainstream Christian tradition in the centuries after Augustine: a hope for this world rather than some transcendent realm. This exemplifies a fundamental division within the Christian world, ancient and modern, and concerns whether Christians believe the kingdom of God involves a hope for the transformation of this world and its structures. Over the first centuries, there was a diminution in the hope of the establishment of God's kingdom on earth and a greater emphasis on the transcendent realm as the goal of the Christian soul.[12]

11.. González, *Story*, 1:217.
12. Rowland, "Eschatology," 68–69.

Rowland argues that the dissonance within the church regarding eschatology has been there since its beginning and moved away from Papias' view that creation would achieve the fulfillment of the kingdom as Jesus instructed his disciples to pray for in the Lord's Prayer. No doubt, Revelation and 1 Thess 4:13–18 provided a source of hope during the intense martyrdom of Christians in the Roman Empire until Constantine in the fourth century, and it would have been easy to pick it up again when Rome fell in the next century. Not only did dissonance pervade the church, but various types of eschatology emerged.

Donald K. McKim offers a definition for various eschatological viewpoints including cosmic, futuristic, inaugurated individual, realized, and symbolic eschatology, and these various views connect with Craig C. Hill's discussion later. Cosmic eschatology examines the "last things" relative to the entire cosmos, including living creatures. In inaugurated eschatology, the eschaton emerges in Jesus' resurrection with other events such as the *parousia* and the resurrection of the dead in the future.[13] Futuristic theology which considers all eschatology as future has been the position of most theologians throughout the history of the church. Individual eschatology looks at the future related to events of individuals such as death and judgment. Charles H. Dodd (1884–1973) introduced realized eschatology which views eschatological events as realized in the New Testament period.[14] Tillich (1886–1965) and Reinhold Niebuhr (1892–1971) introduced symbolic eschatology which argues for the eschatological passages symbolically rather than literally. They indicate that human existence can never be fulfilled within history alone. Teleological eschatology contends the events of eschatology are occurring in human history and not in the future with every generation experiencing its eschatology.[15] Realized eschatology appears more consistent with the eschatology of Polkinghorne and also consistent with the realization of the kingdom of God. It also goes a long way in reconciling the views of science with the promises of God.

William J. Abraham expands regarding personal eschatology.

> In the case of personal eschatology, there is the fact that a human person is intimately related to the range of physics and chemistry that constitute one's body. Thus, it would appear that we cannot survive the dissolution of our body. In this instance, we are dealing with a philosophical challenge that has been with us for centuries and shows no signs of being resolved. Contrary to popular

---

13. Eschaton refers to a period where God's activity in creation changes.
14. McKim, *Westminster*, 92.
15. Ibid., 93.

opinion and to some philosophical circles, this is not simply a scientific problem that can be decided by more scientific research. Precisely because it is philosophical in nature and heavily contested, its weight as a source of cognitive dissonance for the robust theist's eschatology is limited. At the very least, it is a problem that everybody has to live with. More positively, the Christian theologian will want to develop an appropriate account of human nature and destiny that will accommodate the best knowledge we have but that will also rest on divine revelation and the wisdom of the church. Currently, mind-body substance dualism, double-aspect (mental/physical) dualism, a retrieval of the medieval vision of the soul as the form of the body, and nonreductive physicalism are in vogue. I leave open how far these options are or are not compatible with divine revelation.[16]

Personal eschatology should have the label as an eschatological species. And even that does not quite fit. Eschatology describes the destiny for humans and for all creation. I contend human destiny is the eschatological hope in the promises of God for all those who answer his call, yesterday, today, and tomorrow and has no relevance to what eventually happens to earth. We should focus only on the present and our present faith relationship with God. What happens to men and women can only be a part of the larger picture. Depending on where and how you look at the Scriptures, the picture can be bleak or hopeful for personal eschatology. I contend the picture is hopeful for personal eschatology.

Polkinghorne discusses the bleak picture in Mark for the future of creation and moves on to discuss the picture in Revelation. Mark 13:24–27 describes a bleak future for the cosmos when taken literally. Few Christians today expect to see Jesus riding in on the clouds like a "Christianized Valkyrie."[17] While it may be a mistake to take these images literally, ignoring them is a mistake.[18] The extended picture in Revelation points to two truths: that the world will not last forever and the reliability of trust in a faithful and loving God. History has shown the finitude of material and biological life. Life cannot go on forever. While life may not last on earth, it possibly may have migrated elsewhere in the galaxy or originated elsewhere. Inevitably, the question arises as to what does God plan? Science does not have the answer which rests finally with God. Jesus answered the question with the Sadducees, "And as for the dead being raised, have you not read in the book of Moses, in the story about the bush, how God said to him, 'I am the God

---

16. Abraham, "Eschatology," 592.
17. Polkinghorne, *Living with Hope*, 7.
18. Ibid., 7–8.

of Abraham, the God of Isaac, and the God of Jacob'? He is God not of the dead, but of the living; you are quite wrong" (Mark 12:26–27). Polkinghorne says if Abraham, Isaac, and Jacob mattered once, they matter always.[19] This verse connotes Polkinghorne's position regarding all creation and not simply humankind. He argues that if creation had importance for God in the beginning, it will always have importance. In other words according to Polkinghorne, God does not give up on creation, an important observation with respect to the pessimistic views of science for the future of the universe. Unfortunately, the bleak picture agrees to some extent with that of science, and theologians must be careful as science continually changes theory which impacts its predictions.

Polkinghorne points out that eschatology seems to provoke a split between theology and science. The majority of the texts in the classical and canonical periods speak of eschatology as continuity and discontinuity as evident in terms such as *"the new earth* and *the new heaven"* (emphasis Polkinghorne's). They say flesh and blood will not inherit the kingdom and talk of a new body altogether. Science and religion both speak about unseen reality. Science does so in the case of nuclear matter which it cannot see. However, scientists can detect its presence through the process of measurement whereas theologians cannot detect God through physical measurement. Physics develops theoretical models to explain the unseen reality of nuclear matter. Similarly, the unseen theologically makes sense from religious experience. In order for the concepts of religion and science to have ontological conviction, they must exceed explanation and carry *"understanding"* (emphasis Polkinghorne's). Scientists study the object within its realm, nuclear physics in quantum theory, and the physics of macro objects in classical physics. Similarly, to understand God requires entering into his realm in the way he has chosen to reveal, and the dialogue between theology and science should have a theological focus. The modern world has devalued cultural memory and replaced it with communal attention to their present and near future, and eschatology promises a good starting point for the discussion between religion and science.[20] Polkinghorne following his critically realistic approach argues for the unseen reality of religion analogous to the unseen reality of the quantum world of nuclear matter. Scientists easily accept this model which should encourage the acceptance for the unseen reality of God's activity and purpose in creation. Unseen reality offers a bridge for dialogue of religion with science, and the dialogue could move into the differing views regarding the future. Such a move has the possibility

---

19. Ibid., 8–10.
20. Polkinghorne and Welker, introduction to *End of the World*, 1–13.

of assisting theologians in examination of Scripture and the future of God. The comments regarding unseen reality also assist understanding how best to commend Christian faith in the contemporary world, the thrust for this work. For me the unseen reality concerns how God sees the ultimate future for creation. Yet, the future with God stands out as the important point and not the future of the material world which will always be subject to decay.

In summary, Zoroastrian thought plausibly influenced late Jewish and early Christian apocalyptic thought. In the instance of Christianity, the apocalyptic afforded the means to offer veiled assurance to Christians facing Roman persecution, and the next section will take up apocalypticism in detail.

Eschatology

Apocalypticism

Hill helpfully explains the difference between eschatology and the apocalyptic: "*Eschatology* is a system of beliefs about God's ultimate victory. An *apocalyptic* eschatology is one such system."[21]

Bill T. Arnold's discussion regarding the nature of apocalyptic literature is appropriate at this point.

> The apocalypse genre denotes literature containing a unique manner and style of communication and having in common a basic content. Apocalyptic books characteristically are visionary, containing an initial revelation that is symbolic and mysterious, requiring interpretation by a heavenly mediator. Most of these writings use *vaticinium ex eventu*, "prediction after the fact," and the name of the author, if given, is assumed to be a pseudonym, most claiming as authors a venerated hero of Israelite faith (such as Enoch, Abraham, Isaiah, or Ezra), who lived centuries before the books were actually written.... Although the ancients did not formulate a list of works identified as apocalypses, contemporary scholars have isolated seventeen books that fit this category, ranging from the mid-second century BCE to the second century CE, in addition to several more from the Dead Sea Scrolls.[22]

Arnold makes a good observation when he says some apocalyptic addresses events after the fact. Such a viewpoint would argue Revelation as likely current with the events of the time of its writing with the purpose to

---

21. Hill, *In God's Time*, 63.
22. Arnold, "Old Testament," 33.

offer comfort to Christians risking martyrdom for their faith. Further, Revelation's author wrote the text 92–96 CE at the end of Emperor Domitian's reign.[23] Therefore, the comfort for today rests in the scriptural evidence that God stands by, particularly in the Johannine texts that begin with John 14.

Hill notes most Hebrew apocalyptic literature does not appear in the Hebrew Bible with the major exception of Daniel. Apocalyptic comes from the Greek *apo*, "from," and *kalypsis*, "covering." It means to uncover or reveal something previously unknown. The old age will soon come to an end, ushering in a new. In the meantime, conflict erupts between good and evil as history moves toward its inevitable deterministic conclusion characterized by judgment.[24] Judaism did not include most of the Hebrew apocalyptic literature in its canon which argues for its lesser importance. The stress between good and evil in apocalyptic literature also suggests that the real interest in play is theodicy rather than absolute prediction. Apocalyptic literature in the instance of the early Christians would have encouraged them to endure the present for a brighter tomorrow. Indeed, such confidence resonates with the eschatological hope of Polkinghorne.

Hill says the name of a noted figure usually appeared pseudonymously as the apocalyptic author, and generally, pseudonymous apocalyptic writings had a hazy character at best regarding the distant past but were increasingly accurate regarding the more recent. Their knowledge of the future appeared extremely speculative and often proved completely wrong.[25] Several features appear in apocalyptic literature including the visionary nature, prediction after the fact, pseudonymous author, and a brighter tomorrow. The early church had a variety of interpretations for the apocalyptic literature.

Daley takes up Hippolytus's exploration of the apocalyptic.

> Tertullian's contemporary, a certain Hippolytus—probably a Greek-speaking bishop from western Asia Minor—took up the tradition of biblical apocalyptic in his treatise *On the Christ and the Antichrist* and in his commentary on Daniel, the earliest Christian biblical commentary. Hippolytus is not a millenarian, and in these works he is mainly concerned with what apocalyptic literature has to tell us about the person of Christ.[26]

Hippolytus reminds us of the importance of revelation to reveal God and in the apocalyptic Jesus Christ. In short, the theologian should not easily dismiss a particular text because he or she does not accept the genre. Instead,

---

23. Brown, *Introduction*, 774.
24. Hill, *In God's Time*, 59–63.
25. Ibid., 99–100.
26. Daley, "Eschatology," 96. Millennium refers to the thousand years in Revelation.

the texts provide an important source for theological reflection regarding Jesus and an important point for the evangelistic aspect of this work. God will stand by as the Scriptures show that he has always done so and promises in eschatological hope to do so for all time. No examination of apocalypticism would be complete without the inclusion of John Nelson Darby and his work, work which remains foundational for contemporary apocalypticism.

Darby, who published his first work on prophecy in 1829, "Reflections upon the Prophetic Inquiry and the Views Advanced in It," influenced apocalyptic thought over the last two centuries.[27] The eschatology and ecclesiology of Darby follow from his dispensational views.[28] Hal Lindsey, Tim LaHaye, and Jerry Jenkins wrote about the apocalyptic in the twentieth century, and Lindsey closely aligns his apocalypticism with that of Darby. As Robert G. Clouse notes,

> Basic to Hal Lindsey's eschatology is his identification of various "signs" that prove we are now living at the end of the age or, as he put it, in the "terminal generation." Behind the miracles and wonders which scripture predicts will accompany the collapse of our civilization in the end times is the power of Satan himself. These wonders include famines, earthquakes, unusual weather, increasing crime rates, and the appearance of "false" religions.[29]

27. Darby was the first to state the doctrine of the rapture, understanding the pre-tribulation rapture comes from the nature of the church as God's special work (Crutchfield, *Origins*, 165–203). John Nelson Darby in his "premillennial dispensationalism" produced much of the interpretation that led to today's premillennial movement. Darby appealed in his day and today to those who follow biblical literalism (Hill, *In God's Time*, 199–203).

28. "As the name suggests, dispensationalists taught that God deals with humanity through a series of distinct periods. Although they differed on the exact number of these eras, most believed that there are seven dispensations: innocence, conscience or moral responsibility, human government, promise, the law, the church, and the millennium. In each of these ages, there is a unique revelation of the divine will, and humankind is tested by obedience to this standard. The seventh dispensation, the millennium, will be inaugurated by the return of Christ in two stages: first, a secret rapture which removes the church before the great tribulation devastates the earth and second, Christ's coming with the church to establish the kingdom" (Clouse, *Fundamentalist*, 264). Traces of dispensationalism appear in the Patristic period. However, Darby becomes the first to systematize dispensationalism (Crutchfield, *Origins*, 16). Charles C. Ryrie, a significant dispensationalist, saw evidence of dispensationalist thought in Justin Martyr (100–165), Irenaeus (130–200), Clement of Alexandria (150–215), and Augustine (354–430) (Eaton, "Beware," 129–40). "Dispensation represents a new period of revelation and God's dealings with humankind, requiring interpretation in terms of the dispensations immediately before and after. Each dispensation has a christological character and looks at God's progressive plan of salvation. Only God's interaction with humankind, not his character, changes" (Eaton, "Beware," 141–42).

29. Clouse, *Fundamentalist*, 267.

Contemporary apocalypticism picked up on the signs and continually looked at world events and world leaders in order to identify the Antichrist associated with millenarian time and the final great battle of Armageddon. Lindsey's work received much attention for its dramatic portrayal of the future.

> In *The Late Great Planet Earth* (1970), Lindsey deals specifically with the signs of the times that make up the prophetic "jigsaw puzzle" of end-time events. The key pieces in this puzzle are the creation of the Jewish state of Israel in 1948; the recovery of the ancient capital city of Jerusalem in 1967; the rise of Russia as a powerful nation and enemy of Israel; the Arab confederation arrayed against the state of Israel, the rise of a great military power in East Asia (China) that can field untold millions of soldiers; the movement toward European integration; the revival of the dark occult practices of ancient Babylon; the increase of wars, earthquakes, famines, and pollution; the apostasy of Christian churches from historic Christianity; the move toward one-world religion and government; and the decline of the United States as a world power.[30]

Lindsey's eschatology is best categorized as apocalyptic eschatology. The public could easily respond to Lindsey's portrayal during the Cold War which saw Russia as the villain and the Antichrist. Revelation discusses the state of Israel, and the early Jewish Christians would have responded favorably, especially those who had expected a Jewish Messiah.[31]

However, these are only a few of Lindsey's details as Clouse continues to explain.

> Other pieces of the puzzle which were yet to fall into place were the secret rapture of the church (which he expected to occur in 1981), the seven-year tribulation period following this event, and the visible return of Christ. The sequence of events that will occur during the tribulation are those which many dispensationalist prophetic preachers tend to identify. Among

---

30. Ibid., 267–68.

31. Rev 7:4–8: "And I heard the number of those who were sealed, one hundred forty-four thousand, sealed out of every tribe of the people of Israel: From the tribe of Judah twelve thousand sealed, from the tribe of Reuben twelve thousand, from the tribe of Gad twelve thousand, from the tribe of Asher twelve thousand, from the tribe of Naphtali twelve thousand, from the tribe of Manasseh twelve thousand, from the tribe of Simeon twelve thousand, from the tribe of Levi twelve thousand, from the tribe of Issachar twelve thousand, from the tribe of Zebulun twelve thousand, from the tribe of Joseph twelve thousand, from the tribe of Benjamin twelve thousand sealed."

ESCHATOLOGY 91

them are the appearance of the Antichrist, who will head up a revived Roman empire composed of the European Community (the United States will have faded from the scene because of its spiritual, political, economic, moral, and military decline), the rebuilding of the Jewish Temple, the assault on Palestine by the Arab-African confederacy followed by the even larger invasion of the region by Russia (the Gog of Ezek 38:16), and the showdown battle of Armageddon where the European alliance, after having defeated the Russians, will be attacked by an army of 200 million Asians. A nuclear exchange will ensue that will kill a third of the world's population, but just as the battle reaches its peak, Christ will suddenly appear to halt the hostilities and to protect believers from total destruction.[32]

As we move into more of Lindsey's thought, we see it can be easy to misuse his work evangelistically to strike fear into those who have not responded to the gospel. Jesus issued an invitation that persuaded one of the good news of the arrival of the kingdom. His call for repentance was not one to strike fear into those who heard the call. He called for those around him to turn from their current practices to those of the kingdom with the realization the current practices did not provide them the meaning and the hope resident in the kingdom. Eschatology offers hope and not the fear of the apocalyptic literature. In eschatological hope, we have the promise of the presence of God for all time, today and in the future.

Exact timing is also important for Lindsey. Clouse comments helpfully on Lindsay's use of the forty-year period.

> The critical point in this scenario is Lindsay's concept that a generation in the Bible is forty years. From Jesus' statement in Matt 24:34—"this generation shall not pass away until all these things take place"—he concludes that all these things could take place within forty years after the founding of Israel. Thus, he predicted the return of Christ in 1988 and the rapture of the church seven years earlier.[33]

The date 1988 occurred forty years following the creation of the Jewish state of Israel in 1948, which Lindsey concluded started the time clock. The tribulation period begins, according to Lindsey, in 1981, and the rapture of the church at the beginning of the seven-year tribulation which he referred to as pretribulation premillennialism. Lindsey contended the church did not go through the tribulation and the millennial period. Still, I cannot

32. Clouse, *Fundamentalist*, 268.
33. Ibid., 268.

overlook the fact Lindsey's thought might work better with the view of science for the future of the cosmos. Astronomers expect the sun will consume most of its hydrogen, that hydrogen fusion will cease, and that the sun will become a red giant star expanding and perhaps engulfing the terrestrial planets. Life will no longer be possible on earth.[34] However, while Lindsey's work might cohere with science, it does not cohere with the position that the apocalyptic Scriptures most likely addressed the times when those texts were written. Even more sensational in the contemporary period were the novels of LaHaye and Jenkins.

As David Wilkinson remarks,

> In 1995, LaHaye and Jenkins wrote the first novel in what came to be known as the *Left Behind* (1995) series (LaHaye and Jenkins 1995).... It is a publishing phenomenon, having sold over 40 million copies worldwide, been translated into over 20 languages, and is a regular feature of the New York Times Bestseller List. It has spawned a children's series of books, movies, games and even calendars.[35]

For some reason, the sensational fascinates the public. Unfortunately, it feeds on their fears and causes them to not look inwardly. They can blame everything on outside influence over which they have no control. But the evangelistic message calls one to look within and to Jesus Christ, an important point for this work. Polkinghorne takes the high road and avoids the apocalyptic in his discussion of eschatology.

From the discussion of historical and contemporary apocalyptic, our discussion now turns to theological examination. Hill has made a major contribution which I examine for its importance to the evangelistic thrust of this book.

Hill says prudent scholarship takes Daniel and Revelation into account with the context of the apocalyptic eschatological tradition of the time and includes other writings such as those of 1 Enoch and 4 Ezra, to mention but two. Clearly, many of the events prophesied in these writings did not come to pass in their time or in later times to the current day. Did the writers incorrectly assess the revelation? At the very least, the writings contain significant theological material the scholar cannot ignore, particularly as regards God's role in human events and history. In the final analysis, Daniel and Revelation are both Scripture and apocalypses, conclusions the scholar must keep balanced.[36] Hill rightly turns to Daniel and Revelation. Eaton

---

34. Palen, *Understanding Our Universe*, 480.
35. Wilkinson, *Christian*, 4.
36. Hill, *In God's Time*, 94–98.

remarks that Darby in his work argued all prophecy required fulfillment.[37] Darby's view that all prophecy required fulfillment drove his apocalypticism and the search for fulfillment of the Old and New Testament prophecies whereas Hill argues that the dates of the apocalyptic can be determined from the accuracy of the events portrayed.

Hill comments scholars choose the date for the writing of a particular apocalypse as the time in the apocalypse when the accurately recorded events shift to the inaccurate.[38] Scholars date the apocalyptic sections of Daniel circa 165 BCE. This date follows the time, 167 BCE, when Antiochus IV erected the altar to Zeus in Jerusalem temple.[39] Approaching Daniel as possibly referring to Antiochus IV makes far greater sense than seeking coherence with Revelation or with looking to a later leader such as one in the contemporary period. Further, the Bible contains a library of books with varying genre and purpose. It seems difficult to argue Daniel received inspiration regarding events 200–250 years later, the date for composition of Revelation,[40] or 2,200 years later to the contemporary period. From Daniel, Hill turns to Revelation.

Hill says with respect to Revelation that like Antiochus IV in Daniel, Caesar Domitian stands out as a likely subject in Revelation. While Daniel and his friends survive the lions' den, the Christians go to their death there. Christendom often divides over whether or not to relegate Revelation solely to the Roman era or to see its prophecy as yet unfilled and perhaps applying in the current day. The former implies one finishes with the book when one completes its interpretation. The second view, while seeing it as applicable to the current context, often does little more.[41] Caesar Domitian martyred Christians, and they were the ones who needed hope in that day, not two thousand years later.[42] Yet Hill's view does not detract from the value of Daniel and Revelation in the current period. It allows for their presentation of how a loving and faithful God responds to his people throughout history.

Central to the apocalyptic was the millennium, the thousand-year period in Revelation. Christopher Partridge points out that "during the nineteenth century, two broad streams of millennial thought emerged, postmillennialism and premillennialism."[43] Timothy P. Weber expands on the millenarian:

37. Eaton, "Beware," 151–52.
38. Hill, *In God's Time*, 100–129.
39. Ibid., 100–102.
40. Brown, *Introduction*, 774.
41. Hill, *In God's Time*, 110–11.
42. González, *Story*, 1:36–38.
43. Partridge, "End Is Nigh," 193–212. Postmillennialists believe Christ returns

> Historically, premillennialists have used both historicist and futurist interpretations of Revelation, though today the futurist approach dominates. Either way, their crucial text is Revelation 20, which includes two resurrections separated a thousand years. Premillennialists take this passage literally and see it as the clearest evidence for an interregnum between Christ's Parousia and the last judgment. They also equate the first resurrection of Revelation 20 and the rapture of 1 Thess 4:13–18. Thus, all the "dead in Christ" and those alive at Christ's coming "will reign with him for a thousand years."[44]

Biblical stories often carried a hero element without great attention to detail. The stories of Samson in the Old Testament supply a good example. In the instance of Greek literature, Thucydides' (ca. 460–ca. 400 BCE) *History of the Peloponnesian War* provides a good secular example.[45] The dramatic style and telling of the story had greater importance than did accuracy, and some scholars make the mistake of applying contemporary standards to ancient literature.

Some in the early church had a different view of the millennium. As Wilkinson notes:

> Irenaeus saw the millennium as a time where God's rule was fulfilled in the present creation and to offer time for the additional spiritual growth most believers needed before they would be ready to enter God's glorious presence. This intermediate state needed the presence of the glorified Christ on the Earth to initiate the millennium, so this general model became known as premillennialism.[46]

Irenaeus differed from Augustine in his view of moral evil, as John Hick points out:

> Irenaeus accordingly thinks of man as originally an immature being upon whom God could not yet profitably bestow his highest gifts: "God had power at the beginning to grant perfection to man; but as the latter was only recently created, he could not possibly have received it, or even if he had received it could he have contained it, or containing it, could he have retained."[47]

---

following the millennium, and premillennialists believe he returns before the millennium, Christ's thousand-year reign in Revelation.

44. Weber, "Millennialism," 367.
45. Thucydides, *History*.
46. Wilkinson, *Christian*, 189.
47. Hick, *Evil*, 212.

Irenaeus argued that man initially immature matures through moral development and growth to the ultimate perfection God intended.[48] Hick says Augustine blamed evil on creation through the free-will defense. That is, God permits human free-will and moral evil results.[49] Hick's proposals regarding Irenaeus offer a possible explanation for his position. Irenaeus viewed humans as gaining perfection through the soul-making experience of evil. The view that the millennium offers a time for future growth fits his soul-making theology.

Then there is the school of thought that does not accept the millennium, the amillennialists. Of this group, Weber states:

> Amillennialism ("no Millennialism"—in Greek putting an alpha [α] before a word negates it) rejects the idea of an earthly millennium at any time. It believes that OT prophecies about a future golden age were fulfilled in the coming of Christ and the Christian church or point ahead to the new heaven and earth to be created after the last judgment. Jesus declared the kingdom was present in his ministry, which was affirmed at his ascension and "coronation" in heaven (Acts 2:36; Eph 1:20–23). Amillennialists claim that, apart from Revelation 20, no other text describes a time gap between the resurrection of the dead and the last judgment or separates in time the resurrection of the just and the unjust.[50]

It seems difficult to ignore Weber's point here. At any rate, this work argues for a general eschatology and not for an apocalyptic one. This view lends greater credence to the evangelistic message of invitation. Nonetheless, a gap exists between the religious view and that of science for the destiny of creation.

Abraham's point, which we cannot avoid, regarding the difference in how religion and science see the future asks to what extent Polkinghorne's work, the subject of this work, responds. Abraham notes:

> The situation with respect to cosmic eschatology is strikingly different. The picture of the future of the universe currently on offer is grim indeed; it is utterly at odds with the optimistic temporal scenario given in the faith of the church. We have an arresting contrast between what is expected on the basis of faith in divine revelation and what is predicted on the basis of science.[51]

48. Ibid., 212–18.
49. Ibid., 3–14.
50. Weber, "Millennialism," 368.
51. Abraham, "Eschatology," 592–93.

Polkinghorne's argument in eschatological hope discussed later responds to Abraham's observation. However, while the creation of the world may seem pointless to us, we do not know how God views it. Tanner, as noted earlier, argues for greater concern for eternal life and less concern for how the world will end.

Abraham, however, continues to point to the dissonance, recognizing the difficulty for theology in the competing views of eschatology and science.

> The universe faces a highly problematic future. Its long-term history is controlled by the competing effects of expansion (the "explosive" consequences of the big bang) and gravity (drawing matter together). These contrasting tendencies are very evenly balanced and we do not know for certain which will win in the end. If expansion predominates (the possibility currently favored by most cosmologists), cosmic history will continue forever in a world growing steadily colder and more dilute. Eventually, all will decay into low grade radiation. If gravity predominates, the present expansion will one day be halted and reversed. What began with a big bang will end with the big crunch, as the universe implodes into a cosmic melting pot.

It is by no means clear that the theologian can make in this instance the kind of obvious revision that was possible in the case of the conflict between evolution and divine creation. The standard scientific account of the *telos* of evolution is compatible prima facie with a high view of human agents as made in the image of God. The standard scientific accounts of the end of the world as envisaged by science are prima facie at odds with the *telos* of the world as gloriously redeemed by God. We have on our hands a source of significant dissonance between theology and science.[52]

Walter Brueggemann reminds us at this juncture of the unique role of the prophet.

"The prophet must speak metaphorically about hope but concretely about the real newness that comes to us and redefines our situation."[53] When I examine apocalyptic literature from the vantage of prophecy, I conclude it addresses the problems in the culture at that time and extends metaphorical language to that of the apocalyptic. Then the apocalyptic literature becomes a form of the prophetic not of future events but of current events, consistent with Brueggemann's remarks.

---

52. Ibid., 592–93.
53. Brueggemann, *Prophetic*, 67 (italics original).

In the context of this work, eschatology does not focus on the apocalyptic aspects. It concentrates on the eschatological hope in the resurrection of Jesus Christ and its promise for Christian resurrection and Christian destiny. Actually, the destiny of the universe does not present a serious difficulty. What presents the difficulty concerns the destiny for our solar system. More than likely, the universe will outlast it for a considerable time. Physicists contend the solar system as we know it will disappear in five billion years or so. In that time, the sun will have exhausted its hydrogen and expanded as a red giant star to at least the orbit of Venus. The sun will likely absorb the planets through Venus and possibly Earth. At the very least, Earth will no longer exist as we know it, and all earthly life will no longer exist.[54]

Jürgen Moltmann and His Significance for Polkinghorne's Eschatological Hope

Polkinghorne read Jürgen Moltmann's *The Crucified God* (1993) when he prepared for seminary, and it had an impact on him.[55] Further, both Moltmann and N. T. Wright are important for inclusion with the work of Polkinghorne to supply as complete a picture as possible for eschatological hope. Polkinghorne approaches the subject as a scientist, Moltmann as a theologian, and Wright as a New Testament scholar. I begin with Moltmann.

> In actual fact, however, eschatology means the doctrine of Christian hope, which embraces both the object hoped for and also the hope inspired by it. . . . Christianity is eschatology, is hope, forward looking and forward moving, and therefore also revolutionizing and transforming the present. Eschatology cannot be excluded or set apart. Christianity is eschatology, the passionate longing for Christ and for his return. Eschatology also includes the God made known in the Exodus and in the prophets of Israel. Theology must be constructed in the realm of its goal and therefore includes eschatology.[56]

Eschatology then is Christian faith and Christian faith is eschatology and more importantly eschatological hope. Eschatological hope can give one strength in the darkest of times whereas apocalypticism cannot. As I have argued, eschatology should be seen as present and not as some far-off time or last thing.

54. Palen, *Understanding Our Universe*, 480.
55. Moltmann, *Crucified God*.
56. Moltmann, *Theology of Hope*, 16

Moltmann goes on to argue against referring to eschatology as doctrine of the last things. The word "eschatology" is incorrect, as a doctrine of last things is incorrect. Such a doctrine of last things ignores the present. Further, it fails to look forward in making statements about Christ in the present without relevance to the future. Christ today points to Christ future. Any statement about Christ includes who he was, is, and will be as in Col 1:27.[57] I agree with Moltmann here. I also agree that humans have more concern for the next hundred years and the end of life issues than some far-off event at the end of time. Jesus' ministry called one to the present and argued for the benefits of the kingdom in the present and not in some far off time. It becomes too easy to replace thought of the kingdom present now with Jesus' future complete establishment of the kingdom. Evangelism proclaims the kingdom as both present and future.

Summary of Polkinghorne's Eschatology

Polkinghorne proposes that we summarize a viable approach to eschatological expectation in terms of four propositions.

1. If the universe is a creation, it must make sense everlastingly, and so ultimately it must be redeemed from transience and decay.
2. If human beings are creatures loved by their Creator, they must have a destiny beyond their deaths. Every generation must participate equally in that destiny, in which it will receive the healing of its hurts and the restoration of its integrity, thereby participating for itself in the ultimate fulfillment of the divine purpose.
3. In so far as present human imagination can articulate eschatological expectation, it has to do so within the tension between continuity and discontinuity. There must be sufficient continuity to ensure that individuals truly share in the life to come as their resurrected selves and not as new beings simply given the old names. There must be sufficient discontinuity to ensure that the life to come is free from the suffering and mortality of the old creation.
4. The only ground for such a hope lies in the steadfast love and faithfulness of God that is testified to by the resurrection of Jesus Christ. Christian belief must not

---

57. Ibid., 17–18.

lose its nerve about eschatological hope. A credible theology depends upon it and, in turn, a trinitarian and incarnational theology can assure us of its credibility.[58]

The previous comments summarize Polkinghorne's position regarding eschatology and point to his development of eschatological hope. His first comment responds to Abraham's earlier challenge that theologians need to work through the dissonance between theology and science regarding the fate of creation. Polkinghorne's point is well taken despite the fact we have no idea how God might transform creation. The Scriptures do not directly address the future of the earth, much less the entire universe. It did not occur until two thousand years later that the earth and the universe had a limited life, and we can only infer God has it all under control. Our future lies not in the material world, but it lies in our destiny with God for eternity. The Scriptures clearly point to the final destiny of Christians with God for all eternity. Polkinghorne points to discontinuity and continuity, a theme which he shares with Moltmann. Simply put, continuity refers to our having lived on earth. Discontinuity means there must be a disconnect between this material body and our new spiritual body. Further, our spiritual body is not a new creation out of nothing but a transformation from here to eternity. God grounds hope in Jesus Christ, the christological emphasis for Polkinghorne.

Conclusion

The apocalyptic always seems to gather the most attention as we saw in the success of *The Late Great Planet Earth* (1970) and the *Left Behind* (1995) series. Hill and others have pointed out the limitations for the apocalyptic literature. It represented the prophetic in a particular time, and the lack of later fulfillment after two thousand years supports that conclusion. Eschatological hope on the other hand does not rely on specific times, places, people, or events. Instead, it rests solidly in the faithful and trustworthy God who suffered with Jesus, stood by him, and stands by us today. It resonates with Paul's comments in 1 Cor 15. With the resurrection as foundation, we too have a future destiny with Jesus in God. Following John 1 and Col 1, he is our beginning and end in whom all things consist and are held together.

I noted earlier the possible misuse of Lindsey's thought. It can be easy to misuse his work evangelistically to strike fear into those who have not responded to the gospel. Unfortunately, some ministers may have done so. For some reason, the sensational fascinates the public. Unfortunately, it feeds on

---

58. Polkinghorne, *God of Hope*, 148–49.

their fears and causes them to not look inwardly. They can blame everything on outside influence over which they have no control. The evangelistic message calls one to look within and to Jesus Christ, an important point for this work. Jesus issued an invitation that persuaded one of the good news of the arrival of the kingdom. His call for repentance was not one to strike fear into those who heard the call. He called for those around him to turn from their current practices to those of the kingdom with the realization the current practices did not offer them the meaning and the hope resident in the kingdom.

Perhaps the greatest difficulty is the fact that science has a different view for the fate of creation than does religion. The crucifixion and resurrection discussed later assure us of God's faithful and loving care. Going back to the Colossians text, Paul declares, "For in him all things in heaven and on earth were created, things visible and invisible, whether thrones or dominions or rulers or powers—all things have been created through him and for him. He himself is before all things, and in him all things hold together" (Col 1:16–17). It does not make sense, despite the modern scientific view, that when God created everything in Jesus and holds it together in him creation has no future, despite the point Tanner argues that eschatology has little concern for how the world will end:

> The scientific view that the world will end differs from the optimistic eschatological view. Christian eschatology has no more concern for how the world ends than Christian creation on how the world begins. . . . Eternal life is now ours in the present as well as the future. Eternal life does not depend on the ultimate fate of the world. Eternal life places one in God and does not depend on the world. Eternal life is also identified with the kingdom of God.[59]

Her point resonates with the eschatological hope of Polkinghorne and reminds the church to place its focus on Jesus Christ and not the sensational of the apocalyptic literature. And Polkinghorne tells us, "If Abraham, Isaac, and Jacob mattered once, they mattered always."[60] Our eschatological hope rests in God who does not forget.

Consistent with the thesis of this work, eschatological hope in Polkinghorne serves to assist the commendation of Christian faith in the contemporary world—apocalypticism should be excluded in the commendation for Christian faith. It does not give hope in the current time or support one in difficulty. Eschatological hope and the kingdom of God do. They do

59. Tanner, "Eschatology," 222–37.
60. Polkinghorne, *Living with Hope*, 8–10.

because they provide the promise of God's faithfulness to those in the present regardless of how the earth will end five billion years hence.

In conclusion, eschatology and apocalypticism in particular can lead to too much emphasis of the future. Jesus called everyone to the kingdom in the present. Eschatological hope in the resurrection points solely to the presence of God now and always. I agree with Dodd that biblical eschatology is realized eschatology and with Moltmann and Wright, as discussed later in chapter 10, that 1 Thess 4:15 in the Greek means presence of Christ and not second coming.

6

Announcement of the Kingdom

Introduction

JESUS BEGINS HIS MINISTRY in Mark preaching the gospel of the "kingdom of God" and calling for repentance as the kingdom has come near. As Raymond E. Brown (1997) points out, the sense of the passage conveys the message that the kingdom has begun to make itself felt with the coming of Jesus.[1] In John 3 and Matt 10:15, Jesus explains one must be born again and receive the kingdom as a child in order to share in the kingdom, and Jesus uses parables to explain the kingdom through analogy. Jesus, following his announcement of the coming of the kingdom in the present time, comments on it in the greatest detail in the Sermon on the Mount which states that kingdom life differs from secular, and he says that many in his presence would not taste of death until they saw him coming in the kingdom.

I believe that Jesus in his life, death, and resurrection conquered sin and evil for all time. In that sense, Jesus establishes the kingdom which has grown over the centuries. While sin and evil continue to persist, Jesus has conquered their impact on those who have turned to him. The first meaning of the Greek παρουσία, *parousia*, in 1 Thess 4:15 is presence; therefore, when I take the interpretation of παρουσία, *parousia*, in 1 Thess 4:15 as the presence of God, the presence of the kingdom now and developing falls into place. Second, the acceptance of the realized eschatology promoted by Dodd reinforces it. My conclusions here suggest the possibility of theologically reexamining the doctrines of eschatology and the kingdom.

Walter W. Wessel (1990) and Raymond E. Brown (1997) explain the character of time in the Mark 1:15 text announcing the coming of the kingdom. "Time" in Mark 1:15 translates the Greek καιρός, *kairos*, which refers to an event in time rather than ongoing chronological time and in the current instance refers to God's action.[2] The translation of the Greek ἐγγίζω,

---

1. Brown, *Introduction*, 128–30.
2. Wessell, "Mark," 618–31.

eggizo, in the same verse implies the kingdom makes itself felt in the world with the coming of Jesus Christ,[3] and the kingdom is both present and future.[4] The "kingdom of God" is manifest in both present and future reality and looks forward to the time when God conquers sin and evil, restores creation, and reigns over new creation. A new relationship with God through Jesus Christ came with the coming of the kingdom, for God appears in Jesus as divine and human, reminding us that he faithfully appeared throughout the Old Testament. His appearance as Jesus led to the establishment of the church whereas his appearance to Moses led to the establishment of Israel.

Two significant events stand out in the Bible. In the first, God appears to Moses and announces:

> I have observed the misery of my people who are in Egypt; I have heard their cry on account of their taskmasters. Indeed, I know their sufferings, and I have come down to deliver them from the Egyptians, and to bring them up out of that land to a good and broad land, a land flowing with milk and honey, to the country of the Canaanites, the Hittites, the Amorites, the Perizzites, the Hivites, and the Jebusites. (Exod 3:7–8)

In the second, Jesus says: "From that time Jesus began to proclaim, 'Repent, for the kingdom of heaven has come near'" (Matt 4:17). Both events are especially significant in that they lead to the establishment of Israel in the first instance and to the establishment of the church in the second. In Luke, Jesus lays out his mission:

> And the scroll of the prophet Isaiah was given to him. He unrolled the scroll and found the place where it was written: "The Spirit of the Lord is upon me, because he has anointed me to bring good news to the poor. He has sent me to proclaim release to the captives and recovery of sight to the blind, to let the oppressed go free, to proclaim the year of the Lord's favor." And he rolled up the scroll, gave it back to the attendant, and sat down. The eyes of all in the synagogue were fixed on him. Then he began to say to them, "Today this scripture has been fulfilled in your hearing." (Luke 4:17–21)

Jesus' first and continuing concern addressed the needs of the people. Jesus pointed to the importance for relationship with God, a fact which stood out in the early church when he responded to the Sadduceean lawyer:

---

3. Brown, *Introduction*, 128–30.
4. Wessell, "Mark," 618–31.

> "Teacher, which commandment in the law is the greatest"? He said to him, "You shall love the Lord your God with all your heart, and with all your soul, and with all your mind. This is the greatest and first commandment. And a second is like it: You shall love your neighbor as yourself. On these two commandments hang all the law and the prophets." (Matt 22:36–40)

Jesus' words here clearly explain that the *Torah* addressed relationship not just morality, and the same extends to the "kingdom of God." Christian faith concerns relationship with God and with one another.

God intervened in Exodus in concern for his people, his relational concern. When God intervened in the Exodus account, he entered into the suzerain covenant with Israel, detailed to great extent in the Torah which outlined the social, ethical, and religious practices for Israel.[5] Similarly, God through Jesus outlined in the fifth through the seventh chapters of Matthew social, ethical, and religious practices of the "kingdom of heaven," referred to as the "kingdom of God" in Mark. In the exodus, God stood alongside Israel as Israel struggled toward the promise. In Matthew, Jesus promises God will also stand alongside his people in the kingdom, particularly in the second beatitude which says: "Blessed are those who mourn, for they will be comforted" (Matt 5:4). "Comfort" in this text translates the Greek παρακληθήσουται from παρακλέω, *parakaleo*. It is verb indicative future passive third person plural and in the first meaning means to call to one's side, summon, invite. The NRSV takes the fourth meaning of "comfort, encourage, and cheer up." Simply translating the Greek as comfort, despite the fact all translations appear to do so, fails to fully capture the meaning of the text. It catches the result without the means, and the means have great importance here. The means for comfort come from the knowledge and confidence we do not face life alone. We have a great God who stands alongside us throughout. Nonetheless, the indicative future passive tense appears to support the translation as comfort. Otherwise, it reads "they will be summoned" which fails the test of context.[6] The Good News translation (1992) makes an attempt with this translation: "Happy are those who mourn; God will comfort them!" Eugene Peterson's *The Message* (2002) makes another attempt: "You're blessed when you feel you've lost what is most dear to you. Only then can you be embraced by the One most dear to you." In order to not confuse the text, I will stay with the New Revised Standard Version translation and interpret it that Jesus says those in the kingdom are happy,

---

5. Suzerain covenant is an agreement between the greater, guarantor, and the lesser. In the suzerain covenant, God guaranteed the covenant with Israel.

6. Bauer, *Greek-English Lexicon*, 622.

μακάριος, *makarios*, can call God to their side in each and every moment, and will be comforted in his presence.[7] While the language may present difficulty in the contemporary world, Jesus spoke in the language those around him understood.

Jesus explained the kingdom in terms people understood, and in doing so he relied strongly on metaphor and parable to illustrate the kingdom through analogy. In parables, Jesus describes the paradoxical kingdom where poor, weak, blind, and oppressed find relief (Luke 4:18). He compares the kingdom with leaven (yeast) and mustard seed sending the message that the kingdom will affect everyone, and it will persist (Matt 13:31–33). In the kingdom, workers receive equal pay for unequal work (Matt 20:1–16), and the Prodigal finds love and forgiveness when he realizes his father's lowest servant fares better than he does (Luke 15:9–32). In the three parables of the Treasure, Pearl, and Fish, Jesus explains the priceless nature of the kingdom (Matt 13:44–48).

In summary the priceless "kingdom of God" advocates relationship with God and with each other at the core of Christian faith as we saw in Jesus' response to the lawyer of the Sadducees. Kushner (1987) tells of watching two children build a castle on the sand. Soon a wave rolled over it completely leveling their work. He thought they would be devastated. Instead, they ran up the beach laughing and holding hands as they ran. Kushner remarks:

> All the good things in our lives, all the complicated structures we spend so much time and energy creating, are built on sand. Only our relationships to other people endure. Sooner or later, the wave will come along and knock down what we have worked so hard to build up. When that happens, only the person who has somebody's hand to hold will be able to laugh.[8]

The Comments of Polkinghorne and Others

Moltmann (1965) says the "kingdom of God" and the Lordship of God provide the heart of eschatology, and the resurrection and Jesus' appearances to the disciples following the resurrection provide new meaning for the "kingdom of God." This "kingdom" of God begins with a new act of creation, and the kingdom in the resurrection becomes present in promise and hope.[9] The

---

7. Bauer, *Greek-English Lexicon*, 487.
8. Kushner, *When All You've Ever Wanted*, 166.
9. Moltmann, *Theology of Hope*, 204–29.

kingdom began with Jesus and continues to evolve. The new act of creation in the resurrection is the new body Paul speaks of in 1 Cor 15. It requires both continuity and discontinuity while in the resurrection God provides a new body. Continuity means Christians continue in the old creation to the point of death. At that point, they experience transformation from a physical body to a spiritual one that requires discontinuation of the physical, a point which the Sadducees would not have agreed with, let alone understood.

While "kingdom of God" and "kingdom of heaven" appear numerous times in the Synoptics, they only occur twice in John—John 3:3 and in John 3:5. The phrase "eternal life" in John corresponds to "kingdom" in the Synoptics, and we see that John speaks of a realized eternal life in the here and now. The remainder of the New Testament speaks of our having been given eternal life where we will be united with Jesus, as in Rom 6:4-5.[10] Jesus began his ministry with the announcement of the kingdom. He spoke in the present to those around him. In announcing the coming of the kingdom he announced the promise of eschatological hope. The fact that the phrase occurs numerous times shows the writers of the gospels considered the "kingdom of God" significant. These texts remind us that if we matter to God once, we always matter. We receive eternal life here and enjoy life in the kingdom now and not in some far-off future. We matter to God now and always for relationship, the core principle of Christian faith and important for the evangelistic commendation of the "kingdom of God" and Christian faith in the contemporary world.

While it does not appear in the New Revised Standard Version Old Testament, "kingdom of God" does appear seventy-one times in the New Revised Standard Version New Testament and is a core New Testament principle.[11] Wessel (1990) says the "kingdom of God," an important theme for Jesus, did not appear in the Hebrew Bible or the Apocrypha. While the Hebrew Bible does not refer specifically to the "kingdom of God," the idea appears in passages such as Exod 15:18, Ps 29:15, and Isa 43:10. Jesus in pronouncing his kingship pronounces the present reality as well as future eschatological hope. Ephesians 5:5 has kingdom of Christ and of God. Second Tim 4:1 states it differently but has the same sense. Jesus tells his disciples in the Sermon on the Mount to seek the "kingdom of God" (Matt

---

10. Polkinghorne, *God of Hope*, 82–84.

11. Perkins, "Mark," 525–47. See Matt 6:33; 12:28; 19:24; 21:31, 43; Mark 1:15; 4:11, 26, 30; 9:1, 47; 10:14f., 23; 12:34; 14:25; 15:43; Luke 4:43; 6:20; 7:28; 8:1, 10; 9:2, 11, 27, 60, 62; 10:9, 11; 11:20; 13:18, 20, 28; 14:15; 16:16; 17:20f.; 18:16f., 24, 29; 19:11; 21:31; 22:16, 18; 23:51; John 3:3, 5; Acts 1:3; 8:12; 14:22; 19:8; 28:23, 31; Rom 14:17; 1 Cor 4:20; 6:9f.; 15:50; Gal 5:21; Eph 5:5; Col 4:11; 1 Thess 2:12; 2 Thess 1:5; 2 Tim 4:1; Heb 1:8; Jas 2:5.

6:33), and Jas 2:5 promises the kingdom to those who love God.[12] Later Christian thought expanded understanding of the kingdom to the kingdom within as Wolfhart Pannenberg points out and not the moral and political position of Martin Bucer.

Pannenberg says:

> The kingdom of God to come, which had been understood in moral and even political terms by Martin Bucer in the sixteenth century and afterward under his influence, had been reconceived later on in terms of the christological doctrine of the kingdom of grace entrusted to Christ by the Father, exercised in the life of the church and to be completed in the future kingdom of glory. The authoritative source for this view was the word of Jesus, according to Luke 17:21, that the kingdom of God is "within you" or "in the midst of you." While the original meaning of this word was that the kingdom of God became already present with the person of Jesus in the midst of his audience, it was later understood as indicating the interiority of each human heart to be a place of the kingdom. Thus, the concept of the kingdom of God got spiritualized, a "kingdom not of this world," as in George Fox and later on by Spener and Francke. Leibniz generalized this idea by relating the kingdom of grace to the moral destiny of all humankind in the design of its creator. The kingdom of God, then, became the goal of human striving and thus the goal of human history.[13]

Unfortunately, faith often turns to a moralistic view as in the instance of Bucer. This interpretation in some instances happened with the Ten Commandments which define relationship with God and with each other but not morality. Although relationship has a moral dimension, collapsing it solely to morality demeans humankind's relationship with God and with each other. Reducing the kingdom to morality fails also to grasp the message of the Sermon on the Mount.[14] There, one sees that life shifts in the kingdom, and the secular values of the culture no longer apply. The church exploded in the first century not because of moral principles but because those outside marveled at how the Christians loved each other, their rela-

---

12. Wessell, "Mark," 618–31.
13. Pannenberg, "Modernity," 493–94.
14. Jean Piaget observes in *The Moral Judgment of the Child* (1932): "A religion that defines morality as obedience to its commands is appropriate to children and immature people. A religion which persists in understanding 'good' to mean 'unquestioningly obedient' is a religion which would make perpetual children of us all" (Piaget, as quoted by Kushner, *When All You've Ever Wanted*, 127–28).

tionship, which came from the transforming power of Jesus Christ in the "kingdom of God."

Augustine (354–430) identified the "kingdom of God" with the elect which later moved to identification with the church in the medieval period. On the other hand, those who equated the kingdom with the sovereignty of God in the context of his omnipotence as did Calvin (1509–1564) view it as both realized and the final completion of world history. However, a large group of Christians who view the kingdom as the elimination of all evil will tend to see the kingdom as future reality.[15] Augustine's position fails because it reduces the kingdom in extent. The church is in the kingdom, not the kingdom, and carries the kingdom message to those outside.

Conclusion

Throughout the Bible, we see God's showing up and expressing care beginning as for example in Exodus and in the coming of Jesus Christ. In the second instance the leadership in Israel rejected him, leading to the crucifixion, but God vindicated himself and human hope when the crucifixion led to resurrection. Jesus began his ministry announcing the "kingdom of God," and in the resurrection God assured the kingdom's continuation and growing establishment. As Moltmann points out, eschatology began with the kingdom which became present in promise and hope.

Visibly, the kingdom stands out in the church, and the local church in United Methodism extends the kingdom into the world. In the kingdom, those destitute in the world rejoice, and those who suffer great loss find comfort. From time to time, Christians will suffer for the sake of the gospel, and in those times in the kingdom, God will stand alongside as God has stood alongside throughout history. In and through it all, the church shares as joint heirs in the kingdom with Jesus Christ as Paul remarks (Rom 8:17).

Jesus told the disciples in Matt 6:33 to seek first the kingdom. In this pericope, Jesus contrasts the things of the kingdom with those of the world and in doing so calls everyone to kingdom life and the life of the Holy Spirit within, and later, Jesus responds to Pilate that his kingdom is not of this world (John 18:36). Earlier, he told the disciples at the inauguration of the Lord's Supper he would not taste of it again until he came in his kingdom (Mark 14:25). From Mark 1:15 through the gospel record, Jesus refers to present and future reality of the kingdom and the reign of God. Jesus refers to a spiritual kingdom, and with the coming of the Holy Spirit at Pentecost, Jesus Christ and the kingdom resides within and without, and Paul points further to the

15. Harvey, *Handbook*, 140–42.

spirituality of the kingdom in Rom 14:17 when he says it is "righteousness, peace, and joy in the Holy Spirit," and those born of the spirit receive it.

Jesus explains one must be born of the spirit and receive the kingdom as a child in order to share in the kingdom (John 3:1–16; Matt 10:15) and states many in his presence would not taste of death until they saw him coming in the kingdom (Matt 16:28). The disciples though they had only spent a short time with Jesus began to expect he made a difference which we see in Martha and Mary's words when Jesus arrives in Bethany following the death of Lazarus: "Martha said to Jesus, 'Lord, if you had been here, my brother would not have died.' . . . When Mary came where Jesus was and saw him, she knelt at his feet and said to him, 'Lord, if you had been here, my brother would not have died'" (John 11:21, 32), and Jesus' presence in the kingdom makes a difference today as it did then. The kingdom brings a new order of love but not a new political paradigm as Israel had expected. Early Christians experienced the kingdom as we do today, and we see in Luke 6:20 the kingdom renounces the things that are wrong in the world and belongs to everyone in the church, regardless of station in life. It promises total liberation from sin and death and restores everyone to community when they profess faith in Jesus Christ as Lord and Savior.

Finally, the "kingdom of God" informs relationship as noted in the following:

> Teacher, which commandment in the law is the greatest? He said to him, "You shall love the Lord your God with all your heart, and with all your soul, and with all your mind." This is the greatest and first commandment. And a second is like it: "You shall love your neighbor as yourself." On these two commandments hang all the law and the prophets. (Matt 22:36–40)

Jesus summarized the law for the lawyer of the Sadducees making it clear that it also referred to Christians and their relationship with God and with each other. Kushner told the story of the collapse of the children's castle on the sand to make the point that relationship sustains us throughout life. The children ran happily up the hill holding hands which reminds us that having a hand to hold can often carry us through difficult times. The one who does not have a hand to hold lacks the support they might otherwise have. Christian faith addresses relationship, and Christians have a divine hand to hold.

7

Resurrection

Introduction

IF WE ARE TO analyze how Polkinghorne's work would contribute to the interpretation and commendation of Christian faith in the contemporary world, then we must discuss the resurrection. Moltmann notes resurrection narratives occur within an eschatological framework, particularly hope. Christian eschatology in its identity with Jesus differs from the Old Testament which identified with promise in the exodus to the promised land. Yet, the New Testament authors constantly asserted the continuity from the Old Testament to the New Testament. Resurrection recognizes the future in God, and promise and hope come alive in the resurrection. The disciples identify with both the crucifixion and the resurrection, particularly in the Pauline corpus, and the Easter event connects the disciples intimately with Jesus and does so for all who follow.[1] Resurrection ushers in the eschaton of hope. From the resurrection forward, God relates with creation through grace and no longer through law which Jesus asserts as a new covenant between God and humankind in the inauguration of the Eucharist, and Heb 7:22 explains Jesus as guarantor of this new covenant as God guaranteed the old, suzerain covenant, with Israel. Eschatology studies the last things with hope important for last things. The contemporary world tends to take the resurrection as settled without consideration of its impact for a new life.

Polkinghorne says that too many Christians take for granted the crucifixion, forgetting the horrendous death it represented, the agony of the wounds, pain from the sun, and great difficulty to breathe. Deep mystery appears in Jesus' death on the cross, and the gospels all tell the same story, with some slight variation in John regarding the date; Jesus died, was buried, and rose from the dead. Jesus' lament from Ps 22 cannot soften the evidence

---

1. Moltmann, *Theology of Hope*, 172–203.

for his agony.² Ironically, Jesus told the woman in Samaria he could provide living water, and now he thirsts. Do the events of crucifixion diminish his authority? No, the writers of the gospels did not see diminishment, but Paul says it best in 2 Cor 5:9 with his declaration God was in Christ reconciling the world. Jesus' death emerges as God's ultimate purpose in this life, and we worship the God impaled on the cross.³ Polkinghorne offers strong commanding highlights here when he points to the horrendous nature of the crucifixion, the mystery of the resurrection, Jesus' diminished authority in the crucifixion, God's act of reconciliation in the crucifixion, God accomplishing his ultimate purpose in the midst of the shame of the cross, its inclusion in the creeds—Jesus died, was buried, and rose from the dead—and that we worship the one crucified.

The hanging of a youth in a World War II concentration camp shadows the crucifixion in a powerful way. Polkinghorne in discussion of God in the crucifixion refers to the Auschwitz experience in Eliezer Weisel's *Night* (1955).

> The SS hanged two Jewish men and a youth in front of the whole camp. The men died quickly but the death throes of the youth lasted for half an hour. "Where is God? Where is he?" someone asked behind me. As the youth still hung in torment in the noose after a long time I heard the man call again "Where is God now?" And I heard a voice inside myself answer: "Where is *he*? He is here. He is hanging there on the gallows."⁴

God does not desert Jesus in the crucifixion. He stands alongside as he later stood alongside the youth in the concentration camp. The pathos of this story and the crucifixion bring to the forefront the evil that existed and exists in the world. Moral evil overwhelms individuals and society at times, times when we need the assurance of God's presence alongside to liberate us from oppressive evil. While Weisel reflected on the events of the Holocaust, one might reflect on the horrific events in the present day where terrorism dawns over much of the Middle East. Christians there experience the genocide Jews experienced in the 1940s, and only hope in the resurrection provides assurance in the midst of such events.

---

2. Brown says: "Many commentators stress that this is the opening of a psalm that continues for thirty verses and ends on a positive tone. That does not do justice to the fact that the most pessimistic line in the psalm is quoted, not a victorious one. See V. K. Robbins, [*Jesus the Teacher: A Socio Rhetorical Interpretation of Mark*], 1175–81" (Robbins, citing Brown, *Introduction*, 147).

3. Polkinghorne, *Way the World*, 69–73.

4. Ibid., 73.

C. S. Lewis captures the deep feelings surrounding the crucifixion in *The Problem of Pain* (2001) and *A Grief Observed* (1976). In the latter, Lewis does not offer an explanation for the events surrounding the death of his wife Joy. Lewis speaks from the heart to the heart when he writes about Joy, and the pinned body of Jesus on the cross speaks to the heart of Polkinghorne.[5] The cross speaks deeply in its signifying that God went to the extreme to reconcile us and the world into relationship with him and others. Too easily, we discard the crucified God for the risen, forgetting its enormous sacrifice to provide for our future destiny in resurrection to be with God, thought that had already emerged in Judaism.

In Judaism, resurrection appeared as both metaphor and metonymy in Israel's return from exile. Resurrection in Judaism referred metaphorically to restoration of Israel. With Paul, resurrection refers to baptism and dying and rising with Christ. Judaism associated resurrection with the Messiah. They did not expect Messiah to die, let alone rise from the dead, and no Jew would have accepted Jesus as Messiah following his crucifixion. N. T. Wright suggests that the previous comments point to the influence of Jewish resurrection thought on early Christian thought. Judaism had a different view of resurrection and considered it meant the restoration of Israel, whereas in Christianity, resurrection referred to individual as well as cosmic restoration. Jewish thought possibly, as Wright notes, influenced the early church, and the early church fathers might have picked up on that.[6]

Irenaeus was the early defender of the resurrection and hope in *Against the Heresies* and argued for the gift of the Spirit to enable the realization of complete human personhood.[7] Brian Daley relates the views of Tertullian, a follower of Irenaeus:

> A generation later, the Carthaginian convert Tertullian (c. 160– c. 220) seems to have been influenced by Irenaeus's work in his own opposition to Marcionite and Valentinian Gnosis, Asserting that "the resurrection of the flesh is the Christian's confidence," Tertullian defends the Christian hope for bodily resurrection in a number of works, appealing to the power of the Creator to reassemble what has been dispersed in death and insisting that a material body is needed if a person is to experience the full retribution that God's just judgment requires. Tertullian's treatise *On the Resurrection of the Flesh* goes beyond apologetics; it offers

---

5. Ibid., 73–74.
6. Wright, *Surprised*, 46–51.
7. Daley, "Eschatology," 91–96.

the first extended attempt in Christian literature to imagine the characteristics of the risen body: still complete, still fleshly, yet perfect in form and "angelic" in its spiritual powers. Tertullian follows Irenaeus in arguing for the necessity of a millennium of earthly reward for the just before the final crisis of history, resurrection, and universal judgment. Before the end, however, Tertullian suggests that the souls of the dead, confined in the various "reception rooms" of Hades under the earth, anticipate psychologically the reward or punishment that will be theirs as whole persons after the resurrection; while they remain there, their condition can apparently be influenced by the prayers of the fellow Christians they have left behind.[8]

Tertullian paints a more graphic picture of the resurrection which fails in the context of 1 Cor 15 that points to a spiritual but not a physical body. When Christians look at the meaning for the life of Jesus, Christians have the tendency to look at his words, actions, and miracles and not so much the crucifixion and resurrection. We tend to only examine Jesus at Easter and when we take Eucharist which some churches celebrate infrequently, and in doing so we tend to dismiss the resurrection the remainder of the time. Christians need to recover resurrection awareness and regain the hope for their future with God. Only then, do we gain the hope which empowers Christian life in the present.

Peacocke says the resurrection stands out for the meaning it attaches to the life of Jesus. In the resurrection and ascension, we find hope that we too will experience heaven which for the Hebrew meant the presence of God.[9]

Evidence for the Resurrection

Hall points out we must learn to live with doubt:

> We shall have to learn to live with doubt. The false triumphalism of the *theologia gloriae* [theology of glory] will not be driven from us until we have realized that the hope that belongs to faith and is not confirmed by sight always lives with the prospect that it never will be confirmed. We have been accustomed to finding metaphors for Christian hope in nature: the flowers that bloom in the spring, the dark clouds that have their silver lining, etc. What we have to accustom ourselves to is that, in history, unlike nature, nothing is "necessary." There is not necessarily a new

8. Ibid., 96.
9. Peacocke, *DNA to Dean*, 89–111.

beginning in every ending, an alpha in every omega. We must live as Christians under the cross without assuming a resurrection that is either logically or existentially necessary.[10]

Hall makes his strongest observation with *theologia gloriae* that too easily Christians look at the resurrection, ignoring the horrendous crucifixion event. Easily, those in the churches gather for the Maundy Thursday service, and then go about their business the next day much as did the male disciples during the crucifixion. Undoubtedly, Christians will not have strong conclusive answers to many questions of Christian faith and learn to live in faith with an element of doubt under the cross as did those early disciples on that Friday long ago. Doubt forces Christians to lean on confidence in the love and faithfulness of God which will see us through. A focus on *theologia gloriae* will not carry Christians when the world turns upside down as in the picture of the youth hanging in Auschwitz, and they find much comfort in Scripture which Polkinghorne examines as evidence for the resurrection. In a sense doubt can be the catalyst for deepening faith. At times, I experienced the challenge to my beliefs as a Christian. I did so when I entered seminary and encountered challenges occasionally of my faith. Those challenges caused me to restate my beliefs which in turn deepened my faith. For me, doubt became an opportunity as it should for every Christian.

In his discussion regarding the Scriptures as evidence Polkinghorne refers to Feynman:

> As Feynman has said, we are asked to believe that the historian who makes a statement about Napoleon simply means that there are books in libraries which make assertions similar to his own. There is no past; there are only sources.[11]

The Scriptures contain the historical evidence for the resurrection, an event no longer available for examination. In a sense, quantum mechanics encounters a similar task.

Polkinghorne says the church reads the Bible for its historical evidence.[12] Jesus, as far as we know, did not write anything, and we depend on these texts for his record. In addition, the texts do not have recorded dates which requires examination of their context for clues regarding dates for their origination. In observational science such as astronomy, scientists draw conclusions from their observations, and the theologian does the same

---

10. Hall, *Lighten*, 145.
11. Polkinghorne, *Quantum World* (1989), 78.
12. Polkinghorne, *Beyond Science*, 100–102.

with the New Testament record.[13] The observations of astronomy extend over distances of billions of light years and rely on light which left distant stars billions of years ago. Astronomers do not question the accuracy and reliability for these measurements which they cannot authenticate through other sources and measurements. Instead, they accept the evidence.[14] Physics asserts that the laws of physics work the same throughout the universe and that what we observe from the earth holds throughout the universe. Similarly, theologians examine the historical texts from analogy with present religious experience. The texts report the reality of the time like the light from a distant galaxy points to the stellar background. As light provides evidence for a distant galaxy, the texts provide evidence for examination. Furthermore, they represent a variety of authors who report their experience, and following Richard G. Swinburne's principle of credulity, we accept the reports.[15] Early texts did not concern themselves with dates or even precise detail. They reported the events in the style of hero stories. Thucydides' (ca. 460–ca. 400 BCE) *History of the Peloponnesian War* (431 BCE) demonstrates the writing of the time. Authors had more concern with rhetorical style than facts.[16] Next, we consider the accuracy of the various texts which are principally the expression of the New Testament faith communities. Therefore, evidence must be found from the reports of the witnesses to the events of the New Testament.

The primary concern comes first not from the conclusions we make for the texts but the accuracy of the texts themselves. Close examination of the Synoptic Gospels indicates a great deal of common material behind the Synoptics such as the Q material.[17] The existence of material in one gospel omitted in another further suggests the presence of earlier literary material used in the formation of the Synoptics. The church pressed its view on the sayings of Jesus, and we need to discover to what extent.[18] The evidence continues to point back. Mark points to the Q source which points further back. Authors in the Hebrew Bible recorded stories which had passed down generation to generation, and it would not be surprising if the New Testament texts recorded the stories, also passed down, about Jesus in the first century. The Q source which predated Mark provides the earliest recording of the

---

13. Polkinghorne, *Way the World*, 33–37.

14. Ibid., 33–37.

15. The principle of credulity requires we accept the testimony in the absence of evidence to the contrary (Swinburne, *Existence*, 293–327).

16. Thucydides, *History*.

17. The Q material represents a lost collection of sayings (Brown, *Introduction*, 7).

18. Polkinghorne, *Way the World*, 37–48.

events for the time of Jesus which is recorded thirty-five or so years after his death, and might allow for some discrepancies. Polkinghorne points to *sitz em liben*, the situation in life, to effectively argue that the stories emerge in the gospels because they were distinctly memorable at the time and later in the community, and these recollections recalled the significance for life of individuals in the time of Jesus.[19] Arguably, we need to thoroughly examine the record. Avoiding heresies required the church to undertake serious examination of Jesus' time on earth, as it did in the Council of Nicaea. The church in the early councils through Chalcedon (451) worked out its understanding of Jesus and his time on earth.[20] Polkinghorne points out the Christian must make the important claims for Christian faith and provide evidence such as Matthew and Luke did for the Davidic lineage for Jesus in Jesus' genealogy.

Matthew and Luke include the genealogy for Jesus. In the former instance, Matthew must establish Jesus' descent from David to satisfy the Jewish mind, and in the case of genealogy, the claim can be made Jesus was a Jew. Second, genealogy indicates, disregarding the accuracy, that he descended from the Davidic monarchy. It seems such a claim meets both the test of verifiability and falsifiability.[21] The genealogical texts in the Synoptics do not agree in lineage. They do agree in the Davidic source which establishes Jesus as a Jew and as a descendent from David, as the Messiah was expected to come from Davidic lineage. Today, people often trace their genealogy and have many tools with which to do so. Those tools did not exist in the time of the New Testament, and it makes sense that errors would exist in genealogies that spanned many centuries. The fact that the texts span several cultures attests to their importance and acceptance in the ancient world as well as their acceptance in the early church.

Polkinghorne notes the accounts in the gospels and earlier Pauline corpus provide evidence accepted by the early and later church for the historical resurrection of Jesus. The point that the accounts differ in detail, in their accounts of persons present, and in related events suggests reality for the story.[22] A similarly nuanced story among the gospels and Paul would not argue as strongly for authenticity, in my view, and the variations in the accounts do not discredit the account as Wright points out in the following.

---

19. Ibid., 38–42.
20. The Council of Nicaea addressed the gnostic controversy which argued for Jesus as lesser deity than God.
21. Polkinghorne, *Way the World*, 33–37.
22. Ibid., 82–84.

Wright reminds us that differing descriptions of an event do not mean the event never happened. On October 25, 1946, Karl Popper met face to face at 8:30 p.m. in Kings College Cambridge with Ludwig Wittgenstein, not knowing that Wittgenstein did not often listen to papers all the way through and frequently exhibited arrogant and rude behavior as he did in Popper's presence when he waved a poker from the fireplace. The several stories of this event differed in their accounts. Wright introduces this story with its varied descriptions to point out that the various descriptions did not mean the event never happened.[23] Wright refers to his description of the Popper-Wittgenstein event and remarks that the Easter accounts vary significantly. As with the Popper-Wittgenstein encounter, the lack of agreement does not mean the event did not happen, and the gospel writers make it clear the resurrection was in accordance with Hebrew texts.[24] The varying accounts of the resurrection did not mean the event did not occur. Moreover, different people see different things at the same instance and experience them differently. Furthermore, the events were described orally before anyone wrote them down which would have easily made for variation. In summary, we can acknowledge the resurrection occurred while the details may not be in complete agreement. Despite the disparity in the accounts, they provide the historical understanding of Jesus.

Moltmann argues historical understanding represents analogical understanding. The resurrection includes expectational and eschatological questions and introduces new possibilities. It becomes a metaphysical question. The Easter faith of the disciples in their embrace of the resurrection stands out, and the interpreter of the Easter texts looks to the existential picture for the disciples. We can grasp the Easter faith of the disciples, its significance, its import for history, and its import for the church. In the end, the resurrection can only be understood in the context of *promise*.[25] The Easter texts paint a dramatic picture for despair turning to hope. The disciples despair following the arrest of Jesus which was evidenced by their absence during the crucifixion; although, undoubtedly, as his disciples, they must have also feared for their lives. In the resurrection and the later experience of Pentecost, they embrace the resurrection and find hope that sustained their lives and evangelism for the early church. I rejoice that when I face difficulty I can rejoice in the hope resident in God's promises in the resurrection that I am with him today and for all time.

---

23. Wright, *Surprised*, 31–34.
24. Ibid., 53–58.
25. Moltmann, *Theology of Hope*, 172–203.

Polkinghorne notes Jesus definitely performed miracles which ranged from restoration of the leper to community to the raising of Lazarus from the dead, and God performs the greatest miracle when Jesus rises from death on the cross. The onlookers and the disciples accepted the miracles all the way through the resurrection. Importantly, they accepted the coming of the Holy Spirit at Pentecost, fulfilling the promise already given to the disciples.[26] Jesus' performance of miracles as well as God's performance of miracles throughout the Bible show God's concern for humankind. In miracles, Jesus demonstrated his and God's compassion for those who suffer. These miracles reassure us that God cared then and cares today. We do not suffer alone.

Just as he restored the leper to community, Jesus assures the brigand alongside him during the crucifixion that Jesus will be with him. Polkinghorne acknowledges the mysterious nature of Jesus' comment to the thief on the cross: "He replied, 'Truly I tell you, today you will be with me in Paradise'" (Luke 23:43), and Paul alludes to Jesus' descending into the lower parts of the earth in Eph 4:9–10. The events remain deeply mysterious and yet form the great foundation for our faith.[27] Jesus' comment to the thief remains a mystery which the church has sought from time to time to explain. Attempts to do so have resulted in the concept of purgatory as well as other concepts such as a period of transformation. These attempts lack scriptural support, and we can only infer that Jesus reassured the thief of his support in a horrific time of agony. On the cross, Jesus says to the brigand alongside him, "Truly I tell you, today you will be with me in Paradise" (Luke 23:43). Nothing in those words infers that paradise differed from the eternal. Too easily, we fall back on seeing heaven and hell as physical places when they are the spiritual world. In my view, hell is the experience eternally of the absence of the presence of God and heaven the experience of the presence of God. The gospels depict a lot of detail for the crucifixion including that of the large stone in front of the tomb.

The Romans placed a large stone in front of the entrance to the tomb making access improbable.[28] This event in looking back appears strange to the contemporary mind as did many of the features in the Easter event. Authorities today do not handle criminals in the same way, let alone block access to their graves. Following execution, family members or others would take care of the deceased as did those around Jesus at the time. What the

---

26. Polkinghorne, *Way the World*, 27–48.
27. Ibid., 78–79.
28. Ibid., 84–85.

circumstances surrounding the resurrection point out is that Jesus was no common criminal but someone to be reckoned with.

Polkinghorne suggests the strangeness of the resurrection would have been as strange then as today. Other stories of people coming back to life appeared from time to time in the ancient world and in the New Testament as well, for example, the raising of Lazarus from the dead. These recoveries were resuscitations as those involved ultimately died. Late Judaism adopted the idea of the resurrection as an eschatological event at the end of time, and the Pharisees endorsed it, but the Sadducees did not. Examination of the historical evidence for the resurrection acknowledges Jesus as a historical figure. The resurrection is trans-historical in that it transcends everyday experience and is an event without comparison.[29] The Jewish world prepared for a resurrection as restoration of Israel but would not have been prepared to receive a Messiah who had suffered the humiliation of the crucifixion, and the gospels later recorded the resurrection event as reported by the eyewitnesses who encountered Jesus. The resurrection transcends every day experience which does not discount its historical nature and events.

Polkinghorne says the argument for the resurrection depends on the interpretation of the events surrounding it which provide evidence for it. The assessment of Jesus must be grounded in much more than the historical record. Yet, the emphasis of Christianity on a particular man cannot ignore history any more than a theoretical physicist can ignore the evidence from his experimental colleagues. If Jesus existed as both human and divine, a new worldview becomes both possible and reasonable. The resurrection then becomes conceivable. Otherwise, the humanist view persists that Jesus was an unusual person who died as do all. Polkinghorne acknowledges the implausibility of one's rising from the dead; however, the potential existed for Jesus as both human and divine. For more evidence, one must turn to the gospels.[30] Jesus' existence as both human and divine makes the resurrection feasible. Therefore, resurrection required Jesus as both human and divine. As human, he died, something we see in the transformation of his body that was apparent in his appearances following the resurrection. Resurrection rather than resuscitation required Jesus also to be divine. A more interesting point concerns the observation that only the women, with the exception of John, stood by Jesus in his most challenging moment.

Wright reminds us of the dominance of the male in the time of Jesus and its significance for the evidence of the resurrection. The presence of women would not have provided valid evidence, as only the testimony of

---

29. Ibid., 78–79.
30. Ibid., 79–80.

men would have been accepted.[31] Only women appeared at the tomb which on the surface seems unusual. However, the males were Jesus' disciples and participants in what might have been perceived by the authorities as a new movement. The threat of death for their leader threatened them as well, and they would have avoided public appearance. Thus, it is significant that the women not the men discover the empty tomb.

Polkinghorne says confirmation for Jesus' resurrection comes with the empty tomb, an important evidential point. The empty tomb, thus his absence from the tomb, suggested he might be alive, which Paul confirms when he reports his experience on the Damascus road as encounter with the risen Jesus and not a vision which characterizes many reported experiences among Christians over the centuries.[32] The empty tomb confirmed Jesus rose from the dead, and the church throughout has focused on the empty tomb.

Polkinghorne notes that Karl Barth states the empty tomb means the Christian statement that Jesus lives takes on greater meaning than just a manner of speaking on the part of Christians. Polkinghorne, following the observation for the transformed body of Jesus as well as his belief that God will transform all creation, believes unequivocally in the empty tomb which says matter has a greater destiny than it would otherwise have. He supports his argument by insisting that it does not make sense that God would allow creation to end. If creation mattered once to God, it matters always. The New Testament does not describe the resurrection itself, as everyone apparently left following Jesus' burial, and Jesus does not appear to have elaborated on it following the resurrection when he spent time with the disciples. The contemporary mind asks how it could have happened whereas the biblical texts appear content with not answering that question and only describe the aftermath.[33] Importantly, the New Testament does not explain what happened in the resurrection or how it took place. It only discusses events before and after. Three pictures stand out. The first is Jesus on the cross, the second, the empty tomb where death has not conquered, and the third, his appearances following the resurrection.

Polkinghorne mentions the appearances of Jesus as evidential. Several accounts in the biblical texts confirm Jesus appeared in person following the crucifixion. The varying, murky discrepancies between the descriptions of Jesus' appearance possibly resulted from the intimacy of the encounters for those who met Jesus again, and the intimacy of the encounter also explains

---

31. Wright, *Surprised*, 53–58.
32. Polkinghorne, *Way the World*, 82–84.
33. Ibid., 86–87.

the lack of formal, detailed description.[34] Jesus' appearance to the disciples following the crucifixion confirms Jesus rose from the dead, and Peacocke concludes that the appearances of Jesus to the disciples are stronger evidence than the empty tomb.[35] The empty tomb is circumstantial at best, as it could not confirm what happened to Jesus in the interim, whereas the appearances provide strong evidence. They provide evidence for the resurrection as well as a new body when Mary and the disciples fail to recognize him and when Jesus appears to walk through walls and appear randomly.

Polkinghorne cites instances in which people recognized or failed to recognize Jesus. The two disciples on the road to Emmaus recognize him at the end of their conversation when he vanishes (Luke 24:30–31).[36] The gospels emphasize the difficulty in recognizing Jesus following the resurrection, an important historical evidential point.[37] A common thread exists among the accounts despite variation in detail. Mary Magdalene (John 20:14–16) mistakes Jesus for the gardener.[38] The beloved disciple recognizes him at dawn on the shore of the lake (John 21:4–7).[39] The failure of Mary and the disciples to recognize Jesus indicates his appearance had altered in some way. Of his appearance to Mary the Scriptures tell us: "Jesus said to her, 'Do not hold on to me, because I have not yet ascended to the Father. But go to my brothers and say to them, I am ascending to my Father and your Father, to my God and your God'" (John 20:17), further evidence that something had changed for Jesus following the crucifixion. Later, the disciples touch him: "Then he said to Thomas, 'Put your finger here and see my hands. Reach out your hand and put it in my side. Do not doubt but believe'" (John 20:27). In summary, the appearances provide strong evidence that Jesus rose from the dead with a different body of some kind. His appearance to Thomas indicates something different regarding his body. It seems unlikely that Thomas could have inserted his hand in the side of Jesus without his side having changed in some way other than physically. It seems that the normal biological processes had changed or ceased, and his body had changed.

Polkinghorne notes Jesus appears and disappears at will and is able to enter locked rooms.[40] The disciples had gathered, and as John relates:

---

34. Ibid., 82–84.
35. Polkinghorne, *Scientists as Theologians*, 74–76.
36. Polkinghorne, *God of Hope*, 70–79.
37. Polkinghorne, *Searching*, 94–95.
38. Polkinghorne, *God of Hope*, 70–79.
39. Ibid.
40. Ibid.

"When it was evening on that day, the first day of the week, and the doors of the house where the disciples had met were locked for fear of the Jews, Jesus came and stood among them and said, 'Peace be with you'" (John 20:19). Something had happened to Jesus to permit his entering a locked room.

Circumstantial evidence for the resurrection includes:

- Jesus was buried in the well-recognized tomb for Joseph of Arimathea, a place difficult to hide.[41]
- The roles of Nicodemus and Joseph of Arimathea in Jesus' burial, followed later by the empty tomb.[42]
- Jews accepted the empty tomb as real.[43]
- The accusation that the disciples stole the body.[44]
- The adoption of Sunday for the Christian day of worship as early Christians perhaps began to gather on Sunday in commemoration of the risen Christ.[45]
- The disciples would not have been willing to die for an event that never happened.[46]
- The church provides witness of the resurrection, and the witness of the church stands out for its character.[47]
- Most significantly, the disciples following the crucifixion were transformed. Something happened. The events surrounding the arrest and crucifixion completely unsettled the disciples as we see in the example of Peter during the trial and in the lack of male presence, with the exception of John, at the crucifixion and later at the tomb. But something happened. Suddenly the demoralized disciples found new empowered life, and it could have been nothing less than the resurrection of Jesus from the dead.[48]
- Jesus was buried according to Jewish custom which included two stages. In the first stage, his body was wrapped with spices and linen and placed on a shelf in a cave. After decomposition, his bones would have

---

41. Polkinghorne, *Way the World*, 84–85.
42. Ibid., 85–86.
43. Ibid.
44. Ibid.
45. Ibid., 87–88.
46. Wright, *Surprised*, 62–72.
47. Polkinghorne, *Way the World*, 87–88.
48. Ibid.

been removed and stored. Wright concludes we have to acknowledge the tomb as empty except for some grave clothes.[49]

- Jews venerated the tombs of martyrs which became sacred places, but this did not happen with the tomb of Jesus.[50]
- The authorities would have produced Jesus' body were he still dead in order to silence the disciples. None of the arguments outside the testimony of those who saw Jesus firmly establish his resurrection, and the church today as then relies on those who witness to the world what they themselves have seen. Any skeptic will argue for the unlikely preservation of the corpse of a criminal so cruelly executed.[51]
- Jewish authorities may not have produced the body of Jesus to offset these claims because it simply was not available.[52]

The amount of circumstantial evidence undermines the argument that Jesus did not rise. Much of the circumstantial evidence involves speculation regarding what happened, seen in the reflection on what the authorities might have done were Jesus actually dead. The Romans crucified Jesus and would have claimed his body were he not dead and would not have permitted his burial by Joseph of Arimathea and Nicodemus. Were Herod or Pilate interested in his body, it would not seem they would have permitted his preparation for burial and his burial. On the other hand, they may have wanted to avoid further conflict with the Jews and hastened to permit the ritual practices associated with Jewish burial. The greatest circumstantial point concerns Nicodemus and Joseph of Arimathea's part. They both held prominent positions in Jerusalem and would have known were something amiss with the treatment of Jesus' body. Further, it seems unlikely the Romans would have placed a large stone in front of the tomb if they had other plans for its disposal. It also seems unlikely that they could have disposed of the body of so noted a figure as Jesus and not have had it discovered. Still, the strongest circumstantial point comes in the fact something happened that resulted in enormous change in the disciples. As Hall pointed out in the introduction to this chapter (chapter 7), we do not meet the resurrection.

49. Wright, *Surprised*, 58–62.
50. Ibid., 62–72.
51. Polkinghorne, *Way the World*, 82–84.
52. Ibid., 84–85.

We meet the risen Lord as did the disciples which we see reflected in the gospel story.

The hard evidence for the resurrection includes the witness of those who saw Jesus alive following the resurrection. The witness of Mary Magdalene, the disciples, and Thomas' examination of the body of Jesus holds up in a court of law, and the circumstantial evidence adds to that evidence.

Despite the circumstantial evidence, despite the similarities in the accounts of the resurrection, the stories may be seen as problematic. Polkinghorne acknowledges the problem with corruption for Jesus' body. What happened to the body of Jesus as human? Further, the problem arises of how Jesus' body avoided the corruption that all human bodies eventually experience.[53] The nonexistence of the body of Jesus raises some questions. Jesus appears to have a different body which permits his entering rooms with locked doors. Then what happened to his physical body? We do not know. It appears from the texts that Jesus' physical body changed in some way which permitted his direct ascension to God in Luke 24:51: "While he was blessing them, he withdrew from them and was carried up into heaven."

In conclusion, following his bottom-up critical realist approach, Polkinghorne provides the strong case for Jesus' resurrection with the great importance for the resurrection and future destiny of Christians. He examines the evidence bottom-up in the texts and interprets the evidence. He notes the strong evidence in the witness of those who saw Jesus, particularly the women. Next he turns to the circumstantial evidence. He interprets it noting the transformation of the disciples and that they would not have been willing to die for something which never happened. His approach is critical and realistic. Equally important is that the evidence in the resurrection includes its consequences not just for God and Jesus but for humankind.

I have always valued the Bible for its contribution to strengthening my faith. In it, I eagerly read the words of those who witnessed to the life and events surrounding Jesus. Without their record, I do not believe my faith would be as strong and grow as it has in reflection on the record.

Consequences of the Resurrection

Polkinghorne states that the cross represented the ultimate purpose of God. Crucifixion would have been considered weakness, and yet, it produced power and hope. Good advice alone will not suffice. Instead, we require the transforming power of Jesus Christ. Only such power will correct the flawed human character all seem to fall prey to at one time or another. How

---

53. Ibid., 85–86.

can the death of one man make a difference, even two thousand years later? The transcendent nature of Jesus' death stood out for the early Christians and transformed their lives. Early Christians found this so empowering they did not question it. Only later did they seek explanation and understanding for something to be true, and the fact Jesus was at the same time human and divine mattered.[54] God purposefully set out in the incarnation to reveal himself, or so it would seem, and to conquer the sin which destroyed relationship. The prophets may have predicted the crucifixion, but it seems difficult to imagine God purposely planned it. The more reasonable argument says God did not plan it but knew omnisciently it would occur because he understood human nature. Or did God intend one great attempt to call humankind to him which failed when evil sought to destroy the Messenger, Jesus the Christ? Polkinghorne goes outside the conservative box when he says the myth of the fall records the fact of human laxness rather than origin. In Jesus, we find reconciliation and our way back to God and begin to understand what the incarnation meant.

Polkinghorne says Christians following the resurrection began to understand the nature of the incarnation. The church examined how human and divine came into union in Jesus, and the church set aside Christmas to celebrate God's great act in the incarnation.[55] Ultimately, the incarnation resulted in crucifixion and resurrection which represented the vindication of God as well as of Jesus. It also vindicated human hopes. In the resurrection, human hope was real and not a delusion.[56] The church made its first statements regarding Jesus in the Council of Nicaea, 325 CE, with the Nicene Creed[57] and later with the Council of Chalcedon, 451 CE.[58] The resurrection vindicates God, Jesus, and human hopes and does so through the conquest of death. The resurrection makes human hope real, empowers hope, and responds to human search for meaning in our world. Without the resurrection, it would be difficult to make sense of human existence. It vindicates God, Jesus, and human hopes because in the resurrection good overcomes evil, and the church through the centuries identifies with the crucifixion and the resurrection.

Moltmann notes the disciples identify with both the crucifixion and the resurrection, particularly in the Pauline corpus. The Easter event connects the disciples intimately with Jesus and does so for all who follow. In

---

54. Ibid., 74–76.
55. Polkinghorne, *Living with Hope*, 70–72.
56. Polkinghorne, *Serious Talk*, 102–3.
57. Latourette, *History*, 154.
58. Ibid., 171.

the resurrection, the eschatological faithfulness of God proves operative with the resurrection which is more than a physical event. It introduces a completely new historical paradigm and points beyond itself to the new regime of God in creation and the heavens. The continued appearances of Jesus point to his continued involvement in creation then and now and for the future. The titles which express Christ point to the future, and the promises in Christ define the future.[59] Resurrection leads to new creation and to God's continued involvement in creation.

In commenting on the aspects of creation and new creation, David Wilkinson says:

> The action of God and the faithfulness of God must be held together in both creation and new creation. As evidenced by the resurrection and the images of the parousia, God's transformative work will be in both event and in process, in the initiative of grace and in the co-operative work of grace with his new community. We differ in emphasis here with Polkinghorne who stresses the faithfulness of God. While there is much agreement between us, we want to stress a little more the specific activity of God in creation and new creation. This reflects more the biblical material and gives a stronger basis for hope.[60]

The faithfulness of God can be seen in his activity in creation as attested in the sacred texts. Wilkinson argues for the transformative work of God as process. However, this point overlooks the fact that the biological aspect of human life ceases with death which means process does as well. Evolutionary events such as stellar and biological ones provide the means to gauge time. Such events do not exist in the spiritual world of eternity, indicating that time differs in eternity. Still, the resurrection reports when Jesus tells Mary he has not ascended to his Father support the point that Jesus' body changed as well as the possibility for process in its transformation and ours as well.

Smith explains resurrection reports make it clear Jesus did not simply resume his original body. His followers experienced him in a new way, and from faith in the resurrection, emerged the church. Neither the words of Jesus nor his actions made a difference. Something else occurred. People experienced transformed lives. The earliest accounts of the early Christians told how they loved one another. The early Christians had release from guilt. Love can only be the power that supports such change, and the Messianic

---

59. Moltmann, *Theology of Hope*, 172–203.
60. Wilkinson, *Christian*, 187.

twist caused these early Christians to see themselves as "called out."[61] People changed following the resurrection. They loved each other and shared things in common, and they experienced release from guilt. Neither the words of Jesus nor his deeds made the difference. Otherwise, they would have made a difference before the crucifixion. Their view of death changed, and the view of death changes for those who have come to God today.

Wright observes when the early Christians said Jesus had risen from the dead, they knew something had happened which had never happened previously, and their idea of death changed. They did not think that Jesus' soul had gone into heavenly bliss or that he had become divine. Most Jews at the time of Jesus believed in an eventual resurrection. Martha echoes that belief in John 11:24 when she says she knows Lazarus will rise again in the resurrection on the last day—what the resurrection meant to the Jews of the time.[62] However, Jesus' rising from the dead meant more than mere resurrection—it meant the assurance of God's faithfulness.

Polkinghorne states the Christian assurance of life beyond death rests in God's assurance of the eschatological sequence of death and resurrection. Such a position coheres with the psychosomatic human personality and some form of a new body following death.[63] The faithfulness of the loving God assures this point. Only God has the power to provide, and he does not do so through duplication of the person as some have suggested. Further, a strong way of expressing the eschatological thought comes through the point of the body of Christ (1 Cor 12:27 and Eph 4:12–13) and the individual incorporation into the body of Christ.[64] The example of the body of Christ offers understanding for how we are incorporated into God now and for eternity. When we embrace Jesus we assume a new position with God now and always. Baptism identified with Jesus which Paul explains several times: "Therefore we have been buried with him by baptism into death, so that, just as Christ was raised from the dead by the glory of the Father, so we too might walk in newness of life" (Rom 6:4). Eschatological hope reassures one of union with Jesus now and always, and I too am immersed in all that Jesus is.

Moltmann mentions the resurrection narratives occur within an eschatological framework, particularly hope. Christian eschatology in its identity with Jesus differs from the Old Testament which identified with

---

61. Smith, *Religions*, 319–38.

62. Wright *Surprised*, 34–38.

63. Polkinghorne rejects Cartesian dualism of mind and body and argues for the unity of soul and body which he refers to as psychosomatic unity (Polkinghorne, *God of Hope*, 104–6).

64. Ibid., 108–10.

promise in the exodus to the promised land. The text referring to Jesus as "the first fruits of them that slept" means the resurrection for Christians has already begun (1 Cor 15:20), and in the Easter appearance, Jesus expresses his universal Lordship over all, and Christian hope for the future begins with this singular event. Recognition of the resurrection points to the future in God, and promise and hope come alive in the resurrection.[65] I cannot overemphasize these words of Moltmann and their importance for life lived fully with God in the present. Anything else seems empty.

Moltmann argues for an understanding of the resurrection for promise as noted previously. Promise conveys the thought of all Scripture when God appears to Abraham in Gen 17 and instructs Abraham to walk before God to Jesus' final words to his disciples in John. As Moltmann says, the resurrection points to the future, a future with God. God through Jesus has initiated the kingdom, and all in the kingdom look forward to the hope of sharing in the resurrection with him and the saints. Even secular Ernst Bloch, the neo-Marxist German philosopher, conceded the significance of the resurrection for Jesus. Moltmann offers the following comments regarding Bloch:

> Ernst Bloch is right about this reading of the history of Jesus Christ in the light of his resurrection: "Indeed, even the end of Christ was nonetheless his beginning." Jesus' resurrection from the dead by God was never regarded as a private and isolated miracle for his authentication, but as the beginning of the general resurrection of the dead, i.e. as the beginning of the end of history in the midst of history. His resurrection was not regarded as a fortuitous miracle in an unchangeable world, but as the beginning of the eschatological transformation of the world by its creator. Thus the resurrection of Jesus stood in the framework of a universal hope of eschatological belief, which was kindled in it.[66]

Ernst Bloch has understood better than some theologians that the hope for the resurrection is not a human hope for good fortune, but is an expression of the expectation of divine righteousness; thus it represents a hope for God, for the sake of God and his right.[67]

Christian hope, not utopian hope, goes beyond human hope in the righteousness of God. Bloch in the three volumes of *The Principle of Hope* (1994, 1995, 1999) argued for utopian hope. The resurrection goes beyond utopian hope or wishful thinking to eschatological hope in human destiny,

---

65. Moltmann, *Theology of Hope*, 172–203.
66. Moltmann, *Crucified God*, 162–63.
67. Ibid., 174.

and the view of life after death changes. The hope which I have and which grounds my faith is real and not mere optimism that things will work out for the better. The utopian hope of Bloch depended on the actions of human beings whereas mine does not. It is guaranteed by God.

Second-century thought turned to resurrection meaning something different than in Judaism. It meant a spiritual experience. Second Temple Judaism accepted resurrection but did not assign it any importance, and the Dead Sea Scrolls do not present a clear picture. Other than 2 Maccabees 7, resurrection remained a side issue. It stood out in both Paul's thought and John's. Clement, Ignatius, Justin, and Irenaeus considered it important. Christianity clearly saw the resurrected body as a transformed one as Paul sets it out in 1 Cor 15. Wright states that Paul argues the new body as simply a spiritual one, a misreading of the text often made by many. Paul argues for transformation from the current body animated by the normal human soul to a future body animated by the spirit of God. God makes a new creation and does not leave an abandoned one as in the view of the Platonists. Daniel 12 talks of the resurrected righteous who shine like stars. Resurrection meant a new existence following death and not just going to heaven.[68] Paul says:

> Listen, I will tell you a mystery! We will not all die, but we will all be changed, in a moment, in the twinkling of an eye, at the last trumpet. For the trumpet will sound, and the dead will be raised imperishable, and we will be changed. For this perishable body must put on imperishability, and this mortal body must put on immortality. When this perishable body puts on imperishability, and this mortal body puts on immortality, then the saying that is written will be fulfilled: "Death has been swallowed up in victory." (1 Cor 15:51–54)

Paul is saying we change at death and obtain a new imperishable body, and its nature remains a mystery. But he says more than that we change. He sets aside the ancient fear for the finitude of death. Finitude has been vanquished, and one rises to a transformed state and resides in intimate relationship with God always. Jesus' response to the Sadducees assures us that God will not forget us in the world of the eternal.

Wright comments that when Jesus responded to the Sadducees, he indicated things would be different in the resurrection. He said people would not be angels and yet they would be like angels. The Matt 13:43 reference mirrors Daniel 12:3 and makes the Daniel verse a reference to the resurrection.[69] Christian hope beyond death comes in developing Jewish thought

---

68. Wright, *Surprised*, 42–46.
69. Matt 13:43: "Then the righteous will shine like the sun in the kingdom of their

from Paul to Tertullian and Origen. When Jesus refers to Paradise in his remarks to the brigand on the cross, he refers to a temporary place rather than a permanent one, as Jesus does not ascend to be with God until later.[70] The early Christian view saw death as two parts—first, of first a temporary change that is, second, followed by new bodily existence in the new creation which has no similarity in paganism and is as Jewish as one can be.[71] When Jesus responds to the thief alongside him in the crucifixion, he does not say what would happen beyond paradise or whether paradise was separate from eternal life. Humanly, we tend to think of events beyond death in worldly terms which include time. Paradise possibly represented a transitory event between death and resurrection in eternity. As I noted earlier, the Scripture does not prove Paradise did not refer to heaven. I think it did, and that Jesus did not remain there whereas the thief did. Jesus returned to earth to later ascend into heaven.

Polkinghorne refers to Paul who provides the most extensive reflection regarding the resurrection in 1 Cor 15. He concludes in v. 14 the resurrection as pivotal for Christian belief. Further, as all die in Adam, all live in Jesus. Paul asserts true eschatological hope must rest in radical transformation as flesh and blood cannot inherit the kingdom of God. Paul's reflections support continuity and discontinuity, and both the old and the new refer to concrete realities. The new body, then, is not simply an ethereal entity. It is a new ontology brought into being through the life-giving spirit of God.[72] The new body represents the heart of Polkinghorne's argument for hope which he argues occurs as transformation, *ex vetere*.

Polkinghorne introduces the expression *ex vetere*.[73] The world beyond death will have a new character as mirrored in Jesus' exaltation. The new

---

Father. Let anyone with ears listen!" Dan 12:3: "Those who are wise shall shine like the brightness of the sky, and those who lead many to righteousness, like the stars forever and ever."

70. Luke 23:42–43: "Then he said, 'Jesus, remember me when you come into your kingdom.' He replied, 'Truly I tell you, today you will be with me in Paradise.'"

71. Wright, *Surprised*, 38–42.

72. Polkinghorne, *God of Hope*, 76–78.

73. Polkinghorne says that it seems that the transformation of the old at death might also be process, *ex vetere*, and not an abrupt snapping of the fingers to produce the new (ibid., 14–16). Polkinghorne takes the position that *ex vetere* might be process which does not cohere with Paul's view when he says: "Listen, I will tell you a mystery! We will not all die, but we will all be changed, in a moment, in the twinkling of an eye, at the last trumpet. For the trumpet will sound, and the dead will be raised imperishable, and we will be changed" (1 Cor 15:51–52). Here, the Greek ῥιπή, *rhipe*, translated "twinkling" has the first meaning of "throwing, rapid movement, e.g. of the eyes; the 'casting' of a glance takes an extremely short time" (Bauer, *Greek-English Lexicon*, 743).

creation is the transformation of the old. It arises *ex vetere* and not *ex nihilo*.[74] Jesus' resurrection, exaltation, and ascension mirror the character of the world beyond death. In this account Polkinghorne makes the clearest statement regarding the new body *ex vetere*. Still, we cannot forsake our earthly bodies.

Wright adds to Polkinghorne. Paul in 1 Cor 6:14 discusses the resurrection as significant for how we think of our bodies in the life to come. The classic Christian doctrine regarding our bodies presents a more powerful and revolutionary view than that of Plato and has a piety that sees death as going on to eternal rest. Wright concludes much of what Christians think about death has come from culture and not from the Scripture, tradition, and reason of the church.[75] Moltmann, Polkinghorne, and Wright pull us away from a secular view of death to the biblical view of hope and a hope which includes all creation.

Polkinghorne extends resurrection to the cosmic where Rom 8:18–25 and Col 1:15–20 discuss cosmic redemption. God cares for all in creation according to their nature, and we expect a future for the material cosmos as well as for human life. As seen in the transmuted form of Jesus in the empty tomb, matter participates in the resurrection.[76] Polkinghorne further argues: "If the universe is a creation, it must make sense everlastingly, and so ultimately it must be redeemed from transience and decay."[77] Polkinghorne argues for the resurrection of all creation, and God remembers the pattern of all creation in the resurrection. How this remembrance will work remains a mystery as life following death is spiritual and not merely physical or merely material. Clearly there are many problems in these discussions. Yet, Rom 8:18–25 and Col 1:15–20 support all creation in the resurrection and that God cares for all creation.

Polkinghorne argues that God cares for creation including all creatures, and that we can expect the resurrection to include animals and all creation. Through his kenotic act, God made way for the created order. The world beyond death will have a new character as mirrored in Jesus' exaltation.[78] Polkinghorne argues here that Jesus in resurrection redeems not just humanity but all creation. Jesus' resurrection, exaltation, and ascension mirror the character of the world beyond death.

---

74. Polkinghorne and Oord, *Polkinghorne Reader*, 220–22.
75. Wright, *Surprised*, 22–28.
76. Polkinghorne, *God of Hope*, 113–14.
77. Ibid., 148–49.
78. Polkinghorne and Oord, *Polkinghorne Reader*, 220–22.

Polkinghorne identifies a new creation in the resurrection. The universe and creation make sense, and the new creation will come from the old. Otherwise the old seems pointless. The new creation will be dramatically different, discontinuity, and Jesus' resurrection was the seminal event. The old and the new exist side by side, a combination of "already and not yet."[79] It does not seem clear how the new creation and the old exist side by side as their existence does not have the same character. Physical creation has limited extent whereas the unique new creation does not.

Andreas Losch agrees with Polkinghorne:

> In the discussion of the importance of uniqueness regarding religion, I would therefore side with Polkinghorne, as the resurrection of Jesus as the beginning of a new creation is an absolutely unique event, and as such the core of Christian belief.[80]

Both Losch and Polkinghorne understand the importance of the resurrection for Christian faith. Further, it supports Christian eschatological hope for future destiny.

In conclusion, the resurrection turns the world upside down for its consequences. The idea of transformation for all creation conflicts with the view of science for the end of first earth and then the universe. Second, it puts too much emphasis on the material. Perhaps these texts should be spiritualized. In that instance, we can argue that God in some fashion returns creation to its character at the beginning of time. Then, we can rest solidly on the promise that we will be with God now and for all eternity, regardless of the circumstances for the remainder of creation. Through union with Jesus Christ and God, one has the promise of eschatological hope, not mere wishful thinking for things to be different, and can leave the "how" to the providence of God. Like for the early Christians, God has removed the fear of death, and death becomes something to look forward to.

I rejoice in the resurrection and in it every time I celebrate Holy Communion. In Holy Communion, I am reminded of the hope resident in my relationship with God through Jesus.

Conclusion

Resurrection ushers in the eschaton of hope reminiscent when Paul says: "For as all die in Adam, so all will be made alive in Christ" (1 Cor 15:22). The circularity in the argument for Jesus' significance and the resurrection

---

79. Polkinghorne, *Living with Hope*, 96–99.
80. Losch, "Origins," 405.

does not dismiss the argument. Science consistently accepts circularity as in the tension between theory and experiment. Through the centuries, the church sees Jesus as the living Lord in the present, and the resurrection compels the writers of the New Testament to consistently speak of Jesus in divine language (Rom 10:9; 1 Cor 12:3; and 1 Cor 16:22).[81] Following the resurrection and the empty tomb, writers of the New Testament consistently spoke of Jesus as divine, and the emerging church worked out what that means through Chalcedon 451.

Polkinghorne says no first-century Jew would have accepted Jesus as alive as long as his body remained entombed. Perhaps that explains why Paul does not mention the tomb. A variety of instances support the resurrection from the appearances to the disciples, the church choosing the first day of the week for worship, and the historical experience of the church. Polkinghorne says the resurrection of Jesus as miracle makes sense in three ways: "(i) it was not fitting that his life should end in total failure, (ii) it was not fitting that God should abandon the one man who solely put his trust in him, and (iii) it is fitting that our deep hopes that death does not have the last word about human significance should be vindicated."[82] Both Polkinghorne and Peacocke see hope for the destiny of humankind in the resurrection. However, Peacocke does not know how it will occur as all the atoms in the body eventually disappear. Too easily, we fall back on seeing eternal things as physical. The eternal world is not physical. While we may not know how God forges our new bodies, we know that he does. Polkinghorne sums up why his position regarding the resurrection makes sense.

Polkinghorne presents a strong case for why the resurrection makes sense, providing both real and circumstantial evidence for it. He approached his argument bottom-up and examined the real evidence first. The witnesses to Jesus' appearances following the crucifixion augmented by the circumstantial evidence provide strong real support for the resurrection. From hard evidence, Polkinghorne moves to the circumstantial. First, given that Nicodemus and Joseph of Arimathea held prominent positions in Jerusalem, they would have known if something were amiss with the treatment of the body of Jesus. Second, it seems unlikely the Romans would have placed a large stone in front of the tomb if they had other plans for its disposal. Further, they could not have done so with so noted a figure as Jesus and not have had it discovered. Third, something happened that resulted in enormous change in the disciples. His carefully developed argument for the resurrection strongly supports commendation of Christian faith in the

81. Polkinghorne, *Meaning in Mathematics*, 124–26.
82. Polkinghorne, *Scientists as Theologians*, 77.

contemporary world. As Hall pointed out in the introduction to this chapter (chapter 7), we do not meet the resurrection. We meet the risen Lord. The stories do not lack some problems. However, doubt or lack of understanding did not imply an event never occurred. In support of his arguments, Polkinghorne consistently referred to Scripture.

Polkinghorne asserts that the New Testament provides a reliable historical record; it is well attested as represented by the many and various texts from ancient times, far more than exist for other major texts from either the current period or antiquity. Examination reveals small differences among the texts, either from scribal variations or otherwise. However, these variations do not detract from the authenticity of the texts and simply indicate editorial gloss. Close examination of the Synoptic Gospels indicates a great deal of common material behind the Synoptics such as the Q material. The fact that the accounts differ in detail, persons present, and events suggests that the story is true.[83] Polkinghorne makes a strong point when he suggests the variety of texts argues for their accuracy regarding the resurrection. Otherwise it would be easy to argue the writers falsified their stories, and thus neither disciples nor we would know eternal life.

Jesus through the resurrection made eternal life possible for the disciples and all that followed. The disciples now understood what Jesus meant when he said that he was resurrection and life. Christian faith stands on the resurrection and its significance for God's triumph over evil. In the resurrection Christians find their future destiny.

God fully restores humankind through the resurrection. Despite the wonder of the incarnation, Easter stands out as the day everything changes. The resurrection moves humankind from the previous status in law to the status where God no longer sees those who come to him through grace as sinner, and Paul eloquently describes the salvific event in Romans. The resurrection of Jesus struck the church dramatically as evidenced through the adoption of Sunday as the day for worship. The timid, fearful disciples became powerful, strong, gifted, and well-spoken leaders for the early church. From that day forward, the church proclaimed what God had done in Jesus through the resurrection.

We wonder at God's mighty act in the resurrection and continually go back to Scripture to celebrate and investigate the events which led to it. Jesus destroyed death for all time. And yet, things did not end there. He goes on to ascend and sit at the right hand of God (Acts 2:34; 7:55–56; Rom 8:34; Eph 1:20; Col 3:1; Heb 8:1; 1 Pet 3:22). He is the head of the church (Eph 5:23). We can all say with Paul we are crucified with Christ and yet live with

---

83. Polkinghorne, *Way the World*, 33–37.

Christ (Gal 2:20). Now we, with assurance in the resurrection, see death as a time of glorious departure when we go to the place Jesus has prepared.

Assurance in the resurrection provides a strong foundation for Christian hope. Assurance comes first from strongly held belief in the faithfulness and trustworthiness of God as evidenced in the historical record of his interaction with creation. Second, assurance rests strongly in the resurrection of Jesus and God's promise that Christians will likewise experience resurrection. In the resurrection, we have the promise of a new body following death, and eschatology tells the fuller story.

Without the resurrection, I would not have Christian faith and neither would other Christians. Polkinghorne's argument for the resurrection presents the strongest case for his work in support of the thesis that his work grounds the evangelistic thrust for commendation of Christian faith in the contemporary world. In addition, his argument for the resurrection leads to eschatological hope for human destiny.

8

Foundation for Christian Hope

Introduction

THIS CHAPTER TURNS TO Polkinghorne's discussion of the foundation for Christian hope. This foundation requires explanation of the anthropic principle which though anthropocentric argues the presence of observers in creation can only mean one thing: it must point back to an ultimate source for all that exists which suggests meaning and purpose in creation. I refer to the ultimate as God, the source of Christian hope as revealed in the sacred Judeo-Christian texts and confirmed in the tradition of Israel and the church. The anthropic principle suggests we look for meaning and purpose. In doing so, we can only find answers that God has chosen to reveal in the historical record as well as in the experiences in the church throughout the centuries.

Hope, the Gift

Huston Smith comments that both Hinduism and Buddhism place the responsibility on the individual for his or her salvation.[1] In Islam, salvation becomes the responsibility of the individual Muslim who does not have the assurance of Rom 8:16.[2] Similarly, other religions such as Confucianism and Taoism place the responsibility on the individual. Christianity, however, is characterized by God's extending hope through unmerited grace to each and every Christian (Eph 2:8).[3]

---

1. Smith, *Religions*, 50–81.
2. Ibid., 221–70.
3. "Is Confucianism a religion, or is it an ethic? The answer depends on how one defines religion. With its close attention to personal conduct and the moral order, Confucianism approaches life from a different angle than do other religions, but that does not necessarily disqualify it religiously. If religion is taken in its widest sense, as a way of life woven around a people's ultimate concerns, Confucianism clearly qualifies. Even if religion is taken in a narrower sense, as a concern to align humanity with the transcendental ground of its existence, Confucianism is still a religion, albeit a muted one" (ibid., 183).

Polkinghorne notes only Judaism and Christianity look to God for hope. In Christianity, hope emerges in the crucifixion and resurrection, and hope beyond death expects spiritual survival and not reassembly of the atoms of the body, or resuscitation. Christian hope rests solidly in the hope of death and resurrection that God will preserve each Christian's soul in the divine memory and raise it in a new body to eternal life.[4] Hope appears over and over throughout the New Testament, clearly a theological motif associated with Christ, the hope within.[5] In Judaism, hope rests in the suzerain covenant. In the New Testament, it rests in grace (Eph 2:8), and Christian salvation results from response to God and acceptance of the gift. Early Christians looked forward to intimately sharing eternity with God.

In conclusion, religions other than Christianity focus on the efforts of the individual to find his or her salvation. In Christianity, God through grace extends salvation to those who respond to him through Jesus Christ, and grace provides unmerited gift.

Hope, the Concern

Christian hope removed the fear of death for early Christians. Smith also commented that early Christians experienced release from guilt. Love can only be the power that supports such change; the Messianic twist caused these early Christians to see themselves as "called out."[6] Then what hope do those on the outside have? Karl Rahner referred to those who found God outside the church as anonymous Christians.[7] Polkinghorne argues God's presence in every place means it is possible for one to come into relationship with God without any other intervention other than God's revelation to the individual. Any other position would mean God lacks presence everywhere and in every instance, and such a position would deny omnipresence.[8] So Polkinghorne points to the omnipresence of God in all creation. Anonymous Christians find their way to God outside Christian community as God is present in the world outside the church as well as inside the church, and those on the outside who find their way to God possess eschatological hope along with those who find their way through the church.

4. Polkinghorne, *Faith, Science & Understanding*, 106–8.
5. Polkinghorne, *Way the World*, 27–28.
6. Smith, *Religions*, 319–38.
7. Karl Rahner used "anonymous Christians" originally, and Vatican II accepted it, and "anonymous Christians" referred to those who turned to Jesus outside the church (Rahner, *Theological Investigations*).
8. Polkinghorne, *Way the World*, 107–8.

Polkinghorne goes further than merely responding to questions from the religion and science dialogue and provides an extremely important exposition of eschatological hope, a core discussion in this work, and in doing so, he examines the evidence for the resurrection as I discussed in chapter 7, and following his examination, he discusses the resurrection in terms of eschatological hope. The discussion includes human destiny and body in the resurrection, the character of resurrection in both its temporal and material aspects, and the dependence on a faithful, loving God. Christians live expectantly in hope for their future destiny with God.

Douglas John Hall in *Lighten our Darkness* (2001) offers guidance for the examination of hope when he says:

> The lesson that is most evident is that the crucial thing about any religion is the *character* of its expectancy. Just what does it offer by way of hope? That it will be, in a basic way, an expression of the human need to hope is a matter of definition. Today, however, it has been precisely the need and the right to hope that has been called into question. As Albert Camus put it, we must now learn to think soberly and hope no more. That is the most succinct expression of experience in our time. If therefore there is any possibility of religious faith beyond this experience (and it is not axiomatic that there is!), it will depend even more than in the past upon the care with which religion defines its expectancy for us and for this world.[9]

The expectancy before the crucifixion centered in the point that Jesus made a difference in the lives of those around him, and that after the resurrection, Christians experienced the presence of Jesus through the Holy Spirit as he promised in John (John 14:16, 26; 15:26; 16:7; 1 John 2:1), and they began to experience the hope of the resurrection.

Hall sets the foundation extremely well for the importance of Christian hope. Otherwise, the contemporary mind asks how Christianity really benefits us and does not waste our time. The contemporary mind does not need help managing the day to day tasks. It needs the knowledge that life in the kingdom makes a difference today as it always has. All the technology available and the means to obtain it will not help when a person faces serious life threatening events. Only the promise of Christian eschatological hope offers the needed assurance.

Benedict T. Viviano notes that Jürgen Moltmann, in his *Theology of Hope: On the Ground and the Implications of a Christian Eschatology* (1965)

---

9. Hall, *Lighten*, 103.

proposed a robust theology of hope,[10] and Moltmann's work provides a seminal basis for Christian hope. He lived through the German Third Reich and knew suffering first hand. He knows as very few know what it means to have God's presence in the midst of the extreme suffering so many endured under the Third Reich.[11] Undoubtedly, the suffering Moltmann saw in World War II Germany as well as his own experience affected his understanding of the suffering in the resurrection. The innocent went to their deaths in the concentration camps as did the innocent Jesus in the cross.

Moltmann discusses the cross and resurrection which stand at the heart of Christian belief and faith. Without the resurrection, faith would stand empty. Further, it represents the core of Christian theology as Moltmann elaborates:

> Jesus' resurrection from the dead by God was never regarded as a private and isolated miracle for his authentication, but as the beginning of the general resurrection of the dead, i.e. as the beginning of the end of history in the midst of history. His resurrection was not regarded as a fortuitous miracle in an unchangeable world, but as the beginning of the eschatological transformation of the world by its creator. Thus the resurrection of Jesus stood in the framework of a universal hope of eschatological belief, which was kindled in it.[12]

Eschatological hope emerged in the resurrection, and following the resurrection, the early Christians understood the context of suffering and of God who stood alongside Jesus and overcame death. They experienced hope in the resurrection and no longer feared death which no longer held a threat for them, becoming instead the time for them to look forward to intimate relationship with God for all eternity. They had an expectancy that the presence of Jesus through the Holy Spirit made a difference. Therefore, Moltmann rightly observed resurrection as standing at the core of Christian faith.

Secular Hope

Ernst Bloch (1885–1977) examined utopian hope in *The Principle of Hope* (1954, 1955, 1955) which discussed secular hope for a better utopian life. Hope outside religion tends to focus on life on earth without regard for life beyond death. Bloch discusses the many things people hope for in order to

---

10. Viviano, "Eschatology," 82–83.
11. Moltmann, *Crucified God*.
12. Ibid., 162–63.

experience a more pleasant life. Consequently, secular hope does not address subjects such as theodicy.[13] Bloch addresses human expectations in the present whereas Christian hope addresses ultimate human destiny. Polkinghorne's argument for Christian hope looks beyond the present to human destiny.

The Anthropic Principle

John Barrow and Frank Tipler point out there are two basic characteristics for the cosmological argument: "1) something exists, and 2) there must be a sufficient reason for everything that exists."[14] The cosmological argument has largely replaced the design argument and avoids the fatal flaw for the design argument of describing God in human terms as a designer. Such a description, they claimed, limits understanding of God who far exceeds the concept of a designer and which did not account for purpose. Not only does the cosmological argument work better, but it leads naturally to the anthropic principle. Further, these discussions show how discovery can mature in theology and philosophy as it does in science.

The anthropic principle in its various forms argues that creation had to be the way it is, that is, given the laws and constants of physics, for intelligent life to evolve. The slightest change in the physical constants underpinning the physical laws would eliminate the possibility of intelligent life as we know it. John Barrow and Frank Tipler helpfully comment regarding the anthropic principle:

> What is the status of the anthropic principle? Is it a theorem? No. Is it a mere tautology, equivalent to the trivial statement, "The universe has to be such as to admit life, somewhere, at some point in its history, because we are here?" No. Is it a proposition testable by its predictions? Perhaps.[15]

The anthropic principle as argued by Barrow and Tipler, despite the fact that science does not identify purpose in the world it observes, argues for the presence of observers pointing back to the origin of the universe and identifies purpose behind stellar and biological evolution and the development of simple cellular life.

Barrow and Tipler note that the self-selection process necessary for the development of human life but not for development of simple cellular

---

13. Bloch, *Hope*, vols. 1–3.
14. Barrow and Tipler, *Anthropic*, 103.
15. Ibid., vii.

life is referred to as the weak anthropic principle (WAP). Barrow and Tipler define WAP as follows:

> *Weak Anthropic Principle (WAP): The observed values of all physical and cosmological quantities are not equally probable but they take on values restricted by the requirement that there exist sites where carbon-based life can evolve and by the requirement that the Universe be old enough for it to have already done so.*[16]

There is nothing random regarding the development of the universe. It can be argued that an even greater selection process exists than that which Darwin imagined, as for example in the formation of matter and stellar evolution. Had the strong force differed slightly, would the atoms that make up the universe today have developed? These considerations led Brandon Carter to propose a more comprehensive version of the anthropic principle, the strong anthropic principle (SAP). Barrow and Tipler state the SAP of Brandon Carter as: "*Strong Anthropic Principle (SAP): The Universe must have those properties which allow life to develop within it at some stage in its history.*"[17] The SAP proposes there exists at least one possible universe with the design and goal for the evolution and sustenance of "observers." This universe requires observers in order for it to come into existence, and an array of other, albeit different, universes must be necessary in order for the universe to come into existence.[18] Carter's version allows for emergent observers at some point in the life of the universe.[19] Physical laws govern the universe from stellar to biological evolution. While we do not know how these laws came into being, we can argue from theology but not from science that God created the laws in such manner to permit purposeful evolution. Barrow and Tipler go further and propose the final anthropic principle (FAP):[20] "*Final Anthropic Principle (FAP): Intelligent information-processing must come into existence in the Universe and once it comes into existence, it will never die out.*"[21]

Polkinghorne also discusses three important anthropic principles. The first requires that the size—approximately 10^{22} stars—and age—approximately fourteen billion years—of the universe be such as it is for life to have developed. It took ten billion years of stellar evolution for the emergence of carbon. The second requires a smoothly homogeneous universe with a ratio

16. Ibid., 16 (italics original).
17. Ibid., 21 (italics original).
18. Ibid., 21–26.
19. Ibid., 4–7.
20. Ibid., 23.
21. Ibid., 23 (italics original).

of 1 to 10^{60} between the explosive force of expansion and contraction of gravity. Otherwise, the universe would have collapsed from the turbulence of a non-smooth universe and there would have been an imbalance of expansion and gravity. Physicists believe a process of inflation occurred when the universe was about 10^{-35} seconds old, permitting the emergence of the smoothly expanding one later, and in this period the universe expanded extremely rapidly. The third principle concerns the size of the cosmological constant to which physicists assign a value of 10^{-120}. The cosmological constant refers to a type of energy called "dark energy." In the early universe, physicists believe an as-yet-undiscovered, highly symmetric Grand Unified Force broke down into such unsymmetrical forces observed today as the gravitational, electrostatic, magnetic, strong nuclear, and weak nuclear.[22] The anthropic principle works well with theology, the evolution of life, and purpose, and theologically, it points to God behind creation. Evolution, stellar and biological, toward greater complexity suggests God behind all that has emerged, and the emergence of greater complexity suggests to many religious people of God as purposeful.

Polkinghorne points out were the universe not the way it is, we humans would not be here discussing it. This is the weak anthropic principle. He proposes the moderate anthropic principle [MAP] which says: "the contingent fruitfulness of the universe as being a fact of interest calling for explanation." The finely tuned laws are not sufficiently clear as to require no further explanation.[23]

The anthropic principle in its forms purposely points to intention and purpose in creation. For human life to evolve required the universe as it is with its physical laws and constants.

Hope in Trustworthy and Faithful God

The texts regarding Jesus' sacrifice for all creation are a challenge to Christian theology. The Genesis story asserts that God created, but it does not say how, a mystery which will continue. God cares for all creation without saying how he will do so in the demise of the solar system, galaxies, and the universe. It seems reasonable the universe will receive a new body of some kind. We do not know how that might occur from contemporary physics; it appears that the universe will greatly surpass life on earth. Consequently, humans will not experience the new creation in the time before the demise of the solar system. So the texts regarding Jesus' sacrifice for all creation

22. Polkinghorne, "Inbuilt," 247–50.
23. Ibid., 250–51.

provide a serious challenge for the theologian. Yet the greater significance occurs in the removal of the fear of death for all Christians.

Polkinghorne remarks that Advent becomes the time to face issues such as death and the moral character of life in judgment and calls us to recall again the coming of Jesus. At his time, Jews in their oppression expected a king and deliverer. Instead, they received a *crucified Messiah*, following the suffering servant of Isa 53. In the expectation of the second coming of Jesus, we need to be prepared for the unexpected. Hope interweaves the first and second coming, the hope of the shepherds at the birth of Jesus and the disciples in the resurrection. Hope intuitively looks forward beyond the suffering and bitterness of the present.[24] The ancient texts clearly prophesied Jesus as suffering, and Jesus prophesied this as well. Human bent toward optimism has trouble with Jesus as suffering. On a positive note, God stood by Jesus in his suffering as he will stand by us, and God will remember the soul's pattern that identifies me to him.

The theme of hope appears constantly throughout the Bible from the time of the exodus to the resurrection, and hope resident in eternal life with God emerges in the resurrection. Ancient Israel did not see beyond an earthly existence, and with the coming of Jesus, we have the promise of life in the kingdom now and always, gift of a faithful, loving God.

Polkinghorne speaks of the faithfulness of God as follows:

> The only ground for such a hope lies in the steadfast love and faithfulness of God that is testified to by the resurrection of Jesus Christ. Christian belief must not lose its nerve about eschatological hope. A credible theology depends upon it and, in turn, a trinitarian and incarnational theology can assure us of its credibility.[25]

Christian theism identifies God as transcendent and immanent who continues to involve himself in creation and to care for creation. He provides the foundation for our hope, a God who is present for his creatures and creation.

While Christian hope emerges in the resurrection, it depends on the presence and faithfulness of God to all who come to him. Without the assurance that God is faithful and loves and cares for Christians and all creation, Christian faith would have no hope. While scientists hold a dim view for the future of the universe, Christians look beyond that to their future destiny with God who will retain their souls in divine memory.

---

24. Polkinghorne, *Living with Hope*, 2–4.
25. Polkinghorne, *God of Hope*, 149.

Hope versus Optimism

Polkinghorne takes up the topic of optimism in relation to hope. Hope means neither optimism based on prediction nor wishful thinking regarding the future. Lack of hope is nihilism, not pessimism, and absence of hope can lead to the despair that nothing will change for the better. Hope in its openness to the future stridently looks to a better world.[26] Despair ends in lack of hope, meaninglessness, and nihilism. The cultural situation hides hope and confuses it with optimism.[27] But hope differs from the optimistic view of progress which sets the future over the past and present difficulties as stepping stones to the future.[28] Optimism addresses circumstance in the world whereas hope looks beyond the material world to life with God for all time, something which, evangelistically, we need to take seriously. Hope offers openness to the future with God and for new creation.

Polkinghorne points to eschatological hope for new creation as Paul explains in 2 Cor 5:17, which includes the cosmos as well as life (Rom 8:19–23). The Romans text agrees with Col 1:16–17 that says it pleased God to reconcile all things to him through Jesus, and Rev 21:1–4 gives a vision of a transformed world in the symbolic New Jerusalem.[29] God cares for all in creation according to their nature, and we expect a future for the material cosmos as well as for human life. As seen in the transmuted form of Jesus in the empty tomb, matter participates in the resurrection.[30] Eschatological hope says life following death means far more than survival of death as Polkinghorne explains:[31]

> Eschatological hope is that nothing of good will ever be lost in the Lord. That thought in it is enough to rebut a kind of other worldly piety that neglects the ethical demands of the present. It assures us that our strivings for the attainment of good within the course of present history are never wasted but will bear everlasting fruit.[32]

Eschatological hope takes into account the new eschaton with the incarnation and resurrection. Grace appeared and prepared Christians for life, and death no longer controlled. Hope unlike optimism has a strong foundation

---

26. Ibid., 28–30.
27. Ibid., 46–48.
28. Ibid., 94–96.
29. Ibid., 84–86.
30. Ibid., 113–14.
31. Ibid., 94–96.
32. Ibid., 102.

that assures it is not futile. The foundation stands strongly in the resurrection and the faithfulness of our God of love.

Utopian Hope in Bloch

It is helpful at this point to review Bloch's *The Principle of Hope* (1954, 1955, and 1959) for its position as the centerpiece for secular hope and for its influence on the work of Moltmann, which in turn, influenced the work of Polkinghorne. Bloch supports Moltmann and thereby Polkinghorne especially with respect to the resurrection which is discussed later in this section. Daniel L. Migliore (1991) observes Bloch in *The Principle of Hope* (1954, 1955, and 1959) developed a neo-Marxist view for hope in freedom from alienation. Bloch concludes the revolutionary proletariat but not God will free one from oppression. Enlightenment thought shunned the apocalyptic and viewed the world as upward-moving progress, but the events of the twentieth century shattered that view. In the context of the nuclear age, we must express Christian hope anew.[33] Migliore's most important statement that, in the nuclear age, we must express Christian hope anew informs the evangelistic task before us if we are to offer eschatological hope in a troubled world torn apart by terrorism, unparalleled mass murders, and the constant threat of war across the planet. Only eschatological awareness can provide hope in the midst of such circumstances.

Moltmann explains Bloch saw that the Bible brought an eschatological awareness to the world which resulted in universal desire for redemption becoming a future hope and that Bloch is right about this reading of the history of Jesus in the light of his resurrection.[34] Moltmann comments regarding Bloch:

> Indeed, even the end of Christ was nonetheless his beginning. Jesus' resurrection from the dead by God was never regarded as a private and isolated miracle for his authentication, but as the beginning of the general resurrection of the dead, i.e. as the beginning of the end of history in the midst of history. His resurrection was not regarded as a fortuitous miracle in an unchangeable world, but as the beginning of the eschatological transformation of the world by its creator. Thus the resurrection of Jesus stood in the framework of a universal hope of eschatological belief, which was kindled in it.[35]

33. Migliore, *Faith*, 234–38.
34. Moltmann, *Crucified God*, 82–111.
35. Ibid., 162–63.

> Ernst Bloch has understood better than some theologians that the hope for the resurrection is not a human hope for good fortune, but is an expression of the expectation of divine righteousness; thus it represents a hope for God, for the sake of God and his right.[36]

No doubt that Moltmann saw eschatological hope as liberating. Similarly, Bloch looked to liberation in his neo-Marxism. However, Moltmann and Bloch saw liberation differently. Moltmann saw liberation in the crucifixion and resurrection whereas Bloch saw it in his utopian concept of liberation from the class contradictions he observed early in life.

The opening to *The Principle of Hope* (1954) notes that Bloch, who was Jewish, was born in Ludwigshafen July 8, 1885, where he early observed the class contradictions between his birthplace and nearby Mannheim. He pursued philosophy and wrote *The Principle of Hope* (1954), an extensive neo-Marxist discussion of secular hope.[37]

Bloch was not without his detractors as Viviano states:

> Bloch was expelled from East Germany as too religious; he settled in Tübingen where he was found to be too Marxist. It was the period of the Marxist-Christian dialogue. Moltmann saw, in his dialogue with Bloch, that the Bible and the church had resources of hope for humanity *even in this world*, resources which were not being used out of fear of disturbing the status quo. Hope for this planet had been handed over to the Marxists.[38]

Bloch notes that the class contradictions between his birthplace and nearby Mannheim influenced his socialist thought. He began work in philosophy in 1911 and developed his key idea of the Not-Yet-Conscious and published in 1918, "Geist der Utopie" ("The Spirit of Utopia"). His interest in religion, which was unusual in a Marxist, appears in this work. He saw Marxism as the synthesis of rigorous and idealistic socialism. In *The Principle of Hope* (1954), he combines socialist thought from the Greeks with present-day socialist thought and seeing Utopia not as an impossible ideal but as achievable politically. The Not-Yet-Conscious consisted in past, present, and future with unrealized meaning trapped in the past. The Not-Yet-Conscious flows over the horizon of each age as "forward dawning" and "pre-appearance." It contains a psychological dimension in addition to the social and political. Bloch investigates the Cabbala rather than the *Torah* in *The Principle of Hope*

---

36. Ibid., 174.
37. Bloch, *Hope*, 1:xix–xxxiii.
38. Viviano, "Eschatology," 82–83.

(1954), in line with the mysticism of his literary exposition which often referred to Johann Wolfgang von Goethe. He considered his work utopian; it was replete with possibility and strongly opposed imperialism.[39] Bloch discusses utopia in a variety of forms and looks at examples in religion.

Bloch turns his discussion to Judeo-Christianity and notes the occurrence and support of a variety of utopias, and he objects to these utopias for their contribution to oppression. First, Bloch says the promised land for Israel illustrated a utopia. Second, a Christian utopia emerges when Jesus announces the kingdom of God.[40] Bloch notes that Christian social principles condoned slavery in the ancient world and supported the ruling class over the oppressed, and such positions did not provide hope for the underclass in society.[41] Interestingly, Bloch comments on the kingdom of God as utopia. However, the kingdom of God does not promise the materialist benefits Bloch champions. That can be seen when Jesus in Matt 6:19-21 points to the frailty of the material and tells his audience to lay up treasure in heaven, and Jesus continued saying one's heart was where their treasure was. Bloch continues noting the utopian conflicts with greed for profit, discussing several utopias as exemplars.

Bloch notes that Joachim of Fiore organized a utopia around 1200 CE, and that Thomas More proposed the utopia of human freedom in the sixteenth century while the bourgeois continued to progress at the expense of the greater population. Wealth made people impudent and arrogant, and ignorant of the needs of others. The condition of the poor became worse the more economically advanced the country as in England for example at the turn of the eighteenth century. In other words misery accompanied capitalistic splendor.[42] Western governments generally sought the betterment of society and those governed. At times, progress was slow, as in the eighteenth century, where Bloch takes note of slavery in America. The wealthy in society do not want to give up their wealth, a position unchanged since the time of Jesus. Jesus in Luke 18:18-25 tells the young ruler who desires the kingdom to sell all he has, give it to the poor, and follow Jesus. The young ruler was very sad because he had extensive wealth. Wealth does not shake off the final fear, the fear that someday all will die.

Bloch turns to the fear of death and asks: "How do we shake off the final fear?" Fear of old age has replaced fear of dying. We do not talk of dying. We do not want to hear of it. Nothing has greater finitude than death.

---

39. Bloch, *Hope*, 1:xix–xxxiii.
40. Ibid., 2:471–624.
41. Ibid.
42. Ibid.

Elaborate rituals for the dead continued over time. Rich images emerged for life following death, and the prospect of an afterlife emerged in many cultures.[43] Life expectancy in the rich world increased to an extent where many feared the difficulties of old age.[44] With the progress of technology in the contemporary world, life expectancy has increased yet again, but with such increases has come the debilitating diseases of the elderly which shatter the idea of utopia in the case of the elderly.

Bloch concludes that everyone looks forward to a better life and that it cannot be accomplished in capitalism; however, it can be accomplished politically. He goes on to suggest the greatest fear continues to be death and not being able to complete one's goals in life.

Undoubtedly, the utopian hope in the secular world will not sustain one in the midst of difficulty. The values of utopian hope are motivating values, values that motivate one to achievement. For example the desire to have a better car might motivate one to take on a second job. It would not motivate one to die for it. On the other hand, our driving values are the values for which we are willing to die—the values of those who faced martyrdom for Christian faith in the early centuries of the church.

Conclusion

The observed evolution of the world physically, chemically, and biologically to greater complexity supports the argument for purpose behind its order and for the existence of a creator whom we identify as God. With such intention and purpose in mind, it does not make sense that God will allow the world to disappear. That is, it does not make sense on a human plain whereas it might make sense to God. Further, it does not make sense that our lives lack meaning for God. Eschatological hope answers the questions these points raise and provides the assurance one will not live a pointless life. While it might provide a good life in the present, the secular hope Bloch proposes will not provide the assurance all ultimately look for and does not address life after death.

God gifts eternal life to Christians when they accept Jesus, and it means we continually remain with God after death in heavenly places. Eternal life assures us that we live with our eternal God now and forever, a God who prepared an eternal place with him, which means we continually remain with God after death in heavenly places. No one is forced to accept Jesus and eternal life; we of our own free-will make that choice for eternal life.

43. Ibid., 3:1103–42.
44. Ibid., 1142–82.

God as the source of all in the physical world and the world of the spirit can freely give eternal life. He gifted life to us from the beginning and calls us to decide for residence with him for now and for eternity. We experience eternal life in the present world through the indwelling of the Holy Spirit and the infusion of God's love within us. As we do so we experience the fruit of the Holy Spirit in our lives of love, joy, peace, patience, kindness, generosity, faithfulness, gentleness, and self-control (Gal 5:22–23). We look forward to eternal life with God.

Only God present in Jesus can give us eternal life. Although a mystery, God promises to raise our entire human being with Jesus to eternal life. Paul explains in 1 Cor 15 that God will transform our physical bodies to bodies that do not perish, a prospect we share with all the saints. We claim eternal life through God's righteousness and prepare for it through sanctification and holy living in response to God who has prepared the way.

God prepares the way as Jesus explains to Nicodemus in John 3 and as Paul clarifies in Romans and Ephesians. We respond, and our response results in new birth. Our salvation only requires response in faith to trust in God through Jesus. God does the rest.

9

Meaning

Introduction

CHAPTER 9 GOES BEYOND Polkinghorne's discussion of Christian hope in order to address meaning. Christian faith as hope only constitutes one characteristic of the Christian life. Meaning in Christian life enables one to find significance for living. Discussion of hope without inclusion of meaning would miss the point evangelistically for commitment of one's life to God. It would also imply such commitment only rests in life after death, ignoring Jesus' declaration of the kingdom and its presence today. In Matt 5–7, Jesus explained meaning in the context of the kingdom in the Sermon on the Mount.

The work of several important scholars is included for their expansion of the work of Polkinghorne. These scholars include Harold Kushner, Langdon Gilkey, and Viktor Frankl, all of whom comment extensively on the subject of meaning. Their work rounds out that of Polkinghorne.

Clearly the sense of meaning varies with context. In the context of this chapter, meaning includes all that provides one with peace, joy, love, hope, faith, purpose, and a general sense of well-being. Meaning also encompasses those things which provide reason for living. The Beatitudes capture it well when μακάριος, *makarios*, translates as happy rather than blessed.[1] While "to be blessed" suggests a greater richness than does happy, the contemporary world does not use the language of "blessed." Happy also has the weakness of temporariness and dependence on current circumstances. Joy provides a better sense despite the point it does not translate the Greek here. The New Testament conveys the message that people sought meaning for their lives and reason alone was not enough.

Reason alone will not suffice and lack of religious experience cannot engender faith-based hope that makes a difference in the way one moves forward in life. The experience of the early disciples made a difference and empowered them to face untold suffering and persecution, and they

---

1. Bauer, *Greek-English Lexicon*, 487.

experienced God through the power of the resurrection, which we experience through the church, the sacraments, and Christian community. So we can say as did Mary and Martha that the presence of Jesus makes a difference (John 11:21, 32). They found meaning for their lives through a new relationship with God through Jesus.[2]

Kushner notes in *When All You've Ever Wanted Isn't Enough* (1987) that religion provides meaning and hope or it is not religion.[3] Further, without a guarantor, religious claims for meaning and hope lack substance. Such a guarantor in the Abrahamic traditions includes the suzerain covenant with Israel and the covenant of grace with the Christian and God as guarantor for the former and Jesus for the latter. Christian life includes far more than final Christian destiny, eternal life. It also includes life in the present. Otherwise, Jesus' explanation of the presence of the kingdom in his time and its characteristic for human life did not make sense. Meaning enables one to live intentionally and purposely.

People turn to religion when they understand it adds meaning to their lives and encourages them for intentional and purposeful living. The Christian life does that as reflected in the Sermon on the Mount (Matt 5–7). Undoubtedly, my Christian faith enriches my everyday life. I cherish my relationship with God and all he is to me.

Meaning

Polkinghorne on Meaning in Religion and Science

The world is ordered, intelligible, and a source of beauty. Polkinghorne moves eloquently to point out a theistic view of God sees God as the source of order, intelligibility, and beauty. In beauty, we experience his joy in creation. In moral law, we experience his divine will and purpose.[4] Beauty slips through the scientist's net. Without saying how and why, Polkinghorne argues that art and music move us. He also acknowledges art out of cultural and time context may be elusive.[5] The laws of physics assure the order seen in the universe, and life forces evolve with the intellectual capacity to develop the mathematics and tools for observation and the ability to interpret

---

2. Meaning in contrast to hope refers to the things which provide significance for one's present life. Christian hope refers to one's future destiny.

3. Harold Kushner is a well-known Jewish rabbi, best known for his book *When Bad Things Happen to Good People* (1981), reflections regarding the death of his son. See Kushner, *When All You've Ever Wanted*, 18–29.

4. Polkinghorne, *Way the World*, 20–22.

5. Ibid.

the findings, the anthropic principle. Beauty in the arts is more subtle and difficult to explain just as it is difficult to explain the experience of the divine, a point science cannot elucidate.

Polkinghorne notes in the Post-Enlightenment world, that society became pluralistic in belief and unbelief which Polkinghorne attributes to science that in its modern form emerged in the seventeenth century. At that time many scientists accepted a religious dimension of life and believed the rational character of creation and its Creator could only be discovered by investigation. The strongly rationalistic Cartesian system, promulgated by René Descartes (1596–1650), disastrously inaugurated duality of mind and matter.[6] Epistemology shifted with Descartes to rationalism, and people began to question religious experience. Moreover, the loss of religious authority in the culture following the Protestant Reformation led to pluralism in Christian belief, an epistemological paradigm shift.

Polkinghorne moves to discussion of natural theology. A religious worldview contends life has meaning and that the unfolding history of the world has purpose. Following William Paley's *Natural Theology* (1802), one could say that the mind and purpose of the Creator could be found in creation's design.[7] Paley's position is associated with the argument from design in nature to God as designer whereas Polkinghorne's approach has the character of a theology of nature as theology and religious faith seek a deeper meaning in science's understanding of nature. A religious worldview should contend life has meaning. Otherwise, it fails. Natural theology looks for such meaning in the natural world and must take care to not label God as designer following Paley. Labeling God as designer pulls God down to the human level, an incorrect move theologically. In this instance, examination makes judgments regarding interpretation.

Polkinghorne refers to value judgments in science and notes that science eliminates value and meaning in its projects in order to focus on the material. Such elimination does not mean value and meaning do not exist, and the absence of value from the description of science does not eliminate it from the scientific method. Science includes value judgments in its pursuit of truth and often refers to equations as "beautiful." The scientific community maintains moral value in the integrity of its work and in respect for the thought and work of colleagues.[8] Value and meaning do not mean the same in science as in religion. Value and meaning in science address the material and the process of science. In religion, they deal with the

---

6. Polkinghorne, *One World*, 1–3.
7. Polkinghorne, *Beyond Science*, 75.
8. Ibid., 104–6.

MEANING 153

psyche and spiritual side of human life. Yet both religion and science pursue understanding for their respective worldviews.

Polkinghorne argues for the necessity to choose a worldview. Despite the unpopularity of metaphysics today, everyone must adopt some view of reality in order to discuss and understand the meaning of the world in which they live. Otherwise, fruitful discourse turns out to be impossible. Immanuel Kant observed the impossibility of knowing things in themselves. On the other hand, quantum theory points to an intrinsic indeterminacy in physical reality. Since Thomas Aquinas, scholars have looked at divine agency through appeal to the distinction between primary and secondary causality.[9] Mathematics did not emerge. Mathematicians did, and created reality included rational, aesthetic, and moral values as developed and accepted by *Homo sapiens*. Human intuition indicated a moral dimension for reality available for examination, and acceptance of reality beyond the material replaced survival in evolution with contentment and joy in life. Such contentment and joy result from the development of the human brain, and they exist at the *dual-monism* pole, material and meaning.[10] Humankind has sought meaning from the very beginning, and science will not quench that drive. Monism asserts reality consists of only one type or essence, and dual aspect monism argues for mind and body together in the same entity without separating the two. Polkinghorne argues for dual aspect monism analogically with the duality of light which can in theory behave as either particle or wave, and dual aspect monism avoids the Cartesian separation of mind and body. Meaning develops in noting that reality includes more than the material world. It also includes those things which provide one meaning for life in the midst of disaster.

Polkinghorne reminds us that hope on the other hand empowers one in the midst of disaster, uncertainty, and finality. Hope answers the deep quest for understanding and purpose, the subject of theological eschatology. In the liturgy of the church, we confess, "Christ has died; Christ is risen; Christ will come again," confirming belief in past, present, and future. Less emphasis is placed on the third, the subject of eschatology, than on the first two.[11] Meaning, then, has to do with life in the present and hope beyond life in the present, both of which maintain importance for life. While hope points to the future with God, it also empowers the present with God. God gives meaning and purpose to Christian life.

9. Polkinghorne, "Metaphysics of Divine Action," 147–51.

10. Polkinghorne, *Exploring Reality*, 56–58 (emphasis Polkinghorne's). Monism says only one substance exists.

11. Polkinghorne, *Living with Hope*, vi–viii.

Undoubtedly, Cartesian rationalism and its influence on science impacted the search for meaning. Science which examines only the material fails to satisfy that search, and it remains the task of religion to continue to pursue questions of meaning. In doing so, religion has the opportunity to dialogue with science and pose answers to such questions as why something exists in creation rather than nothing, why order exists rather than disorder, and why we are here talking about it, the anthropic principle. The importance of the added dimension of religion comes in its expanding our view of the material world to include purpose and meaning for human existence.

Meaning in Religion and Science

Evangelism today needs to address concerns of the culture which have changed dramatically in recent years. In earlier times, most people looked to religion for answers of meaning and purpose and turned to their faith for support when difficulty struck. Since then, the ever-greater availability of more sophisticated tools of technology has eradicated many of the difficulties of earlier times. As a result, more and more people turned from religion to science for answers, as the great success of technology in all areas, particularly medicine, made many less dependent on religion for support. Nonetheless, science failed to provide answers to questions regarding meaning and purpose and could not answer important questions of why the world exists rather than nothing and why we see order in the world around us rather than disorder. We cannot avoid response when a person asks why we need God today and argues that the sciences from medicine and psychiatry to biology and physics provide all we need for a successful life. The church cannot avoid that question. Evangelistically, we look at the questions these fields do not answer such as questions of meaning, hope, and purpose.

Gilkey (1965) says Christian thought argues that the world has purpose through its understanding of creation, and the divine will and wisdom caused the world. Scientific inquiry does not exhaust the intelligibility of the world but intends to make the world intelligible. Concern comes in whether or not truth discovered in science can be reconciled with the Christian worldview's understanding of creation. Faith delineates creation from the creator, and religious truth has ultimate concern for the Christian since religious truth deals with God alone. Religious practice studies God and the evidence associated with him in order to discover truth whereas science studies only the material world. Consequently, Christians must take specific historical events into account, particularly as revealed in the Judeo-Christian texts. Every mode of inquiry has an existential aspect and must make certain assumptions before it can begin. Second, philosopher and scientist determine the type of reality the world provides. Philosophy not only searches the structures of reality; it searches the underlying structures for meaning as well.[12] Gilkey notes the dissonance between religion and science in their respective examinations of reality. Religion which relies on God's revelation easily knows God as creator. Science, because it does not in many instances accept the reality of God's revelation, does not see God as creator. In general, science does not claim any scientific knowledge for God as the scientist who only examines the material world cannot answer questions of meaning.

Gilkey suggests humans cannot answer the questions of meaning in the context of materiality. Being a finite human means contingency, contingency from dependence and experience. When people do not find an answer to the questions of meaning, they often become cynical, and acquisition of the means for material satisfaction and security do not provide meaning for one's life. Questions of meaning, particularly in times of stress and suffering have caused human discomfort and confusion in previous generations. Coherence came in the realization that human origin and final existence comes from the Creator. Such confidence in God provided confidence for successful living, and secularity did not provide such confidence. In faith, Christians approach God, the Sovereign in whom all existence and experience has meaning. Biblical creation sets humankind coherently and significantly with meaning in creation, and God's act in creation addressed not only the form of creation but also addressed meaning in creation as one sees in the Genesis account, particularly in establishing humankind's place in creation. In summary then, the Doctrine of Creation provided meaning for human existence within creation.[13] We find meaning in God where existence and experience have meaning and can find meaning in day to day living. Meaning goes far deeper and requires one in relationship with God. Without relationship, we do not have meaning for successful living which does not always stand out in examination of the world. My relationship with God empowers each moment of every day. I arise rejoicing in God and end the day on the same note. God provides companionship throughout every day.

Gilkey emphasizes that experience of the world as contingent implies its order and meaning are not always evident. Nowhere is this truer than in the problem of evil which presents the greatest issue for Christian faith and its explanation to the secular world. Matter provides one of the greatest contributions to evil. The second source of evil in Christian thought comes

12. Gilkey, *Maker*, 125–62.
13. Ibid., 163–207.

from free-will. Human nature is dependent yet has free-will to choose relationship with God and with others, and human dependence and freedom are inherently good. Wrong exercise leads to difficulty, and the first rupture occurs in the break of the human spirit with God's spirit which leads to humankind's becoming less than it can be. Whitehead points out that "why" questions do not work, as when we ask, "Why this world rather than another?" we have no other world for comparison.[14] At the most, science can suggest a major event resulted in the formation of the universe around us. Further observation shows purposeful evolution first in the stars and second in the ever greater complex biological life we observe. While science does not discuss the origins, it cannot answer the questions of theodicy. Christianity does so and points out the Creator limited his involvement in creation to permit free-will and free-process, but free-will and free-process resulted in moral and natural evil. Without free-will and free-process, humans would lack freedom to experience novelty in creation and the world would lack freedom to change. If order and meaning are not always evident, we find other means to discover it as in prayer. In prayer, we take time not only to approach God but to listen.

In addition, science cannot answer questions regarding our place in time. Gilkey says our place in time remains a mystery. Time exists in our very being as it pulses through life to the final end for our existence. From awareness for the temporal nature of life comes our search for meaning in life, and such meaning did not emerge in the Hellenistic period when the Greeks saw meaning in the order of the cosmos. In the Christian view, human life merges with the divine, breaking the cosmic order of death and rebirth to move on to answer questions of meaning in life. Two problems developed from science. First, creation did not start instantly in time. Second, time did not exist before the beginning of creation, threatening understanding for the eternal nature of God. Judeo-Christian thought explains the mystery of time and creation through myth, what theologians refer to as speaking of God in terms of history, eternity in terms of time, and transcendence in terms of existence. The point for the first moment in chronological time concerns the astrophysicist, and time for the origin of the first *Homo sapiens* concerns the anthropologist.[15] Time always seems to raise the most questions, hence its mystery as Gilkey notes. Examining and explaining biological process requires time; otherwise, time does not matter. In the human realm it governs the day-to-day patterns of life as well as the more involved such as the gestation of an embryo. Christianity explains time for humans

14. Ibid., 209–46.
15. Ibid., 287–318.

in eschatology, the eschatological hope for human destiny, and Christians see time moving forward to eternal time with God. That eschatological hope provides meaningful Christian life.

Frankl's *Man's Search for Meaning* (1968) discusses the importance of meaning for life. Frankl compiled his observations from three years in Auschwitz and other German prison camps. Prisoners continued to survive the harsh conditions of imprisonment as long as they could find a scrap of meaning for their existence. When they could no longer find any such meaning, they often turned their face to the wall and died. Why should one care about the preservation of the species through procreation if there is no meaning to life? It would seem lack of meaningful existence makes life empty and fails to encourage progress. Something that exists in the human psyche beyond reason compels us forward. Sometimes we refer to this as the human spirit, the drive to move on beyond despite the pain to something greater. Christian hope points to the greater as God. Without question, the presence of Jesus in one's life through the Holy Spirit provides meaningful human existence.

Peacocke remarks Jacques Monod's theories of chance at the molecular level for evolutionary development had completely ruled out any importance for meaning in human existence,[16] and only *Homo sapiens* asked questions regarding meaning of existence. Consequently, humans had to learn alongside chance as a reality of life with an element of interwoven causality.[17] Monod's view of evolution obscures meaning that makes a difference in one's life. However, because it can be argued that restricting evolution to the molecular level eliminates meaning in selection, and in examining evolution on the level of humans, it becomes reasonable to assert the influence of meaning for the choice of a mate. Relationship, not money and power, provide meaning in everyone's life.

Kushner says when you ask someone what is important and then see where they invest their time and energy, the two do not agree. Money and power do not satisfy the deep yearning of our soul.[18] Kushner notes that Carl Jung states in *Modern Man in Search of a Soul* (1933): "About a third of my cases are suffering from no clinically definable neuroses, but from the senselessness and emptiness of their lives. This can be described as the general neurosis of our time."[19] Frankl, Jung, and Kushner agree—intentional, purposeful, joyful life requires meaning.

16. Peacocke, *God*, xiii–xxi.
17. Ibid., 87–102.
18. Kushner, *When All You've Ever Wanted*, 15–18.
19. Jung, as quoted by Kushner, *When All You've Ever Wanted*, 18.

Kushner further remarks lack of meaning prevents living a life full of joy. A psychotherapist can unlock the blockage for meaning in our lives but can take us no further. Psychotherapy can tell us what it means to be normal, but we must look elsewhere to find what it means to be human, a religious question. Kushner notes Jung says in *Modern Man in Search of a Soul* (1933): "We overlook the essential fact that the achievements which society rewards are won at the cost of a diminution of personality. Many aspects of life which should have been experienced lie in the lumber room of dusty memories."[20] The need for meaning is neither a biological nor psychological need. It is a religious need.[21] Evangelistically the Christian message answers such questions of meaning. Jesus did so in Matt 4:17 with the announcement of the kingdom of heaven and went on in the following chapters to explain in detail what it meant. Jesus pointed to the temporality for material things and told his hearers to seek first the kingdom of God, and in doing so they would receive everything else (Matt 6:36). Jesus spoke of a new way of life and not of faith based on morality. When Jesus speaks of the new covenant he echoes Jer 31:33, the covenant of the heart.

Unfortunately, some view religion not as relationship in the kingdom but as morality which Kushner discusses. He noted Jean Piaget's comments regarding religion as morality:

> Jean Piaget in *The Moral Judgment of the Child* observes that "a religion that defines morality as obedience to its commands is appropriate to children and immature people." . . . A religion which persists in understanding "good" to mean "unquestioningly obedient" is a religion which would make perpetual children of us all.[22]

Religion which demands strict obedience to a set of "dos and don'ts" does not provide meaning. Kushner says there must be more to morality than obedience. Fear of God in a biblical sense means awe which inspires obedience far more than does simply being afraid. Fear is a negative feeling and awe positive. Religion should call on us to grow not to obey. Drawing on Scripture, Kushner notes the relationship God had with Abraham when he instructed Abraham:

> "Go forth into an uncharted world where you have never been before, struggle to find your path, but no matter what happens, know that I will be with you." Like a father who is genuinely proud

---

20. Ibid., 23.
21. Ibid., 18–29.
22. Ibid., 127–28.

when his children achieve success entirely on their own, God is mature enough to derive pleasure from our growing up, not from our dependence on him. . . . Authentic religion does not want obedient people. It wants authentic people, people of integrity.[23]

We all want to find our path in life. God wills that for us as well and the means to find it when we live in strong relationship with him through Jesus and the Holy Spirit which encourages us in our path. Kushner notes: "'Encourage' is such a good word. Religion should not be in the position of giving us answers. It should give us courage to find our own way."[24] True religion empowers everyone to find their individual path to God, and does not dictate a path like a nagging parent. Kushner develops this idea by pointing toward religion as a refining fire, not nagging parent:

> God's first words to Abraham, "Go forth out of your land, your birthplace, our father's house, to the land which I will show you," can be understood to mean, "Follow Me and obey Me without question." But they can also mean, "leave behind all the influences that keep you from being the person you are capable of being, so that the real Abraham can emerge."[25]

Abraham's great faith and confidence in God enabled him to follow God toward the promise. In doing so, he grew in relationship with God, and the Abrahamic religions look to him for the source of their faith. He did not pursue the dream to be more than God offered, something we could all learn.

Kushner continues to point out the things in life which people often mistake as providing meaning. In some instances, people are driven by the dream to achieve high status, either socially or economically. Dr. Daniel Levinson calls that the "tyranny of the dream" as Kushner remarks:

> In *Seasons of a Man's Life* (1986), Dr. Daniel Levinson sees middle adulthood as offering the opportunity to renounce the "tyranny of the Dream" and become successful on more realistic terms. He writes, "When a man no longer feels he must be remarkable, he is more free to be himself and work according to his own wishes and talents." At one point, the sages of the Talmud say something remarkable. They say, "One hour in this world is better than all of eternity in the World to come." What do they mean? I take the passage to mean that when we have truly learned how to live, we will not need to look for rewards

23. Ibid., 132.
24. Ibid., 130.
25. Ibid., 134.

in some other life. We will not ask what the point of righteous living is. Living humanly will be its own reward.[26]

Unfortunately, the world around us encourages everyone to pursue the dream. Advertisers continually put the dream out front. Politicians talk about the dream, the prosperity gospel advertises the dream. Israel pursued the dream at the time of Jesus, and Jesus told them of another, one that emphasized relationship.

Too often, we overlook relationship in our drive to achieve success. Then, we have not one to turn to when success does not occur, or even worse, when disaster strikes. When Kushner told of watching the collapse of the children's sand castle on the beach, he concluded that only the person who has someone's hand to hold can laugh in adversity.[27] If anyone knew that point, Kushner did. He experienced the dark night of the soul with his son's death.[28] Gerald G. May comments that this dark night gives one understanding that one does not need to be in control, but he notes that few had explored this night in detail until Kushner did so in *When Bad Things Happen to Good People* (1981), in which he wrote about the death of his son from progeria, rapid aging. At the end of this text, according to May, Kushner points out that achieving understanding in such a situation can mean response as well as explanation, and he emphasizes that God's role in suffering is to stand alongside. The dark night, an ongoing spiritual process, provides meaning to life. In this night, we turn from concern about suffering to understanding its meaning.[29] When we face difficulty, we search for meaning of the circumstances in our own dark night, our need to find the meaning our soul seeks.

Strassberg (2010) provides a good conclusion for this section:

> Hefner maintains that the human spiritual quest for meaning is an effort to answer three ultimate questions: Where did we come from? What should we do? Where are we going? The most important question is the middle one, the moral question, but the answer to that one depends on the answers to the other two.[30]

Actually, eschatological hope answers all three questions. In the first question, we examine the Judeo-Christian texts to understand our origin, and we discover God. Continuing in the texts, we discover the two great commandments,

26. Ibid., 151.
27. Ibid., 166.
28. Kushner, *When Bad Things Happen*.
29. May, *Dark Night*, 1–13.
30. Strassberg, review of *Religion-and-Science*, 523.

love God and neighbor, which directs us to relationship and ultimately to the kingdom of heaven. Finally, we discover human destiny in the crucifixion and resurrection. All three provide the meaning everyone seeks.

Conclusion

Polkinghorne pointed out that a religious worldview takes the position life has meaning, and he argues well for hope to empower and provide meaning in one's life. Hope answers humankind's quest to understand the world and find purpose. Polkinghorne answered that question in the liturgy which confirms "Christ has died; Christ is risen; Christ will come again." While Polkinghorne did not go into the depth of meaning as did Kushner, he pulls us back in statements like the preceding to the meaning in Christian faith that sustains one in the everyday and eliminates the despair that nothing will change for the better.

All want to avoid hopelessness, the despair that nothing will change for the better, but people tend to invest their time and energy in the things that do not satisfy their deep soul's yearnings. Evangelistically, we offer them Jesus, the one who makes the difference, satisfies their soul's deep yearnings, and leads to relationships that govern and sustain meaningful life. Christianity, when not lived according to "dos and don'ts" leads to one's finding the path that makes a difference. In relationship with God through Jesus Christ, one has the companion who stands alongside in the important moments of life and provides peace, love, and joy.

10

Hope

Introduction

Self-conscious Humans Became Aware of Their Mortality

POLKINGHORNE OBSERVES AS HUMAN self-consciousness developed, consciousness of God also developed as well as estrangement from him, referred to as original sin, and self-conscious humans became aware of their mortality. Humans have seen death as the bottom line for life and have moved toward the thought of a "good death" and the welcomed idea of a quick death. In doing so, humans demean the thought of continuation beyond death. Such a view denies death and places it in some isolated, far-off hospital ward. However, the more appropriate move addresses the reality of death.[1] Douglas John Hall reminds us: The last word of the gospel is one of triumph. People do not meet the resurrection; instead they meet the risen Lord.[2] Hall's words remind me that I do not fear death but instead look forward to meeting my risen Lord in death. We need to recover hope in death, not demean death, and can do so through eschatological hope for the future of humankind. Many avoid speaking of death and never come to terms with their mortality. When the time comes to face their mortality, they despair. Evangelism should not avoid death but should speak positively regarding the promise of our faithful, loving God. Then, when the time comes for one to face mortality, he or she is prepared. That preparation also reassures his or her loved ones who know that death does not have the final word.

Polkinghorne insists that death did not have the final word for Jesus and neither does it for humankind; those who come to Jesus will be made alive in his death. While discussion of death has become taboo for many, it is nonetheless a prominent thought—perhaps out of sight but definitely not out of mind. Humans may seek to prolong life and even to prolong life after death through large memorials. These actions only put off the inevitable.

1. Polkinghorne, *God of Hope*, 126–28.
2. Hall, *Lighten Our Darkness*, 139–45.

The solar system has a limited life expectancy, and sooner or later, all must disappear.³ Following Augustine, the prevailing Christian tradition associated death with sin, detailed by Paul in Romans 5:12. Current evolutionary understanding as well as the regularly anticipated death for all species has disassociated death from sin.⁴ Interpreters of the third chapter of Genesis often made the point that sin resulted in death. Genesis did not say God created man and woman as immortal. Instead, Gen 1:26–27 says God made humankind in the image of God, *imago Dei*, and in Gen 2:7, the text says God formed humankind from the dust of the earth.⁵ Thus, God formed humankind from the elements in creation in his image. As God does not have physical attributes, the image refers to the spiritual and relational aspects of God which is in keeping with the Ten Commandments when God first tells Israel the nature of their relationship with him and next their relationship with each other. It also fits Jesus' comments:

> He said to him, "You shall love the Lord your God with all your heart, and with all your soul, and with all your mind." This is the greatest and first commandment. And a second is like it: "You shall love your neighbor as yourself." On these two commandments hang all the law and the prophets. (Matt 22:37–40)

Therefore, the great sin in Genesis meant humankind turned from God, concluding they could manage on their own, and consciousness of mortality emerged. God called me through hope in the resurrection to abide with him now and always. I answered that call and pray all will hear his call and respond.

In conclusion, death, then, does not have the final control of our lives. Faith and recommitment to relationship with God pulls us out of the despair that death controls our future, and our future rests with God in relationship with him. Death will not have the final word for me nor for you. You and I may look forward to death as the time when we meet the risen Lord and rise to dwell in the arms of a loving, faithful God for all eternity. In hope, I do not fear death.

---

3. Polkinghorne, *Way the World*, 90–92.
4. Polkinghorne, *God of Hope*, 126–28.
5. The Hebrew אָדָם, *adam*, in Gen 1:26, 27 and 2:7 can have the meaning man, mankind, or human being. The NRSV translates it as Adam in Gen 4:25 (Brown, *Hebrew and English Lexicon*, 9).

Death as Falling Asleep

The consciousness of mortality seems to dominate life, particularly beginning in midlife. In early life, it does not seem to occur to most that life has an end or that death is possible. As creatures grow older, they become aware of the death of people around them and realize they are changing with aging. While the changes that occur with aging cause concern, the finality of death causes even greater anxiety as well as the end of what one has achieved in life. Then, the fear emerges that all one has accomplished will end, and people seek to preserve memory in one way or another. Those close to them do not help and assist the denial for the reality of death. Death only has reality for those who have not answered God's call. Death has no reality for me as I have answered God's call and cherish the time when I move from my physical body to my spiritual one.

Preparation for Reality of Death

Polkinghorne contends Christians accept that more exists for humans than mortality. Their destiny ultimately resides in their resurrection to life after death. Christianity does not deny the reality of death; it simply denies death as the final reality.[6] Attention paid to life's attractions and temptations pulls one away from facing the reality of death. Then one day all achievements and acquisitions fail in the moment of death. Instead, one should wisely use the time available to explore the reality of God's faithfulness which prepares one for death.[7] Polkinghorne encourages everyone to prepare for the reality of death. Such preparation should begin early in life. Preparation when one is in one's forties for example, assists accepting the mortality of human life and enables one to live life expectantly and not in fear. No one wants to face a terminal illness unprepared. Preparation early permits us to live out our lives in hope putting life first and death second. It sounds easy to suggest one should prepare for death earlier in life. However, the question comes as to how does one prepare for the unknown. Without my faith as a Christian, I would have no understanding for what death means. Christian faith, and only Christian faith, tells me that death opens the door to eternal life for the Christian with God. In eternal life, I rest in the arms of a loving and faithful God.

Jürgen Moltmann states the significant human experience is life, while death is secondary, and the New Testament biblical record points to death as the doorway to life with the living God in contrast to the thought that sin

---

6. Polkinghorne, *Way the World*, 90–92.
7. Polkinghorne, *Living with Hope*, 18–20.

results in death, and human life ends in death. The church in the development of doctrine identified three forms of death: death of the soul (*mors spiritualis*), death of the body (*mors corporalis*), and eternal death (*mors aeterna*). The view that death came into the world through sin restricts death to humans. On the other hand, the death of a large number of people whether through moral or natural evil does not result because of their sin. The philosophical position going back to Plato views the soul as immortal, and death simply separates it from the body. In both the Old and New Testaments, the Spirit gives life to all creatures. When we understand death as the transformation to life with God, we experience a "second presence" of those who have died and can continue on with our lives.[8] Moltmann supports the point that physical death for humankind did not result from sin, an important point for evangelism. Yet, sin does result in a kind of death, the death of relationship with the eternal, and evangelism seeks to bring those on the outside back to life, life with the living God who paid the price on the cross for relationship with humankind. Yes, undoubtedly my self-centeredness tends to pull me away from relationship with God and with others. However, as I have given myself unreservedly to God, I feel the life which he gives me both today and for all time. I fear death of relationship more than I fear death of the physical, a fear which I suspect others share as well. God reassures me that he partners with me in the journey toward the goal of life with him for eternity. The call of evangelism calls all to come to God to share the confidence for hope in the resurrection.

Humankind early became conscious of mortality. In earlier times, people did not have the resources in medicine available today and did not understand why illness could come from out of nowhere, striking down loved ones. As they became conscious of mortality, they sought answers. Jesus appeared and gave the answer when he announced the kingdom present and coming. The kingdom pulls us away from those things that would destroy us and gives life.

The advance of technology threatens those things which sustain human psyche in the modern world. The enormous advance of medical science has delayed the finality of death for many. I have lived far longer than I imagined at an earlier age and still have years ahead. Nonetheless, death lies ahead, and technology has not prepared me to face it. Hope and assurance in the resurrection for eternity has prepared me, and I rejoice at the prospect of entering through death's door to be with my Father.

---

8. Moltmann, "Is There Life After Death," 238–55.

Eschatology

Theology of the Cross

Introduction

Douglas John Hall concurs with Martin Luther, for whom the theology of the cross, *theologia crucis*, was the way of speaking about the entire realm of Christianity. It provided the means of doing theology as well as the means to conceive of the content of faith. Protestant piety sees the cross as empty whereas Luther does not by any means.[9] Protestant piety needs to recover the crucifix. Otherwise, Protestants forget the hope in the resurrection and fail to see the suffering God. Restoring *theologia crusis* can facilitate the church's memory of what God has done and lead to transformed lives in the experience of hope. I have Salvador Dali's print for his *Christ of St. John of the Cross* in the center of the living room. It reminds me daily that God stood alongside Jesus in the cross, that the cross assures me of hope in death, and that I too will rise to be with God. Somehow, the empty cross, while it speaks of victory over death, does not capture the deep meaning of the crucifixion, death, burial, and resurrection of Jesus.

While some have differed with Luther on this point, *theologia crucis*, Hall offers this counterpoint:

> On the contrary, what makes Luther's theology a theology *of the cross* and not, in a round-about manner, a theology of glory is that the gospel is for him not the good news *of deliverance from* the experience of negation so much as it is the permission and command to enter into that experience with hope.[10]

Theology of the cross does not look only at the suffering Jesus. It also looks at the assurance which comes in knowing that God was willing to face such humiliation in the cross in order to pull humankind and all creation to him.

The cross stands out in everything the church does, calls the world to come to the God who cares, and reminds the world that the presence of God makes a difference. The early church looked forward to presence once again with Jesus, something those of us in the church look forward to as well.

The point of the humiliation in the cross stands out for me. No Jew, as Wright reminded us, would have accepted a crucified Messiah. For me, it stands out even stronger that God would suffer humiliation in the face of those whom he sent Jesus to reclaim. It takes immense love to stand in the

---

9. Hall, *Lighten*, 109–15.
10. Ibid., 117.

face of such accusation and humiliation as God did through Jesus. Yet, Jesus never faltered. Even in the passion of the cross Jesus loved those around him as I see in the example of the brigand alongside him on the cross. Such love, care, and faithfulness does not just call me, but it assures me of my hope in the resurrection for my death to open the door to my God.

Parousia—Presence

Moltmann notes in Christian faith, we turn to God and live with him in the present. YHWH, the God of promise, promises his presence both now and future, and the Greeks would have understood the use of *parousia* in 1 Thess 4:15 also as the presence of God. Therefore, the Christian looks not only to the present but also to the future.[11] For me, the thought of presence says it all. I do not have to wait for some far-off event which may or may not occur in my lifetime. Instead, I have Jesus by my side each and every moment. He assured me in the last chapters of the Gospel of John of his presence through the Holy Spirit. Today, Jesus through the Holy Spirit reminds me that he is here, a source of hope for me in his resurrection that I too will experience resurrection exchanging my frail physical body for a body incorruptible. While apocalypticism led many to see *parousia* in 1 Thess 4:15 as the taking up of the church in order that the church avoid the tribulation, an eschatological view without the apocalyptic sees the second coming of Jesus as his presence.

Wright who agrees with Moltmann regarding *parousia* as presence explains that the idea of the second coming develops in the rest of the New Testament and not in the gospels, principally with Paul. *Parousia*, usually translated "coming," means "presence." It appears in two important passages, 1 Thess 4:15 and 1 Cor 15:23. Christian theology here develops in the political context of the Roman Empire and insists on the strongly held belief of Jesus as Lord of the world. In 1 Cor 16:22, Paul uses the Aramaic, μαράνα ἀθα, *Maran atha*, "Our Lord, come!" and Paul speaks further of Christian hope in Col 3:4.[12] Wright makes the most important assertion for the meaning of *parousia* as presence rather than coming. The Greek παρουσία, *parousia*, translates as presence in Matt 24:27, 37, 39; 1 Cor 15:23; 16:17; 2 Cor 7:6; 1 Thess 2:19; 3:13; 5:23; 2 Thess 2:9; Jas 5:8; 1 John 2:28, 2 Cor 10:10; and Phil 2:12.[13] Wright has the same view that Moltmann does of *parousia* as presence, a view that does not rule out the second coming of

---

11. Moltmann, *Theology of Hope*, 30–32.
12. Wright *Surprised*, 128–36.
13. Bauer, *Greek-English Lexicon*, 635.

Jesus. The disciples believed Jesus' presence made a difference for them, and the church's believing Jesus is present makes a difference for believers today.

I cannot conceive of anything greater than the knowledge of the presence of Jesus today and not in some far-off time. His presence with me today strengthens and reassures me of the faithfulness of God, and it is God's love and faithfulness that assures me that I possess hope in the resurrection.

Eschatological Hope

Polkinghorne notes that Kathryn Tanner (2000) says our experiences of joy represent the reflection of eschatology into the everyday. Tanner argues for eschatology as life lived with God in the present and not some far-off time beyond death. Further, Tanner calls us to right the wrongs of the present. Transcendent present and not transcendent future provides the good of hope. Everyone dies with unfinished business, and there must be more to hope than that.[14] Eschatological hope frees Christians from worry, worry about what lies ahead. When I reside through the Holy Spirit in faithful relationship, I know the peace that eschatological hope provides. Such relationship in the Holy Spirit results in the experience Paul refers to in Gal 5:22–23: "By contrast, the fruit of the Spirit is love, joy, peace, patience, kindness, generosity, faithfulness, gentleness, and self-control." Eschatological hope and the Holy Spirit lead to a joyful life in relationship with God.

Polkinghorne argues that eschatological benefit comes only from God and from a relationship with him. Sacramental Christian life brings balance of past, present, and future as in the prayer "Christ has died, Christ is risen, Christ will come again." The Orthodox emphasized sacramental presence even more strongly, understanding the earthly congregation's participation in everlasting worship of heaven. Further, Paul reminds us that in baptism we experience the eschatological act of death to the present and rising to life in Jesus, as he says:

> Do you not know that all of us who have been baptized into Christ Jesus were baptized into his death? Therefore we have been buried with him by baptism into death, so that, just as Christ was raised from the dead by the glory of the Father, so we too might walk in newness of life. (Rom 6:3–4)

God stands as the God of hope through his being the God of past, present, and future.[15] The church experiences the presence of God in worship, par-

---

14. Polkinghorne, *God of Hope*, 98–100.
15. Ibid., 100–101.

ticularly in the Eucharist. Jesus celebrated communion with the disciples the night he was arrested and led toward the cross, and the Eucharist reminds us of it and that we will celebrate Eucharist with him in the future. That presence strengthens us and connects us every day as we experience eschatological hope. Reflection on these comments reminds us of the importance of Christian community. Christian community sustains me as nothing else can. I cannot forsake Christian community, worship, and the Eucharist and remain at peace.

Hope by itself does not work. It has the risk of becoming a slogan where church members fail to understand what it really means. Or even worse, it becomes no more than just another theological term thrown about with little significance. As Wilkinson states:

> Yet that hope has to engage with the reality of what experience presents to us. It needs to be earthed or it simply becomes an "opiate of the people." The end of the Universe helps us to work this out. It shows decisively that the myth of human progress is extremely limited and cannot give hope in the cosmic sense. I have argued elsewhere that such optimism in future technology and indeed a critique of it is a major feature of recent science fiction [Wilkinson's reference to his previous work] (in Wilkinson 2000). In particular the *Star Wars* movies of George Lucas suggest that the myth of human progress is inadequate and hope needs to be based on the belief in transcendence. Neither the despair of Weinberg nor the confidence in human progress of Dyson and Tipler give the hope that faith in a transcendent God gives. Tipler is striving for such a thing in his "Omega Point theory," but he ultimately fails.[16]

All agree that Christian hope provides expectancy and not wishful optimism. Otherwise, it would come and go with each new event. Because of its nature as expectancy, it is imperative for the church to celebrate continually eschatological hope for unceasing strengthening of its members and for the promise of a new creation to come, the resurrection of the old creation. The church does so in the Eucharist. In the Eucharist, we celebrate Jesus in our midst. We celebrate his flesh and blood given for us that we might have life. In the Eucharist, the Holy Spirit reminds me of eschatological hope in the resurrection.

Polkinghorne contends that the world to come must be temporal without continuing the old creation. As Revelation says: "He will wipe every tear from their eyes. Death will be no more; mourning and crying and pain will be no more, for the first things have passed away" (21:4). In new creation,

---

16. Wilkinson, *Christian*, 178.

God will wipe away every tear, and a new kind of matter will exist. The act of creation occurs in two steps. The first includes God's kenotic act of love allowing creatures to be themselves. Such an evolutionary world that ensues is one of transience and death. This first stage must be followed by a second in which God consummates his will so that creatures may enjoy the everlasting presence of God. Christians believe the world to come began with the resurrection of Jesus,[17] but God who acts temporally in process in the old creation will do so in the new.[18] I contend in disagreement with Polkinghorne that God acts temporally in the old creation but not in the new. The new contains "spirit matter," and humans reside with God in spirit. Temporality has no meaning in new creation and only has meaning in our interactions in old creation. Further, God does not act in process in the new creation. Since such processes as biological in the old creation, will not continue in the new, temporal will have no meaning, and eschatological hope has already inaugurated its presence known through the coming of Jesus.

Polkinghorne helpfully explores the significance of inaugurated eschatology:

> Hope based on an inaugurated eschatology is the foundation of a moral view that supports and enables the costly demands of fidelity and duty. A person's loyalty to an aging and debilitated parent or to a partner whose nature falls short of some notional ideal or to a handicapped child cannot be discharged without demands and restrictions being imposed upon the life of the one so committed. Hope can sustain the acceptance of such limitation by delivering us from the tyranny of the present, the feeling of need to grab as much as we can before all opportunity passes away forever. We are enabled to live our lives not in the spirit of *carpe diem*, but *sub specie aeternitatis* (in the light of eternity). Hope enables the acceptance of existence and its possibilities and impossibilities as they actually are. In that acceptance, and not in some willo'-the-wisp illusion to unrealistic and unattainable immediate perfection, lies the possibility of entering already into joy in this life. Realised eschatology finds its enabling in the hope sustained by a realistic futurist eschatology.[19]

Jesus strongly asserted the coming kingdom, identified its presence with his coming, and for its completion as continuing into the future. He did not see it as some far-off event occurring in later generations, and the same

---

17. Polkinghorne, *Science and the Trinity*, 164.
18. Polkinghorne, *God of Hope*, 118–22.
19. Ibid., 48–49.

is true for eschatology. Eschatology is not a prophetic association but an association with present reality. It embraces the presence of Jesus today and not some far-off tomorrow, reminding that God does not forget us as Polkinghorne notes with respect to the Sadducees.[20] When we move away from apocalyptic eschatology, we move away from only looking to the future. Then, eschatological hope comes alive in the present. I agree with Polkinghorne and with Dodd that eschatology is realized today. Jesus ushers in the new eschaton whereby God extends grace and eschatological hope in which we rejoice with the realization that life with God begins now and not in some far-off event. That knowledge empowers my Christian life. Not only do I experience God's presence, but he is available to me whenever I call.

Polkinghorne notes that Jesus entered into conversation with the Sadducees, the most conservative group in Israel and a group which only accepted the first five books of the Hebrew Bible, the *Torah*. They concluded that the *Torah* did not say anything about life beyond death and dismissed it all together. It was natural for them to come to Jesus to challenge him on the subject. Jesus refers to Exod 3:6 and argues the God who so honored Abraham, Isaac, and Jacob in life will not forget them in death. We have no idea of anything ultimate beyond death without God, and we have the assurance God is our destiny beyond death. If we matter to God today—and we do—we will certainly matter to him after death, and the basis for our hope lies in the faithfulness of a loving God.[21] Jesus in Mark 12:18–27 remarks that God is the God of the living, not of the dead. Patriarchs who mattered to God once matter to God always and so it is with us.[22] The strong assurance of eschatological hope comes in noting that God continually showed up throughout the Hebrew Bible and showed up ultimately in the incarnation. From the suzerain covenant with Israel to the covenant of grace with Christians who responded to him, God stood by and continues to stand by. Such faithfulness of a loving, trustworthy God assures me that I have eternal hope in the resurrection and will abide with God for all time.

The Judeo-Christian texts constantly speak of God's appearing, often when least expected, as when God appears to Moses in Exod 3 and when he appears in Jesus in the gospels. He would not have continually made himself known had he not retained all creation in his divine memory. That recognition assures everyone he will remember our souls.

Polkinghorne next takes up the subject of the soul. Hellenistic thought argued for the intrinsic immortality of the soul, and the Apocrypha Wisdom

---

20. Polkinghorne, *Living with Hope*, 42–44.
21. Ibid.
22. Polkinghorne and Beale, *Questions of Truth*, 22–24.

3:1, 4 speaks of immortality. These views continued to develop to the point where the Pharisees accepted eternal life at the time of Jesus.[23] Later discussion of immortality usually takes up the Platonic concept of soul.[24] The Bible does not consistently use soul in the same way. In Gen 34:3, נֶפֶשׁ, *nephesh*, its first appearance in the NRSV, it appeared to refer to the person's psyche.[25] Later in Gen 35:18, it referred to one's life. It occurred the first time in the New Testament in Mark 12:30, ψυχή, *psuche*, and appeared to refer to one's psyche as in Gen 34:3. Peter says in his sermon: "For you will not abandon my soul to Hades, or let your Holy One experience corruption" (Acts 2:27). Here soul clearly referred to that of the human which was immortal and survived physical death. Paul uses both spirit and soul in 1 Thess 5:23: "May the God of peace himself sanctify you entirely; and may your spirit and soul and body be kept sound and blameless at the coming of our Lord Jesus Christ." In a later text "soul" appears in the words of Jesus to refer to psyche: "Now my soul is troubled. And what should I say—'Father, save me from this hour'? No, it is for this reason that I have come to this hour" (John 12:27). In one of the later New Testament books, Revelation, it appeared to refer to psyche: "The fruit for which your soul longed has gone from you, and all your dainties and your splendor are lost to you, never to be found again!" (Rev 18:14).[26] It seems difficult to establish that the biblical authors consistently used soul the same way. While the New Testament understood that a person's soul survived physical death, they did not often refer to the soul. Paul refers to the body that survives death as a spiritual body, translation of the Greek πνευματικός, *pneumatikos*: "It is sown a physical body, it is raised a spiritual body. If there is a physical body, there is also a spiritual body" (1 Cor 15:44).[27] Instead of referring to soul, Paul refers to immortality: "For this perishable body must put on imperishability, and this mortal body must put on immortality" (1 Cor 15:53). God will not only remember me in death, but he will gift me a new spiritual body. I will reside with him in an imperishable body free of the pain and suffering often experienced in my earthly body.

In conclusion, the New Testament definitely stated that a person survived death in the resurrection but did not consistently refer to the resurrected body the same way.

23. Polkinghorne, *God of Hope*, 56–58, 94–96.

24. Ibid., 104–6.

25. Brown, *Hebrew and English Lexicon*, 659.

26. Brown dates Mark 60–75, Acts 85 ± 10 years, 1 Thess 50 or 51, John 80–110, and Rev 92–96 (Brown, *Introduction*, 127, 280, 457, 334, 774).

27. Bauer, *Greek-English Lexicon*, 685. Brown dates 1 Cor at 56–57 CE (Brown, *Introduction*, 512).

Wright (2008) adds that belief in the soul was rare in early Christian writings. Peter, in 1 Pet 1, refers to the "real you" which will one day receive full salvation and is also being saved now. Psyche in the 1 Cor 15:44, 46 text means soul and not body. Origen (182–254) pointed out that our physical bodies constantly change, with which Aquinas (1225–1274) later agreed. Today, with our understanding of molecular biology, we know the cells of the body die to be replaced by new. The new body will be immortal in the sense of passing from mortal life to everlasting life where sickness and death no longer affect it.[28] The new body Wright refers to is the spiritual one that Paul notes in 1 Cor 15. Even though the use of soul was rare, the New Testament understood our spiritual nature survived death in the resurrection in the memory of God. Again, the important point is that God has assured me of my hope in the resurrection. I rest in the knowledge and assurance that God is faithful and loving. I only need that assurance and nothing more. However, I do understand that those we seek to evangelize may want more. While I might have the temptation to suggest Polkinghorne's position regarding pattern might lend itself to evangelism, I am stopped by the concern that his position lacks evidence in the revelation. Otherwise, we risk god of the gaps, falling back on god for things we do not understand. Only the promise of God to each and every Christian has evidence in the revelation, the foundation for effective evangelism.

Polkinghorne initially explores continuity and discontinuity as noting it is theology that tells the story of hope for humanity beyond death, a subject about which science lacks any information. Yet, science can participate in the discussion which addresses continuity and discontinuity.[29] Acceptance of humans as psychosomatic beings requires reconceptualization of life following death. Regarding continuity, humans must exist in the old creation before the new creation. Discontinuity requires discontinuing old creation and establishing a new creation in the resurrection.[30] The old creation refers to our bodies before death, while the principle of discontinuity signifies that the old body is replaced with the new. The acceptance of humans as psychosomatic leads to seeing life after death as spiritual rather than physical. This position requires redressing the doctrine of hell. Given that the physical body does not survive death, a person cannot experience physical anguish in hell. The anguish must be spiritual in order to remain consistent with Paul in 1 Cor 15. I contend the anguish develops from lack of relationship for humans who are relational by nature. For hell, human

---

28. Wright *Surprised*, 147–63.
29. Polkinghorne, *Theology in the Context of Science*, 150–52.
30. Polkinghorne and Beale, *Questions of Truth*, 22–24.

agents lack any relationship with God. Those who have rejected God in their life on earth will not have relationship with him in death. Further, they lack eschatological hope in the present. I cannot imagine a worse fate both in the present world and in the world to come.

Finally, we address God's concern for matter-energy. Polkinghorne explains continuity/discontinuity in the resurrection through analogy with matter-energy. For life to continue in the world to come, matter-energy must assume a different character.[31] Paul clearly states in 1 Cor 15 we are raised a spiritual body and the physical stays behind. Matter-energy as known in the old creation is not involved. We mistakenly conclude the laws of physics apply in new spiritual creation. The laws of physics apply in the natural world and are responsible for its origination and the continued process of evolution. Modern physics contends the universe will not last indefinitely. Polkinghorne argues that it will take on a new character as God will not dismiss it. That argument lacks evidence. We simply do not know what God intends for the universe hundreds of billions of years from now and it may be a mistake to go in the direction that Polkinghorne suggests when he argues the universe will possess a new character.

Polkinghorne argues for process in the new creation, hence his concern for temporality as well. Finite embodied beings are expected to participate in process in the new creation as in the old. Polkinghorne views the new creation as imperishable. Finite beings do not participate in the new creation as in the old. Jesus also insists that things will be different in Matt 22, Mark 12, and Luke 12 when asked regarding the widow's remarriage. The argument here does not resonate with Paul, particularly in 1 Cor 5:51–52: "Listen, I will tell you a mystery! We will not all die, but we will all be changed, in a moment, in the twinkling of an eye, at the last trumpet. For the trumpet will sound, and the dead will be raised imperishable, and we will be changed."[32] The natural world requires process as observed in evolution. The eternal world does not. Death happens instantaneously and one's soul moves to reside with God for eternity, an event that does not require process. God wills the Christian to instantly reside with him, the ultimate will of God. Polkinghorne's argument makes the mistake of extending our knowledge of how the physical world works to that of the spiritual. We have no way to measure things in the spiritual world of God and can only rely on his revelation. At this time, he has not revealed how the spiritual world works. The biblical record uses metaphorical language to describe the spiritual world as did Jesus in John 14. In the religion and science dialogue, we

---

31. Polkinghorne, *End of the World*, 29–41.
32. Polkinghorne, *God of Hope*, 144–45.

need to stay close with what is and avoid the speculative moves here. Finally, I do not need to know what the spiritual world is like. I only need to know that I possess hope in the resurrection to abide eternally with a loving and faithful God who will take care of my soul.

Polkinghorne states that theology makes claims for the ultimate will and purpose of God rather than the fate of the physical world. Reasonable eschatological hope must include continuity and discontinuity. Hope for this creation beyond its death requires continuity. A lack of discontinuity means one experiences resuscitation with restored life, hope does not exist, and endless meaningless repetition ensues from life to death to life, whereas a sane theology will say that the new emerges from the transformation of the old, and science has opportunity to explore how such transformation comes about.[33] Theology does not need to say more than what it says regarding God's revelation. God has not chosen to reveal his ultimate purpose for the material universe. He has only revealed his will and purpose for humankind. Polkinghorne says there must be sufficient continuity of the old body that humans share the resurrection and do not simply have new names. Discontinuity assures the life in the resurrection separates from the mortal who is subject to suffering. Continuity assures God's remembrance, and discontinuity assures one does not continue to live to die again. Instead the soul now resides with God.

Polkinghorne continues with discussion of the soul by talking about physical incidents in which the destruction of parts of the brain while the person continues to survive have encouraged a psychosomatic view of the human person, leading to the observation that humans look more like animated bodies rather than incarnated souls. Instead, an information carrying entity appears.[34] Polkinghorne states pattern carries the real me, the soul.[35] The final hope of the Christian rests in the resurrection, and God will eschatologically re-embody our "information-bearing pattern" in the new creation.[36] Polkinghorne suggests revision of the Thomistic-Aristotelian idea of the soul as pattern.[37] Following Thomas Aquinas, the soul represents "form, or "information-bearing pattern," of the body."[38] God remembers the soul, the pattern, and gives it new properties following death.[39] Such a

33. Ibid., 12–13.
34. Ibid., 104–6.
35. Polkinghorne uses "real me" to refer to person.
36. Polkinghorne and Beale, *Questions of Truth*, 22–24.
37. Polkinghorne, *End of the World*, 29–41.
38. Polkinghorne, *God of Hope*, 106.
39. Polkinghorne, *Scientists as Theologians*, 54–56.

concept permits change as well as specific markers of the particular person. Still, this view does not solve the mystery of immortality. For resolution, the argument moves to the divine memory and the suggestion pattern with specific markers resides in divine memory.[40] God will preserve my soul in the divine memory and raise it in a new body to eternal life.[41] Brain damage evidence implies the mind does not control a person's emotional state, and that conclusion suggests the emotions have a different origination in the human person. It makes sense in that for some instances of emotional instability, people do not appear to be able to reason out of difficulty. In summary, Polkinghorne suggests part of the human person includes an entity which we refer to as the soul and which Polkinghorne refers to as containing the "information-bearing pattern" for the person. In doing so, Polkinghorne seeks to explain how God will remember the human person following death. Polkinghorne is not diminishing the Aristotelian view of the soul. Instead, he builds an argument for how God will remember the person that is the real me. He argues for an evolving soul rather than a static soul. Such an evolving soul contains the information that is the human person, and the soul evolves throughout life as it gains new experience and new information.

The pattern idea in Polkinghorne explains the soul's information that God remembers. A better alternative identifies the "information-bearing pattern" as the characteristic of the soul which God remembers in eternity. Pattern then is a characteristic of the soul as red hair might be a characteristic of a human person. Neither diminishes the soul nor the person. Instead, the characteristic pattern offers one explanation of how God remembers the human person following death. However, we do not know how God remembers the human soul, and projecting human thought not contained in biblical revelation risks the criticism that God becomes a creation of the theologians, an outcome that would undermine the evangelistic task. The revelation of eschatological hope in the resurrection of Jesus is more than sufficient to assure me that I will reside with God for all time. Ultimately, faith rests in the experience of God both personally and in the biblical record, tradition of the church, and the sacraments. When a Christian ceases to participate in worship, Christian community, and the sacraments, he/she risks losing eschatological hope.

Yet, it is not necessary to discuss the soul as "information-bearing pattern." For example, the license plate number on my car identifies my car uniquely. It does not provide any additional information regarding the car

40. Ibid., 106–8.
41. Polkinghorne, *Faith, Science & Understanding*, 106–8.

and its ownership. The state stores that information elsewhere. God only needs to know my unique identifier. However, through omniscience, he simultaneously knows everything there is to know about me. God does not forget the physical as that would deny his omniscience. He simply chooses that the physical not survive. Were it to survive, it, being biological, would face an infinite series of deaths. In its place, God will give us a new body of his choosing.

Paul says in 1 Cor 15 if there is a physical body, there is a spiritual body. When the physical body dies, the spiritual body rises and receives an immortal, imperishable body. When Paul speaks of spiritual body he speaks of the real me. It never dies. The new body, in order to be imperishable, cannot be matter as we know it and must be spiritual as Paul says. Further, in 1 Cor 15, Paul indicates the change as instant, in the twinkling of an eye, and not process as suggested by Polkinghorne.

We can rely on the faithfulness of God to remember the pattern that is the individual, the soul. However, as I have argued, the more consistent position sees the "information-bearing pattern" as a characteristic of the soul and not the soul itself. Further, God more than likely remembers us in a different way. Polkinghorne is correct when he argues that God must have some basis for remembering an individual. The argument has the problem as stated earlier of projecting human thought on God. Further, it overlooks that God far exceeds anything we can imagine, and that would include how God can remember an individual. I doubt God requires the pattern for which Polkinghorne argues. All we need to remember is that God retains us in divine memory in both the present and in death.

Knowing the souls of those who have died are held in the memory of God encourages prayer to embrace both the living and the dead. God acts through grace to purify and transform all souls, living and dead.[42] God holds all in the divine memory. When we pray, we pray with the knowledge that God holds the souls of the living and the departed in memory. Memory works here, for God as omniscient must have some means of knowing and memory seems a suitable synonym for God's knowing as long as it does not imply God has a mind and a brain. In other words, we accept that God has an omniscient memory that we do not have human capacity to grasp. We do not know the "what, how, or where" for the divine or for those who have died. Instead, we accept in faith that God prepares us for our soul's transition.

Polkinghorne says Christian hope lies in the resurrection to a new body and not in survival of the current body as in the Cartesian view for

---

42. Polkinghorne, *God of Hope*, 110–12.

existence without a body.[43] Life in the world to come does not just repeat life here. It must be a new creation as Paul says in 2 Cor 5:17. God as noted in 1 Cor 15:50 provides a new body from new matter which he creates. Creation makes itself through God-given freedom, evolution means suffering exists in creation with death as inevitable, and our hope rests in our destiny beyond death.[44] But a problem also develops with the thought for a new body and requires examination. When Paul discusses the new body in 1 Cor 15, he makes the point that the soul does not wander endlessly off into eternal space. Instead it has a new non-physical place. In John 14:1–4, Jesus makes a similar explanation:

> Do not let your hearts be troubled. Believe in God, believe also in me. In my Father's house there are many dwelling places. If it were not so, would I have told you that I go to prepare a place for you? And if I go and prepare a place for you, I will come again and will take you to myself, so that where I am, there you may be also. And you know the way to the place where I am going.

God has prepared a dwelling place for our new body, and somehow the new body, spirit, soul, and dwelling place are all wrapped up together in some mysterious way in the resurrection, which does not deny the present life and body.

Paul in 1 Cor 15 argued flesh and blood could not inherit the kingdom, and while the old creation eventually dies, Christian hope rests in the new creation which begins in Jesus, whose seed provides genesis for new creation.[45] In death, God does not create a new body for Christians. Such creation, *creatio ex nihilo*, would imply a physical creation as in the Genesis account. Additionally, it would imply a new soul and a new person. Paul suggests this creation involves the transformation of the old to the new. In salvation, we experience the hope for future destiny which does not mean we cease to enjoy present life. Hope enriches present life. Jesus used parables to explain the kingdom to the disciples. The authors of the New Testament often explained difficult concepts metaphorically. Physicists use models to explain physics such as the Standard Model in particle physics. Physicists know that the models are not reality, and neither are the metaphorical pictures in the New Testament reality. The theologian must be careful to not see the eternal world as a material one with material characteristics, another reason to avoid the use of "information-bearing pattern."

Moltmann (1965) states that hope does not cheat us of the present. Hope must embrace and transform human actions. When hope brings faith

---

43. Polkinghorne, *Science and Providence*, 20–22.
44. Polkinghorne, *Living with Hope*, 46–48.
45. Polkinghorne, *God of Hope*, 116–18; Polkinghorne, *Searching*, 54–56.

into life, it becomes directed to the new creation of everything through the God who raised Jesus. It opens the future and connects everything including death.[46] Hope brings intention and purpose into the current life and expands the future for Christians who live the rich life of the kingdom in expectancy for the future, looking forward to the time when Jesus will transform our bodies to the new and to his return. Eschatological hope pulls us away from only looking to the future in Christian faith. Otherwise, we miss the empowerment of the current presence of God in our lives. Reflection on God's presence today greatly enhances the prospect of his presence with us for all time.

Wright says when Paul speaks of Christians as citizens of heaven he means Jesus will come from heaven in order to transform our bodies through his making all things in subjection to himself. In Col 3:1–4, Paul says:

> So if you have been raised with Christ, seek the things that are above, where Christ is, seated at the right hand of God. Set your minds on things that are above, not on things that are on earth, for you have died, and your life is hidden with Christ in God. When Christ who is your life is revealed, then you also will be revealed with him in glory.

Wright says Rom 8:9–11 provides an even stronger passage:

> But you are not in the flesh; you are in the Spirit, since the Spirit of God dwells in you. Anyone who does not have the Spirit of Christ does not belong to him. But if Christ is in you, though the body is dead because of sin, the Spirit is life because of righteousness. If the Spirit of him who raised Jesus from the dead dwells in you, he who raised Christ from the dead will give life to your mortal bodies also through his Spirit that dwells in you.

The first letter of John also confirms that we will see Jesus as he is, that we will be like him, and that heaven means the riches are our being in the presence of God as opposed to a physical place.[47] Obviously, Paul's comments create some difficulty. First, Paul's comments imply we do not immediately receive our new body which contradicts his comments in 1 Cor 15. Second, Paul says these events occur when Jesus returns. I take Paul's comments in 1 Cor 15 as paramount. Then Paul is saying in Colossians that we in the bodies we have already received will be revealed together with Jesus. In Matt 6:36, Jesus also argues that we should direct our attention to the things that are above. The things of the world no longer control for the one who is now

---

46. Moltmann, *Theology of Hope*, 33.
47. Wright *Surprised*, 147–63.

in Jesus. Jesus indwells Christians through the Holy Spirit, and eternity for the Christian intimately embraces the presence of God and is more than the pursuit of the everyday such as playing golf.

Polkinghorne comments that heaven is certainly more than such earthly pursuits as playing golf every day. It involves the everlasting presence of God. Heaven waits for us in the inexhaustible richness of God, and the picture of unending fulfillment seems the most satisfactory in the discussion of heaven.[48] Perhaps we come closest to the experience of heaven in worship and the practice of piety. In worship and spiritual practices such as prayer, fasting, and contemplative practice, Christians turn their thoughts from the everyday to God. In doing so the Holy Spirit leads us into intimate fellowship with the divine as we celebrate the presence with God and look to the future for eternal life with God.

Hill remarks that first-century Jews believed God would raise the faithful to eternal life. The heart of this understanding rested on belief of the inseparable nature of body and soul. Our soul inherently makes us human, and humanity, we have come to believe, continues after physical death. But for the Christian, resurrection represents more than just the miracle of God in Jesus. It represents for all of us eternal hope that we too survive death to live with him for all eternity. From here, we form endless questions regarding the nature of this afterlife.[49] The New Testament moves away from the unity of body and soul. However, the New Testament does not suggest priority to the mental over the physical body as Cartesian dualism might suggest. In the New Testament view, the soul separates at death to receive a new, imperishable body for eternal residence with the divine. But the prospect of the everlasting presence with the divine does not diminish life in the present because creation would not make sense.

Objection to hope argues that only the present has significance. However, the real present rests in the hope for the future and an eternity immanent in time.[50] The heart of evangelism exists in a transformed creation and looks to the future from the platform of history. Evangelism calls the world to the God of hope, and hope alone makes reasonable the expectations of the creature.[51] The New Testament did not diminish the present nor life in the present. Otherwise, Jesus' Sermon on the Mount loses relevance in the Christian life lived on earth. Instead, it called the Christian to the present, kingdom living through the Holy Spirit.

---

48. Polkinghorne, *God of Hope*, 134–36.
49. Hill, *In God's Time*, 1–11.
50. Moltmann, *Theology of Hope*, 26–28.
51. Ibid., 262–303.

Eschatological hope enriches the present while looking forward to the future secured by our faithful, loving God. It does not demean life today, but instead requires life today for continuity; any other position is not reasonable. God does not act temporally in eternity where processes such as the biological processes in this world do not occur. Still, God's activity with creatures in this world requires a temporal aspect, and God can be temporal and atemporal. Eschatology, then, has begun, and Christians have the confidence God will omnisciently remember their pattern in their soul and raise them to new life.

Eschatological Promise in Faithful, Loving, Trustworthy God

Polkinghorne notes theology's claims lie in the hope of a loving and faithful God.[52] The Old Testament continually noted the faithfulness of God. Some of the various texts that referred to his faithfulness include the Psalms of Lament and their expressed conviction for the faithfulness of God as in Ps 13:1, 5. In addition, Isaiah, Ezekiel, and Jeremiah spoke of the exile and Yahweh's repeat of deeds of the past. And invariably, the prophets spoke of God's intention to restore Israel. Third Isaiah, Isa 65:17, 25, spoke of restoration, setting the stage for new creation thought in the New Testament.[53] Many of these passages have significance for their impact on New Testament thought. For example, the Songs of Lament support trust in the faithfulness of God, and Isa 65 supports the New Testament discussion of a new creation:[54]

> Everlasting faithfulness of God is far and away the most rationally credible basis for the possibility of a human life post mortem, and so experience of such a life would seem, in itself, at least strongly suggestive of the existence of a benevolent deity.[55]

And we see that at the heart of all these texts stands God as faithful, trustworthy, and loving. However, a difference emerges with the coming of Jesus. In the Hebrew Scriptures, the texts consistently cried out for God. With the death, burial, and resurrection of Jesus, we have God continually present with us. We rejoice continually in his presence. We no longer have a high priest who sacrifices for the sins of the people on Yom Kippur. We go directly to God

---

52. Polkinghorne, *Serious Talk*, 62–66.
53. Polkinghorne, *God of Hope*, 58–60.
54. Ibid., 94–96.
55. Ibid., 146.

through Jesus, our high priest. Without this God, eschatological hope would not have promise in the God who reveals himself in his faithfulness.

Moltmann (1965) adds that God becomes known when he reveals himself in his faithfulness. The history of promise in the Old Testament texts reveals God and makes him known to humankind, and the faithfulness of God makes hope possible. Moltmann concludes our experiences do not make faith and hope. Instead, faith and hope become our experiences.[56] God reveals himself the most significantly to Abraham, to Moses, and through Jesus. In the first instance, the promise to Abraham leads to Israel. In the second, it leads to the establishment of Israel as a nation. In the third, it leads to the establishment of the church and to eschatological hope. God makes himself known through the Holy Spirit to Christians today. Not only can we call God to our side at any moment, but we can live expectant lives in the knowledge of God as faithful, expectant faith.

Daniel L. Migliore (1991) characterizes Christian faith as expectant faith. Eschatology represents Christian hope for the completion of God's purposes in creation and in our lives in fellowship with God; without hope, Christian doctrine would become distorted. Beginning with Abraham and Sarah, Israel trusted in the faithfulness of God to complete his promises, and prophets as in Isa 2:4 look to a time of glorification. Similarly the New Testament rests in hope when death will be no more, as stated in Rev 21:4. And Rom 15:13 speaks of the God of hope. Events such as the two world wars, the Holocaust, and the nuclear arms race greatly diminished hope in the twentieth century.[57] No doubt, the continued problems of humankind suffering at the hands of others can lead to despair that the world will never improve. We can choose to look at the problems in the world of both moral and natural evil or look up. When we look up, the presence of God in our lives sustains us and carries us through each day. Hope in the promises of God enables Christians to rise above such despair, live in the present, and look forward to the future.

Future hope rests on the faithfulness of God. To confirm his faithfulness we rely on his revelation as William J. Abraham notes::

> As John Polkinghorne remarks, "If, as I believe, any hope of a destiny beyond death can ultimately rest only on the faithfulness of God the Creator, then appeal to the revelatory insights by which the divine character has been made known is absolutely fundamental to the discussion."[58]

---

56. Moltmann, *Theology of Hope*, 116–20.
57. Migliore, *Faith*, 231–34.
58. Abraham, "Eschatology," 589.

Scientist-theologians should begin with revelation and not science despite the point that revelatory top-down insight presents a problem for Polkinghorne's argument which espouses bottom-up investigation. While we might be tempted to speculate on the nature and purpose of God, we do far better following what the revelation says. Insight gained in the exploration of the revelation enables one to live optimistically in the present even in the darkest of times.

Janet Martin Soskice (2000) notes religious hope does not just address the future; it resides in the trust of the faithful God even in the darkest of times. Hope in God does not mean optimism. Lack of hope is nihilism, not pessimism. Hope in its openness to the future stridently looks to a better world.[59] Hope emerges in relationship with God. When we come to him and commit our lives all things change. We take up a new path as Paul says: "So if anyone is in Christ, there is a new creation: everything old has passed away; see, everything has become new?" (2 Cor 5:17). We wake up in God reminiscent of waking up to a fresh morning with the dew on the roses. Soskice reminds us that hope is life changing, and Polkinghorne notes hope negates presumption which assumes fulfillment always available and despair which denies possibility of fulfillment as in the Holocaust.

Incidents such as the Holocaust require that hope does not look to the future in denial of the past. Hope rests in the Hebrew *chesed*, the steadfast love of God. Only such a God as the one who raised Jesus from the dead can be the source of deep hope. Therefore, theology must move beyond merely seeing God as behind cosmic history and beyond merely seeing Jesus as no more than a minimalist teacher. We must talk of God continually active and involved in the cosmos and in human life as written in Rom 4:17: "I have made you the father of many nations"—in the presence of the God in whom he believed, who gives life to the dead and calls into existence the things which do not exist. This same God uses his powers to bring everlasting good to humankind.[60] Nothing challenges hope more than events such as the Holocaust, the inexplicable murder of millions of Jews, and understanding such events requires moving more deeply into theology. And events like those continue in the modern world with no let up. The secular world cannot solve the problems or turn the world around. Only God can, the God who suffered the humiliation of the crucifixion. Moreover, examination of the events behind the crucifixion assists one in this instance. In the crucifixion, God suffered the outrageous actions of the Jewish and the Roman leaders, making it clear the world cannot escape such tragedies. The

---

59. Ibid., 78–87.
60. Polkinghorne, *God of Hope*, 94–96.

source of strength in the midst of those times comes from God who through eschatological hope strengthens one in the midst of disastrous events.

Moltmann comments that faith rests in hope, and that lack of faith rests in hopelessness. Despair lacks hope yet includes hope as the solution. Despair can lead one to hope for faith which leads to eschatological hope.[61] Sometimes we need to experience the pathos of despair in order to recover hope. When one is in the depths of depression and can go no further down, one may realize the current state as unacceptable and rise above it to turn to God. When that happens, hope can emerge, and such hope can lead to faith to eschatological hope in God.

Polkinghorne contrasts the religious and scientific views when he states the only real hope lies in God. However, Christian eschatological hope rests strongly in hope in a God who is active and interactive in creation today. Hope in a God who acts and interacts provides far stronger reassurance than coherent possibility in a scientific worldview.[62] Despite the great technological success of science in the contemporary world, science does not satisfy the human quest for understanding and meaning. In addition, science cannot explain events like the Holocaust. Eventually, we find the material world with all its accomplishments will not satisfy our deep need for the assurance that there is greater purpose than can be discovered in a purely material worldview. Only a God who is active and interactive in creation has the answers to the human quest.

In both the suzerain covenant with Israel and the covenant of grace in the New Testament, God assures us that he cares and will be here for us. In conclusion, the faithfulness of God assures the foundation for hope. Hope leads to faith to hope, and Christians have the expectancy for their future destiny with God. This confidence carries one in the midst of difficulty and avoids the despair that nothing will change for the better.

Faith in God

Polkinghorne's Christian hope consists in understanding God as companion,[63] so that despite suffering and pain in the world, hope prevails.[64] To see God as companion fits with the Greek παρακαλέω, *parakaleo*, although translated as comfort in NRSV Matt 5:4, has the literal meaning to call to one's side. It means that we can call God to our side at any moment,

---

61. Moltmann, *Theology of Hope*, 22–24.
62. Polkinghorne, *Science and Providence*, 95–99.
63. Polkinghorne, *Science and Christian Belief*, 64–66.
64. Ibid., 14–16.

and he will be there. Christians who passionately recognize eschatological hope and understand God as companion live passionately for the possible.

Moltmann notes that hope exhibits passion for what is possible. Passion becomes resonant through faith in Jesus in expectation for what God has promised. Faith remains primary, and without faith, hope can be no more than utopia. Hope expands the dimension of faith in Christian life, and faith in Jesus then leads to belief in the goodness of the present, the hope of the present, and the hope of the future. The resurrection, then, becomes not the symbol pointing to heaven but to the future of the earth. Therefore, when we have peace with God, we inevitably have conflict with the world which does not reside in the faith and hope of Jesus.[65] Hope can lead to new possibilities. However, the only hope which leads to a way out is faith in Jesus. Any other path is an illusion. Realistic hope does not take things as they are; hope looks to the future.[66] However, "now" means much more. "Now" includes the presence of God and not only the present ontology of man and woman.[67] Hope encourages passionate living for God in the present world with the assurance of what God has promised, and life without such passionate living in faith is empty. Hope leads to peace, peace with God, and faith engenders the confidence that all works with God and involves commitment of one's entire being. I cannot imagine living without God in my life. He enables me to live expectantly.

Conclusion

Too easily, we might conclude hope does not require anything from us. Polkinghorne quickly corrects such a supposition on our part. Hope requires work, as Polkinghorne rightly concludes.

> Now hope that is seen is not hope. For who hopes for what is seen?" (Rom 8:24). For the Christian, hope arises out of endurance in the face of adversity, based on trust in the love of God (Rom 5:3–5). Hope is essentially moral in its character, for it is a good future for which we may dare to hope. If that is the case, we should be prepared to work for what we hope for. Of course, human striving cannot bring about our ultimate destiny, for that lies in the hands of God, but spiritual formation can fit us for what that final destiny is hoped to be. Moreover, to the extent that hope is partially realisable within present history, it is a realization that

65. Moltmann, *Theology of Hope*, 20–22.
66. Ibid., 24–26.
67. Ibid., 28–30.

> is to be striven for. As Jürgen Moltmann says of the theology of hope, it is "a theology of combatants, and not of onlookers."[68]

Hope involves participation, and one does not sit on the sideline as a spectator. Christianity is not a spectator proposition. When we participate in the community of the church and the sacraments regularly, we grow closer to God. When we pursue such pietistic practices as regular biblical reading and study, prayer, and contemplative practice, we come closer to God in each and every day with the full knowledge that God travels with us as companion. To live in hope means to engage in the life of the kingdom. Life's experiences form us as they must have for Moltmann.

Often life experiences impact how we view the world, and sometimes it means being in the right place at the right time. Benedict T. Viviano says regarding Moltmann's experience as a prisoner of war:

> It did not happen by accident. Moltmann's mind was prepared by the biblical theology movement initiated by Karl Barth and continued by Cullmann, transmitted to Moltmann by his Heidelberg teacher Gerhard von Rad. Moltmann's experience as a prisoner of war had already deepened his character. The final mental push was provided by the thought of the Jewish, Marxist, atheist religious thinker Ernst Bloch, especially his major work, *The Principle of Hope* (1995).[69]

Moltmann would not have escaped the experience as a prisoner of war unaffected. As a prisoner of war, he saw firsthand the kind of evil that resulted in the crucifixion. He would have understood what Eliezer Weisel meant when Weisel says God hung with the dying youth in the concentration camp.[70] Knowing God as companion in every day grounds us in the expectancy that his presence makes a difference. His presence makes such a difference that we wake up each day expectantly, wondering what God has in store today. Yet, such experiences as the Holocaust can make the crucifixion very real in the modern day.

Moltmann's argument for hope moves from his view not only of the crucifixion as central to Christian faith, but it also moves from his eschatology, and Bauckham provides a summary for eschatology in Moltmann. "Moltmann's emphasis on hope and his claim that eschatology must be universal, suggests a thorough engagement with the theme of the physical

---

68. Polkinghorne, *God of Hope*, 30.
69. Viviano, "Eschatology," 82–83.
70. Polkinghorne, *Way the World*, 73.

universe. Richard Bauckham [Wilkinson quotes Bauckham] summarizes Moltmann's eschatology as":

- Christological
- Integrative
- Redemptive
- Progressive
- Theocentric
- Contextual
- Political and Pastorally Sensitive[71]

Bauckham comments that Moltmann agrees with his summary:

> This summary, which has received Moltmann's own approval (Bauckham 1999), does sound all embracing. The resurrection of Jesus Christ from the dead is the starting point of Moltmann's eschatology. Hope is based on the future promised and entailed by the resurrection of the crucified Christ. In this, Christology and eschatology are in a mutually interpretive relationship. The history of Jesus can only be understood against the eschatological background and eschatology gets its character and content from the history of Jesus (in Moltmann 1990: xiv)."[72] Wilkinson cites Moltmann (1967) . . . "It is this fundamental link which distinguishes true Christian eschatology from Utopian dreaming (in Moltmann, *Theology of Hope: On the Ground and Implications of a Christian Eschatology*, 17).[73]

Wilkinson's excellent summary of Moltmann's eschatology provides a basis for discussion of eschatology in evangelism. We have hope in the resurrection in gaining the knowledge of Jesus as Christ. Christology was extremely important to the early church in its drive to understand Jesus in the early councils through Chalcedon 451. We can do no less. The more extensively we probe Jesus, the greater he will impact our faith.

Moltmann does not limit Christian hope only to future destiny. Instead, he reminds us that Christian hope frees us for openness to a present of love. Moltmann provides:

> As a result of this hope in God's future, this present world becomes free in believing eyes from all attempts at self-redemption or self-production through labour, and it becomes open

---

71. Wilkinson, *Christian*, 28.
72. Ibid.
73. Ibid.

> for loving, ministering self-expenditure in the interests of a humanizing of conditions and in the interests of the realization of justice in the light of the coming justice of God. This means, however, that the hope of resurrection must bring about a new understanding of the world. This world is not the heaven of self-realization, as it was said to be in Idealism. This world is not the hell of self-estrangement, as it is said to be in romanticist and existentialist writing. The world is not yet finished, but is understood as engaged in a history. It is therefore the world of possibilities, the world in which we can serve the future, promised truth and righteousness and peace. This is an age of diaspora, of sowing in hope, of self-surrender and sacrifice, for it is an age which stands within the horizon of a new future. Thus self-expenditure in this world, day-to-day love in hope, becomes possible and becomes human within that horizon of expectation which transcends this world. The glory of self-realization and the misery of self-estrangement alike arise from hopelessness in a world of lost horizons. To disclose to it the horizon of the future of the crucified Christ is the task of the Christian Church.[74]

Possibility forms the heart of Moltmann's thought here. Idealism failed with the events of the Holocaust as Jesus' mission could have failed in the crucifixion. Instead, the crucifixion and resurrection opened up possibility, and with possibility, came the emergence of the church. Despair turned to hope, hope which we possess in the contemporary world, hope which sustains us in the midst of joy as well as calamity. Bloch could not provide such hope. Only eschatological hope does so and empowers one through Christian faith.

Polkinghorne's point augments the previous one of Moltmann. Hope empowers the present and not just the future. Polkinghorne says:

> Those who embrace hope place themselves in the hands of the Lord of the open future. To do so is an act of total commitment to the One who is faithful. In the words of Gerhard Sauter, "This is when eschatology finds its proper subject: the perception of the living God who by his promises discloses a way that we can go without being clear about where it may lead us and without being given any means to measure distances." There is an apocryphal saying attributed to Martin Luther, in which he declared that if he knew that tomorrow the world would end, he would plant an apple tree today. Eschatological hope is that nothing of good will ever be lost in the Lord. That thought in it is enough to rebut a kind of other worldly piety that neglects the ethical

---

74. Moltmann, *Theology of Hope*, 338.

demands of the present. It assures us that our strivings for the attainment of good within the course of present history are never wasted but will bear everlasting fruit.[75]

Polkinghorne's emphasis of eschatological hope means nothing good will ever be lost in God. Eschatological hope for Polkinghorne includes the entire creation and not just Christians. It does not make sense to Polkinghorne that God created the world and will not intervene in some way to prevent its demise. Polkinghorne takes hope to faith. Hope sustains us when we do not know what the future may hold. The future rests in God, and hope empowers us to live in hope for both the present as well as future destiny.

We do not know what God intends for the future of creation. Theology and science differ regarding the outcome for creation which presents a difficulty in understanding the Scripture references which indicate God will restore all creation and not just humankind. It does not seem reasonable that God's concern extends to the material world. It seems more likely that the texts point to a restored humanity in relationship with God, our hope in the resurrection.

---

75. Polkinghorne, *God of Hope*, 102.

11

Theodicy, Divine Action, and the Trinity

Theodicy

Introduction

AMONG THE INSIGHTS POLKINGHORNE provides is a strong response to the position of some that a loving God would not permit the pain and suffering that exists in today's world. Second, he presents a coherent argument for divine action as well as a defense of trinitarian thought.

John Hick works out an interesting theodicy in his efforts to reconcile the existence of evil with the existence of God. He does so by means of a soul-making theodicy. Hick attributes his soul-making theodicy to Irenaeus whereas the Augustinian tradition through Aquinas associates evil with the fall and the misuse of free-will.[1] Michael L. Peterson suggests hope, Christian hope, is unappreciated, and Christian theodicists see something beyond the struggles of the daily world.[2] Theodicists continually struggle with the questions that arise when the God of love does not intervene to prevent pain and suffering. Evangelism cannot avoid that question either as many people criticize the idea of a loving God who permits suffering through natural and moral evil.

Polkinghorne

Polkinghorne notes that a totally risk-free world would be bland. The Christian response to suffering sees God present in suffering as in the crucifixion. God gives creation the ability to make itself and does not act in creation to overrule.[3] Assessing Polkinghorne's comments about the doctrine of the

---

1. The fall refers to the Genesis account of Adam and Eve's disobeying God.
2. Peterson, "Eschatology," 518–33.
3. Polkinghorne, *Science and Theology*, 94–95.

Trinity and how that doctrine addresses such contingency, as in Polkinghorne's *Exploring Reality* (2005), Keith Ward comments:

> With elegance and concise prose, he [Polkinghorne] shows how the doctrine of the Trinity might express the essential "rationality" of the being of God. He suggests that God may be temporal, in the sense of gradually unfolding the divine purpose in relation to the free acts of creatures. He suggests that the spirit can be seen at work in diverse religious traditions, so that Christianity will not exclude non-Christians from the saving love of God. And he proposes a free-process defense for the existence of natural evil in the world—seeing such evil as "the necessary cost of a world allowed to make itself." These chapters are rather breathless, but they have a beauty and clarity that makes them models for reflection and debate.[4]

God created a world with free-will which creates itself, and that position resulted in human suffering, moral and natural. Polkinghorne uses free-process as justification for natural evil. Were the life spans of all life unlimited, the planet would have become overpopulated, and overpopulation would soon eradicate plant and animal life required for support. It seems reasonable that life spans have limits and that makes Christian hope as the final destiny for humankind all the more rational. Despite these limitations, God does not will pain and suffering for humans.

Polkinghorne concludes that "God no more expressly wills the growth of a cancer than he expressly wills the act of a murderer, but he allows both to happen. He is not the puppet master of either men or matter."[5] Polkinghorne makes the most important point that God does not will the evil that often confronts humankind. Instead, evil is a by-product of the way the world is. It always seems to me that it is fruitless to fall back on theodicy and attach the word evil to those things which contribute to human suffering. Theologians need to reexamine the language of theodicy here. Is it outdated in the modern context? Did the ancients simply attach the word evil to any harm they did not understand? It would seem so as analogous to the instances when theologians in recent times used "god of the gaps" to explain gaps in knowledge with respect to science.

Something in humanity results in suffering and oppression, from stark terrorism to hateful comments made to another person from resentment. Christians refer to these tendencies in human nature as sin, and the effect of sin is human suffering and oppression. Paul explains the conundrum

---

4. Ward, review of *The Intertwining*, 55.
5. Polkinghorne, *Scientists as Theologians*, 50.

in Rom 7:21–23.[6] Attributing evil to sin fails in the circumstances when hundreds die in a natural event or as the result of a moral event such as terrorism. We need to avoid making such moves, particularly in evangelism. Certainly, natural events are not evil. While moral evil can be attributed to the sin of the person or persons who create it, the person who suffers does not do so because they have sinned; although, in certain instances moral evil results from sin. Certainly, the Holocaust did not occur because of the sin of the oppressed, an approach sympathetic with that of Augustine.

Polkinghorne discusses the problem of evil and cites Augustine's comments in *The Confessions* (ca. 397–400) in which Augustine argues for evil as the absence of the good. He questions how one can point to evil as no more than the absence of good, particularly to someone experiencing pain and suffering.[7] Appeal to the absence of good and the reality of sin both cause problems in theodicy. It seems that we run into difficulty when we attempt to attach meaning to natural and moral evil. Instead, a better move acknowledges the presence of natural and moral evil in a world of free-process and free-will. The meaning then is that God created a world with the freedom to create itself, a world which he chose not to control in its evolutionary process. In both instances, it implies evil as discriminatory rather than random, but acts referred to as evil occur randomly. The traditional free-will defense has a similar difficulty.

Recent work discards the free-will defense in theodicy in light of the point the world came into existence far before the emergence of humankind. However, such a point does not examine the free-will defense in terms of morality.[8] Free-will only applies to humankind and to evil surrounding humankind, and free-will comes into play when *Homo sapiens* appear. No moral evil occurred before. Neither did natural evil. We speak of evil with respect to those who suffer, animate objects, and particularly humans. A kenotic view suggests God limits himself in creation when evil occurs. Otherwise, the picture would be of God as the puppet-master who controls creation in order to eliminate suffering.

The problem of suffering received constant attention through the centuries and even more so after the twentieth-century experience of the Holocaust. "The problem of suffering is not simply a rational conundrum; it is a deep existential challenge to human trust in the value and victory of goodness."[9] Yet, we look no further than the crucifixion to discover a

---

6. Polkinghorne, *Living with Hope*, 28–30.
7. Polkinghorne, *Way the World*, 28–30.
8. Polkinghorne, *Reason and Reality*, 42–48.
9. Polkinghorne, *Belief*, 43.

fellow-suffering God and not a spectator God.[10] God as fellow-sufferer and the acceptance that random events will cause suffering sets the stage for answering questions regarding evil when they occur. It seems unnecessary to use the word evil in the modern period. When Moltmann examined suffering, he concluded God was a fellow-sufferer with Christians, and they do not suffer alone but share with God in both creation and in suffering.

Shared creation also has significance for theodicy, and humans can no longer hold God responsible for all that happens. The classic confrontation between the claims of divine power and love dissolves when we consider God's kenotic acts. The kenotic Creator cannot overrule creatures and must interact in continuing creation.[11] Similarly a free-process defense responds to the problem for natural disaster. Disease and disaster in creation result from chance and necessity in a world in process. The doctrine of creation contains two important theological concepts. The first asserts the self-limiting of God in creation, kenosis. The second, evolution, points to God acting in a natural way through its processes.[12] Kenosis provides the strongest argument in responding to the problem of evil. God has so limited himself in creation that he does not interfere nor overrule. Kenoticism does not rule out his response to prayer or in miracles, providence, and the resurrection.

In conclusion, Polkinghorne's free-will and free-process defense answers the questions of theodicy without shifting the blame for evil to God. God does not will pain and suffering. To eliminate it requires a different kind of world, one in which novelty could not evolve. Further, the elimination of death would soon result in overpopulation and a world that could no longer support life.

Others

Marilyn McCord Adams (2007) says Hick in *Evil and the God of Love* (2007) suggests Augustinian theodicies take their source from primeval beginnings. God made a perfect world and evil emerged in Adam's rebellion. On the other hand, soul-making theodicies look forward. God created immature persons who mature in lifelong process. Augustinian theodicies move the blame for evil from God to creation, and soul-making theodicies hold God responsible for evil. In creating the world in the manner he did, evil naturally evolves, both moral and natural. Hick argues in favor of soul-making theodicies and shows how Irenaeus reads the Genesis story as an episode of the childhood

---

10. Ibid., 43–44.
11. Polkinghorne, "Kenotic Creation," 96–98.
12. Polkinghorne, *Meaning in Mathematics*, 82–84.

of humanity opening up a soul-making theodicy, and soul-making theodicies are superior for those reasons.[13] Some difficulty develops here. In the first instance, the Genesis account did not imply early humankind as immature. Second, a soul-making theodicy treats God as parent. Third, and most important, it fails to take sufficiently seriously the *imago Dei* of Gen 1:26 and would imply also that God is immature. Fourth, the Bible does not record instances where evil leads to maturity. Augustine's approach meets Occam's razor requirement for simplicity relative to Irenaeus.[14]

The Augustinian approach asks what the nature of evil is, and second what its source is. Augustine rejects the Neoplatonic view that evil is a metaphysical necessity and argues that both moral and natural evil result from the wrong choices of humans. He contends evil results from free-will and the associated wrong choices with suffering as the consequence. In doing so, humans turn to the lesser good from the greater good of God. Augustine thought the free-will act was not one compelled externally but resulted from nature and the will of the free agent.[15] Augustine presents a simple straightforward answer to the question of evil. However, natural evil does not necessarily involve wrong human choices. It might in the case of global warming and not in the case of an earthquake. Plate tectonics generate earthquakes, and they happen independent of human involvement. Hick comments:

> In what has become one of the key sentences in the whole literature of theodicy, Augustine says, "God judged it better to bring good out of evil, than to suffer no evil to exist." Again, "For God would never have created any, I do not say angel, but even man, whose future wickedness he foreknew, unless he had equally known to what uses in behalf of the good he could turn, thus embellishing the course of the ages, as it were an exquisite poem set off with antitheses."[16]

Aquinas separates evil into evil that affects creatures and that which affects the rest of creation. Aquinas generally follows Augustine except that he gives priority to "deprivation" and "defect." Evil is the absence of the good, and Roman Catholic writing on evil usually follows Aquinas.[17] Today, we would expand on Augustine and point out the necessity of evil given the fact

---

13. Adams, foreword to *Evil*, xviii–xxii.

14. Occam's razor says one should discard more complex arguments when a more simple one works as well (Haught, *New Atheism*, 40–52).

15. Hick, *Evil*, 46–69.

16. Ibid., 88.

17. Ibid., 90–114.

of evolution. Further, as already pointed out, a world without sickness and death would soon overpopulate leading to a world unable to support life.

Hick argues for the soul-making theodicies of Irenaeus and notes that:

> Irenaeus accordingly thinks of man as originally an immature being upon whom God could not yet profitably bestow his highest gifts: "God had power at the beginning to grant perfection to man; but as the latter was only recently created, he could not possibly have received it, or even if he had received it could he have contained it, or containing it, could he have retained."[18]

Irenaeus argued man as initially immature matures through moral development and growth to the ultimate perfection God intended.[19] I concluded that this position fails as it puts morality at the heart of Christian faith and holds God responsible for evil. Further, it sets religion up as a set of dos and don'ts, a disagreeable outcome as noted earlier in Jean Piaget's comments.

Augustinian theodicy relieves God as responsible for evil whereas Irenaeus holds God responsible. Augustine uses the philosophy of evil as nonbeing whereas Irenaeus sees theodicy as strictly theological, and Augustine looks to the past whereas Irenaeus is eschatological and looks forward. It does not make sense that God deliberately created evil in the world. Such a move implies an evil side to God. On the other hand some pain protects humans from making wrong choices.

The existence of evil in the world causes many to question the omnipotence of God. Why does an omnipotent, loving God allow evil in creation or at the very least not intervene to prevent the occurrence of moral and natural evil? Ian G. Barbour notes:

> The problem of evil (theodicy) is another reason for questioning divine omnipotence. Why would a good and all-powerful God let evil and suffering persist? How could God allow the slaughter of Jews at Auschwitz or the torments of children with AIDS if God had the power to prevent them? Suffering may sometimes lead to courage and moral growth and may evoke sympathy in others, but these positive consequences can hardly justify the prevalence or intensity of suffering. The answer given by both Peacocke and process thinkers is to suggest a limitation of God's power rather than of God's goodness. In addition, for the Christian, the cross is a symbol of God's participation in suffering and

---

18. Ibid., 212.
19. Ibid., 212–18.

God's ability to transform evil by love rather than to prevent it by an exercise of power.[20]

Kenosis avoids discarding divine omnipotence as it suggests God does not lose omnipotence and merely chooses not to act. His not acting does not imply he causes evil. It simply means he has provided freedom within the world which makes the world more appealing.

The strong answer to the question of why God permits evil in the world responds that God stood alongside Jesus in crucifixion and also stands alongside those who suffer today as fellow-sufferer. Ted Peters notes the same when he quotes George Murphy: "Here is Murphy again: 'The only real Christian theodicy is the passion of Christ. This is not an explanation of evil but a claim that God suffers with the world from whatever evil takes place.'"[21] The strong counter to the theodicy question argues God as fellow-sufferer. He has created a creation which creates itself, and which sets up men and women as cocreators. Humans share creation with God in the kingdom, and sometimes that includes sharing suffering. When they suffer, God does not disappear; he stands alongside even in the midst of natural disasters. As Francisco J. Ayala points out these come about through natural processes:

> However, we now know that tsunamis and other "natural" catastrophes come about by natural processes. Natural processes don't entail moral values. Some critics might say "that does not excuse God, because God created the world as it is. God could have created a different world, without catastrophes." Yes, according to some belief systems, God could have created a different world. But that would not be a creative universe, where galaxies form, stars and planetary systems come about, and continents drift causing earthquakes. The world that we have is creative and more exciting than a static world. This argument will not convince all, but is a valid argument for some as an account of physical evil; and many theologians use it, whether implicitly or explicitly.[22]

The contemporary world has a better understanding of natural processes than did the world of the Bible. God created a world which evolved through the control of natural laws. These laws do not change, and an evolving world often results in disruptive events that lead to human pain and suffering. Barbour contends process better correlates with God who stands alongside in the midst of such events.

20. Barbour, "Remembering," 99.
21. Peters, "Constructing," 933.
22. Ayala, "Evolution," 331.

Process theology has the advantage in theodicy that it removes God from responsibility for evil. Polkinghorne has dismissed process thought as inadequate whereas Barbour did not. Barbour notes:

> Alfred North Whitehead criticizes the monarchial model of God as "imperial ruler" and speaks instead of "the fellow sufferer who understands." I cite Charles Hartshorne, who offers an extended critique of traditional concepts of divine immutability and impassibility, which he says were drawn more from Greek than biblical sources. Polkinghorne criticizes process thought for giving "an inadequate account of divine action that seems to be restricted to the role of a powerless pleading from the margins of occurrence." I believe it would be more accurate to say that process thought points to a different form of power: not unilateral control over another, but response to and empowerment of another (as feminists have suggested)—which is neither omnipotence nor impotence.[23]

Both Polkinghorne and Barbour through free-will, free-process, and process thought remove God as responsible for evil.

Daryl Koehn does not address evil in relation to God and points out that discussing evil with respect to God avoids our looking at ourselves, and suffering decreases as we know ourselves better.[24] Aristotle fits associated evil with voluntary human action. The church fathers later identified evil with human action, sin. Voluntary actions according to Aristotle are the actions within our control. These views locate evil within the agent. Reducing evil to vice reduces it to deviance which is a mistake.[25] We forget too easily that blaming other sources for our troubles avoids our looking within which in some situations results in our escaping the problem. Further, assigning the label evil to events, particularly natural ones, creates problems in many instances. Free-process does not point to a world that is evil nor free-will to humankind as evil. In free-will, people make wrong choices that result in events referred to as evil. The evil in that case comes from a person's discarding relationship with God to make other choices that also result in a person's discarding relationship with others.

Polkinghorne's free-will and free-process position works well, fits well with the views of Augustine and Aquinas, does not hold God responsible for evil, and acknowledges that the world is more interesting than otherwise it would be. Discarding the soul-making proposal does not eliminate

---

23. Barbour, "John Polkinghorne," 250.
24. Koehn, *Nature*, 1–13.
25. Ibid., 16–34.

Christian growth. Christians through the aid of the Holy Spirit grow toward Christian perfection which the church refers to as sanctification. Sanctification encourages us to grow closer to God, whereas soul-making theodicy emphasizes personal growth but not sanctification.

Divine Action

Polkinghorne argues divine action will always be hidden, and we will not be able to attribute one event to providence and another to divine agency. While divine action may not be determined by experiment, it may be intuited through faith. In the second instance, the mechanical nature of the universe points to the faithfulness of the Creator. Third, the picture points to a world which is becoming. Novelty and top-down causality in such a developing world goes against the Laplacian view of a mechanistic, bottom-up, and deterministic future for the world and presents a problem for theology. In a becoming world, God will not know the future. He will know the world in time, which implies a temporal aspect to God. His lack of knowledge of the future for a becoming world does not mean God is imperfect. It simply means he is involved temporally in the becoming world.[26] In his arguments, Polkinghorne argues God as cocreator kenotically necessarily self-limits his knowledge of the future. This position disavows classical theology's position of omniscience. Further, it has the failing that if carried to the extreme, God could not possibly have known to what creation would evolve much less how. God must possess omniscience in order to have created the world. His involvement in the world does not require omniscience. In this instance and from the argument of Occam's razor, the simpler argument allows for God being omniscient with respect to creation without choosing to intervene and with his actions hidden and not readily apparent. However, God's actions are not always hidden as for example in the resurrection.

The argument for the hiddenness of divine agency counters the suggestion from the new atheists that God is an hypothesis which can be tested in experiment. Clearly this position for divine agency, a becoming world, lack of omniscience regarding the future, and the temporal aspect for God is at odds with classical theological thought.[27] No doubt, contemporary understanding that the world evolves requires reexamination of classical theology. However, it presents a far more intriguing view than the classical thought, as it permits the understanding of God's continuing involvement

---

26. Polkinghorne, *Quarks*, 72–74.
27. Ibid.

in creation via *creatio continua*. Given this, it becomes easier to understand God as fellow sufferer understood analogously with human agency.

An important strategy for understanding divine agency relates divine agency to human agency. When we act, our entire being acts. That view of human agency encounters top-down as well as bottom-up causality, and such top-down causality suggests an analogy for God's divine action in creation.[28] Polkinghorne departs from his usual bottom-up approach to argue for a top-down understanding for divine agency, and he must make this move to fit our understanding of revelation. He extends it further to information input and discusses the theological consequences for a top-down approach.

Polkinghorne says that God's top-down action with the world results in a number of theological consequences.

1. One of the dilemmas of talk about divine agency has been to find a path between the ineffable mystery of the claim presented by the idea of primary causality and the unacceptable reduction of the Creator to an invisible cause among competing creaturely causes (making God just a physical interventionist poking an occasional divine finger into the processes of the universe). The continuous input of active information appears to offer the opportunity of such a tertium quid. It is the translation into the mundane language of conjecture about causal joints, of a long tradition of Christian thinking that refers to the hidden work of the Spirit, guiding and enticing the unfolding of continuous creation.

2. If it is the unpredictabilities of physical process that indicate the regions where forms of holistic causality can be operating, then all such agency, including divine providence, will be hidden within these cloudy domains. There will be an inextricable entanglement—it will not be possible to itemize occurrences, saying that God did this and nature did that. Faith may discern the divine hand at work but it will not be possible to isolate and demonstrate that this is so. In this sense, the causal joint is implicit rather than explicit. The veiled presence of God, discreetly hidden from contact with finite human being, may be held to require divine actions to be thus cloaked from view. The theological assessment of the balance between what God does and what creatures do, is the old problem of the balance between grace and freewill, now being considered on a cosmic scale.

28. Polkinghorne, *Belief*, 54–60.

3. There are, of course, predictable aspects of natural process that the divine consistency can be expected to maintain undisturbed as signs of God's faithfulness. The succession of the seasons and the alternations of day and night will not be set aside.

4. Considerations of divine consistency lead us to expect that in comparable circumstances God will act in comparable ways, though the infinite variety of the human condition means that no simple lessons can be drawn from this about individual human destinies. In unprecedented circumstances, it is entirely conceivable that God will act in totally novel and unexpected ways. That is how I try to understand claims about divine miracles, a subject which lies outside the humdrum limits of the present discourse, but one which is of central importance to a Christian thinker because of the pivotal role played by Christ's resurrection.

5. If the physical universe is one of true becoming, with the future not yet formed and existing, and if God knows that world in its temporality, then that seems to me to imply that God cannot yet know the future. This is no imperfection in the divine nature, for the future is not yet there to be known. Involved in the act of creation, in the letting-be of the truly other, is not only a kenosis of divine power but also a kenosis of divine knowledge. Omniscience is self-limited by God in the creation of an open world of becoming.[29]

Polkinghorne's argument for hidden divine action fails, particularly in the resurrection where divine action raises Jesus to life. However, it works with the amendment that we observe the result of God's divine action without understanding how God acts. That position certainly fits with the mystery that surrounds the appearances of Jesus following the crucifixion when he tells Mary not to touch him.

Polkinghorne makes an interesting move here of suggesting divine agency as the continuous input of information into creation. However, he does not suggest how this works and what it might involve. While it avoids the causality difficulty as he points out, it does not posit a clear picture for how God inputs information. He does successfully argue for the unpredictableness in creation hiding God's activity and this fits well with chance and necessity in evolution. However, it continues to imply God's continuous

29. Ibid., 72–74.

intervention in creation. From there, Polkinghorne moves to the question of consistency. On one end, God maintains consistency through his faithfulness. On the other, he must act in comparable ways which means that if he chooses to act to stop a specific event, he must always intervene when those specific events occur. Yet, this argument seems at best to grasp at straws. Kenotically limiting omniscience seems unnecessary as God did not have to restrict omniscience in order to provide free-will and free-process.

Polkinghorne offers an interesting picture for divine action. He makes the move to resolve the causality question of not attributing everything that happens to God which also solves the theodicy problem as well. His argument works, and he does not need to limit God's omniscience to do so.

Trinity

Polkinghorne remarks that Thomas Kuhn argued that dramatic change leads to scientific revolutions which alter the scientific paradigm, and quantum theory brought on such a change in physics. Theologically, the crucifixion lead to the development of the theology of the Trinity.[30] The church has accepted revelation as complete in the canonical texts of the Bible and the Apocrypha and has interpreted the revelation over the centuries in the tradition of the church. The Trinity presented an initial difficulty to interpret the dual divinity and humanity of Jesus which the church resolved in its early councils, and the events following the resurrection suggested a significance for the life of Jesus that exceeded his actions before the crucifixion.

Something must have gone on in the life of Jesus to explain what follows after the crucifixion and resurrection, and explanation requires theological reflection. To begin with, the gospel writers used theistic language to speak of Jesus as did Paul, who uses Lord more than two hundred times which soon resulted in the church's trinitarian position. Still, the strongest evidence comes from both the historical facts coupled with individual and corporate experience of encounter with the divine.[31] The high Christology of the early church appears first in John and in the Pauline corpus. The writers appeared to have wrestled with how to understand God as Son and as Holy Spirit. It seems God as Holy Spirit led them in their reflection as well as the church which Jesus had promised in John 14:26, 15:26, and 16:7. The Holy Spirit leads the church to truth and its grasping the meaning of the Trinity.

A bottom-up thinker focuses on the economic Trinity and also sees benefit for the immanent trinity. The church explored the Trinity in order to

---

30. Polkinghorne, "Inbuilt," 48–50.
31. Polkinghorne, *Exploring Reality*, 88–89.

understand its experience of the divine nature. In science, the emergence of an idea clarifies the phenomenon and so it does in theology with respect to the Trinity. The three-person Trinity assists, for example, our understanding of the transcendent God as also personal and expands our view of God as love.[32] The economic Trinity concerns the events of God's revelation, and the immanent Trinity represents the indwelling of the three persons of the Godhead. The economic Trinity does not sufficiently describe the continuing work of God in the contemporary world. On the other hand, the immanent Trinity does, and the economic Trinity provides the starting point for bottom-up reflection.

Bottom-up thinking seeks to move from the evidence and experience to the higher level of theological thought. Bottom-up thinking moves from the economic Trinity, the revelatory acts of God, rather than the essential Trinity, to the divine nature.[33] The essential Trinity, as the words suggest, includes the divine nature. These various versions of the Trinity illustrate the multiple facets for God acting in creation. First, he is divine. Second, he acts in revelation. Third he continues acting in creation. Yet, some approach the Trinity bottom-up from soteriology, and early trinitarian thought emerged from the church's encounter with God.

Importantly, trinitarian thought develops from the encountered reality with God in the early church. A scientist would approach the Trinity from below which would proceed from soteriology, the economic Trinity. However, Catherine LaCugna cautions in *God for Us* (1991) against overemphasis on trinitarian thought from below and argues that trinitarian thought cannot be reduced to soteriology. Nonetheless, Polkinghorne argues the church's experience of both soteriology and doxology nudges it in the direction of the Holy Trinity. Bottom-up thinking is not the same thing as basing the final conclusion on a particular starting point. Karl Rahner offered a good strategy when he identified the immanent Trinity (God in the Godhead) with the economic Trinity of God known through creation and soteriology.[34] Conflict occurs here. The revelatory acts of God are top-down and not bottom-up. They include information from God about creation. Only in the sense that God's revelatory acts are seen as evidence can they be considered bottom-up. Bottom-up does not refer to starting at the bottom but to the examination of the evidence, or especially religious experience.

The doctrine of the Trinity emerged from experience rather than from metaphysics. In other words, one's experience of God spans many

---

32. Polkinghorne, *Science and Christian Belief*, 154–56.
33. Polkinghorne, *End of the World*, 202–4.
34. Polkinghorne, *Science and the Trinity*, 100–102.

dimensions, across time, and through the various senses as well as the inner self. We also experience God as God, Jesus Christ, and Holy Spirit.[35] Polkinghorne speaks well when he says in expansion of his earlier christological view: "I believe, therefore, the doctrine of the Trinity is not so much an attempt to construct a metaphysics of the divine nature as to do justice to the richness and complexity of the divine revelation."[36] Polkinghorne moves away from the voluminous statements of the Trinity such as in the *Quicunque Vult* in the Athanasian Creed to the economic Trinity and says the Trinity does not provide a blueprint for God. It provides the revelation of his nature and character.[37] The richness of the revelation refers to the various descriptions of God immanent in creation, as God in Genesis, as Holy Spirit in the conception of Jesus, and as Son in the incarnation.

In conclusion, Polkinghorne does not argue for revised trinitarian thought. In the Trinity, we have the picture for the intimate relationship between God as God, Son, and Holy Spirit. It suggests God as loving and relational and contrasts sharply with the Old Testament picture which at times pictured God as vengeful, and the richness of trinitarian thought strongly supports the evangelistic mission of the church in the contemporary world.

Conclusion

Polkinghorne begins his discussion of theodicy by noting the boring features of a totally risk-free world. He argues from the standpoint of shared creation that both God and humankind share in creation in both its benefits and its disasters. Pain and suffering appear of necessity in an evolving world of free-will and free-process, but such a world does not hold God responsible for pain and suffering but sees that God chooses kenotically not to interfere. Yet he remains alongside as fellow-sufferer. Hick's position does not make sense. First, it overcomplicates theodicy. Second, it does not make sense God deliberately created evil. Such a move requires God to have an evil nature which defies all we know.

Polkinghorne provides insight for God's actions in the world, his argument works extremely well, and it does not require his arguing God of necessity limits his omniscience. In this instance, his argument risks taking the analogy of the human to the divine too far.

---

35. Polkinghorne, *Way the World*, 98.
36. Ibid.
37. Ibid., 98–101.

12

In Conclusion

Introduction

Earlier, in the introduction to this work, I drew attention to Peacocke's comments on Leslie Newbigin's *Foolishness to the Greeks* (1986): "No-one concerned with the future of the Christian, or indeed any other religion, can avoid facing up to the impact of science on faith. This encounter is identified by Newbigin as the crucial point at which the gospel is failing to have any impact on 'Western' men and women."[1] The work of Polkinghorne offers a credible singular response to the problem that Newbigin identifies and assists the evangelistic spread of the gospel message as well as catechesis.

Evangelism has not only the crucial task to spread the message, but it also has the task to assure that those making a new or renewed commitment are linked into the church through discipleship and catechesis. Evangelism announces the message of the kingdom, spreads the message of expectancy and eschatological hope, both present and future, and invites everyone to meet the risen Lord. Polkinghorne's work invites everyone to eschatological hope and reminds the church of the future destiny for those committed to God in the present.

Evangelism in too many instances presents the good news of the gospel in a negative framework and often rejects reason and appears anti-intellectual. Moreover, some evangelists oversimplify the message and present inadequate content. In doing so, the evangelist turns good news into bad news and provides no element of hope. The work of Polkinghorne offers the evangelist the positive framework of hope whereby an informed evangelist can invite those outside to the kingdom as does Jesus when he announces the kingdom in Matthew and says: "Repent, for the kingdom of heaven has come near" (Matt 4:17). Repent, μετανοέω, *metanoeo*, here calls one to turn from the world to the kingdom and away from one's past sins.

---

1. Peacocke, *Theology*, 1.

IN CONCLUSION

This final chapter of this work sets out the major contributions of John Polkinghorne to theology, particularly his work on eschatological hope. The chapter assesses how well Polkinghorne's work responds to Leslie Newbigin's assertion that the church needs to respond to the impact of science in the contemporary world. Polkinghorne's work succeeds. Not only does it succeed, it provides a strong, singular amendment to evangelism, hope for human destiny, both present and future.

Polkinghorne

Polkinghorne approached theology as one might expect for a scientist of his stature, always separating epistemology from ontology or the actual reality.[2] He readily examined the evidence from the bottom-up and was decidedly critical realistic as seen in his discussion of the resurrection. This approach commends him to the broader culture.[3] His process of thought resembles the process of the scientist who carefully looks at the experimental evidence to interpret the result. In doing so, the scientist also asks what might have been overlooked and does not accept any new discovery as absolute.

In short, Polkinghorne's life experiences in both the world of the Anglican Church and physics provides the preparation he needed to extend more deeply into the world of the church. His methodical approach which does not accept things as necessarily settled makes it easy to argue that his work supports and augments material for evangelism.

Evangelism

Successful evangelism responds to the culture and does not ignore important questions. In doing so, it responds to the expectancy in the culture and reaches out to each new generation. Jesus went to the people as did Wesley later, reached out to where the people were, spoke in language they understood, and supported his message with the use of parables. Billy Graham did similarly in the contemporary world. In these instances, people responded and followed. The message always relied on Scripture, and Graham frequently spoke with an open Bible in his hand, inviting people to kingdom life.

Jesus began his ministry with the announcement of the kingdom, and those around him experienced the kingdom (Luke 6:20). Evangelism today can do no less. People around Jesus expected his presence to make a

---

2. Polkinghorne, *Physicist to Priest*, 131–56.
3. Polkinghorne, *Faith, Science & Understanding*, 32–34.

difference, an expectancy evangelism needs to have out front. Evangelism should go to the people as did Jesus and speak to the people in contextual language that they may understand and respond. Sometimes we forget that those outside the church do not have biblical understanding, and the biblical language in evangelism may not resonate with them.

Epistemology

Polkinghorne supported his critical realistic approach with Scripture, reason, tradition, and experience, readily suggested the verisimilitude character of discovery to point out that science did not claim absolute truth.[4] Polkinghorne carefully worked systematically through questions in religion and science. His best work for evangelism addressed the factual and circumstantial evidence for the resurrection which lead to his systematization of eschatological hope. He also addressed side issues such as the problem of evil, and here too his bottom-up examination of the evidence worked extremely well.

The discussion earlier in this work of Polkinghorne covered a range of themes to support the claim that Polkinghorne's work is a good source for evangelism. First, it established his approach as a bottom-up thinker who looked at reality in a critical realistic manner which the scientific community he addresses would find acceptable. This gives him the starting point for examination, bottom-up in both religion and science.

We saw in the discussion earlier that greater congruity would develop when scholars seek to develop thought that includes both the bottom-up and top-down approach. Sole bottom-up does not accommodate divine agency, and bottom-up must also accommodate top-down. Fear of shortfalls such as Polkinghorne's fear that a total top-down approach results in gaps in knowledge should not discredit such an approach. Instead, shortfalls call for examination and modification.

In summary, Polkinghorne epistemologically approaches questions in religion and science from a bottom-up, critical realistic position. He acknowledges that discovery in both religion and science has a verisimilitudinous character, representative of reality. This conclusion agrees with his experience in particle physics where the Standard Model models reality and yet is not a full account of reality. It would work well to use bottom-up and top-down as complementary. In the instance of divine revelation, revelation is top-down, from God to creation, and requires top-down exploration, and complex biological systems require top-down exploration as well.

4. Ibid., 73–80.

Kenosis

God's greatest kenotic act occurs in the crucifixion. Polkinghorne argues that God did not need to create the world, but once he did, it became intrinsically important to him, and he remained involved in its fate.[5] God self-limits his omnipotence in creation to permit free-will and free-process. This move gives creatures freedom, enables a world that makes itself through natural law, and allows for creatures as co-sharers of creation through free-will and free-process. Moreover, this position greatly assists evangelism's response to questions from the culture regarding God's activity in creation and also discounts the criticism of how a loving God could permit suffering.

Polkinghorne argues that creatures become cocreators with God.[6] Unfortunately this argument has the problem that *Homo sapiens* did not emerge until two hundred thousand years ago, after the universe had aged 13.7 billion years or so and could not have been cocreators. Further, the creaturely scale is vastly smaller than that for the universe, limiting the extent to which creatures can cocreate. This argument for co-sharing should be scaled down in order to be credible in the contemporary world.

More importantly, the co-sharing frees God from responsibility for moral evil; however, the free-will defense does so as well. While God chose to kenotically limit his activity in the world even in the midst of disastrous events such as the Holocaust or the tsunami that enveloped Japan in recent times, it does not mean that God willed these events. Polkinghorne points out that everything occurs according to the providence of God but not always according to the will of God.[7] God's kenotic limitation in creation means some events happen within God's providence but not according to his will. Further, Polkinghorne also argues God self-limits his knowledge regarding future events, thereby limiting his omniscience.

Polkinghorne makes his strongest move away from classical theology when he argues the necessity for God's kenotic limitation of omniscience.[8] No necessity for such limitation appears, particularly in Scripture. Had God done so, at the beginning, he could not have known how the world would evolve, a threat to the observed purpose in evolution. The position of not limiting God's omniscience does not affect kenosis, free-will, free-process, or co-creating with humans. Instead, self-limiting kenosis means God as cocreator does not override creatures. The idea that God self-limits om-

---

5. Polkinghorne, *Science and Creation*, 62–64.
6. Polkinghorne, *Faith, Science & Understanding*, 126–27.
7. Polkinghorne, "Kenotic Creation," 102–4.
8. Ibid., 104–8.

niscience in creation is unnecessary and its elimination does not restrict kenosis or the thought of *creatio continua*.

Temporality connects with his argument for omniscience when he argues God knows all that can be known, meaning past and present; God cannot know the future for it has not yet developed.[9] God interacts temporally in creation through his connection with creatures and through *creatio continua*. His act of creation began with its beginning and the setting in place of natural law which governs the evolving world; consequently, with laws in place to assure a world that creates itself, God maintains a position as overseer and not as one who continues to effect change in creation. On a human level, this argument for limited omniscience is true. Humans lack omniscience for the future. God does not have that limitation, and applying kenotic limitation to omniscience goes too far. However, God's knowledge of the future would not impact his kenotic self-limitation in creation.

Overdoing kenosis risks the same error as the pursuit of "god of the gaps" and does not cohere with the observed purpose in an evolutionary world. A complicated kenotic model fails Occam's razor, and a Trinitarian Model of Kenosis (TMK) works extremely well and makes for a better fit with classical theology. The premises for such a model might include the following:

1. A single source exists for all that we observe in the universe.
2. Space-time expands without limit.
3. The source, also infinite in presence, occupies all space without somehow impinging on creation.
4. Observations in the universe suggest the universe possesses "the footprints" of its creator; i.e., the character of the universe and its inhabitants suggest aspects of the creator.
5. The creator is the god of the Abrahamic religions whom we call God.
6. God's activity is constant and consistent everywhere in the universe. From time to time, he may intervene directly in the universe as in the incarnation and resurrection as well as with Jesus' meeting with Paul on the road to Damascus.
7. God created a world which makes itself, *creatio continua*; he kenotically self-limits himself in creation to permit free-will and free-process; he acts temporally in creation and atemporally in the eternal. However, God

---

9. Ibid., 118–20.

IN CONCLUSION

retains omnipotence and omniscience. In the case of the former, he chooses not to exercise omnipotence in order to permit free-will and free-process.

8. Creatures share in limited extent in creation as cocreators with God.
9. God has revealed himself to humankind on the earth which does not eliminate the possibility that he acted and revealed himself elsewhere in the universe.
10. God interacts trinitarianly with creation, sometimes as God, sometimes as Jesus Christ, and sometimes as Holy Spirit.

These premises develop from what we observe about our world, what God revealed in the Judeo-Christian texts, and the continued experience of the church. In the universe, we observe order throughout the cosmos and do not see conflicting laws of nature. Observation indicates that the natural laws apply equally throughout the universe, which points to a single source for their initiation in support of the first premise.

The universe has expanded from an infinitely small size to its current size of 13.7 billion light years across. Physicists believe it will continue to expand for billions of years, and the rate of expansion is accelerating.[10] That can only occur when there is no limit to the expansion, the second premise.

The source for creation must also be infinite in extent in order to exceed the limits of an expanding universe. As the detail of the watch in Paley's *Natural Theology* (2006) suggested the skills of the watchmaker, the details on multiple levels in creation point to an incomprehensible source for all that exists which has revealed itself in the Abrahamic religions, and we call the source for all that exists God, premises 1, 3, 4, 5.[11]

Since God has infinite extent, his activity must be constant and consistent throughout the cosmos. The observed order and evolution we observe supports such a conclusion, and his revelation to creation reveals some of his nature, premise 6. This picture of infinite extent complicates the assertion of immanence in a creation infinitely smaller. However, God as Holy Spirit can interact immanently in creation on any level which he does as we see in Gen 1, John 1, and Col 1. Not only does he act through the Holy Spirit, but the picture, particularly in Col 1 indicates God acts simultaneously trinitarianly as God, Jesus Christ, and Holy Spirit analogous to light as simultaneously wave and particle.

---

10. Wilkinson says recent evidence shows the universe's rate of expansion is accelerating (Wilkinson, *Christian*, 29–52).
11. Paley, *Natural Theology*, 7–10.

God of necessity in his divine will self-limited omnipotence in creation in order to not tyrannically overrule creation. His self-limitation permitted free-will and free-process, a world which makes itself, and creatures in limited extent as cocreators and co-sharers with God, premises 7, 8. His move here permitted a far more novel world where art and beauty emerge, and creatures share in the joy of co-creation.

God has revealed himself on earth, and we retain the record of his revelation in Scripture. The great extent of the universe makes it possible life evolved elsewhere, but we have no evidence whether it has or has not. Therefore, we must assume the likelihood it did and that God has possibly revealed himself to others beyond our earth. If so, we can expect to encounter others from outside earth in eternity, premise 9.

The Trinity provides the wonderful model for God's activity in creation. In Scripture, we have the record that God acted as God in the Old Testament period, as Jesus in the gospels, and as Holy Spirit in the remainder of the New Testament, premise 10.

The perturbation model in quantum physics suggests how God might interact in creation from the infinite to the infinitesimal. He can possibly act through infinitely small perturbations that disturb systems to change the normal course of nature. While we might not know exactly how, contemporary science has the lens to suggest possibilities for interaction that do not overturn the laws of nature. Both perturbation and chaos theory have that possibility.

My suggestions for the revision of kenosis do not detract from Polkinghorne's argument for eschatological hope, and my revision suggests a more credible argument for the commendation of the Christian faith in the contemporary world.

Craig A. Boyd and Aaron D. Cobb (2009) earlier summarized Polkinghorne's kenotic thought in this way.

As Polkinghorne uses the term, it refers to four different—but related—kinds of kenosis:

1. Kenosis of omnipotence;
2. Kenosis of simple eternity;
3. Kenosis of omniscience;
4. Kenosis of causal status.[12]

Polkinghorne in the first instance argues God self-limits omnipotence in order to not overwhelm creation. In the second, kenosis of simple eternity and omniscience refers to Polkinghorne's view that God self-limits omniscience and cannot know the future which has not developed yet. In

12. Boyd and Cobb, "Causality," 396.

the case of kenosis of causal status, Polkinghorne argues that the God of love allows special providence as a cause among causes.[13] Kenosis of omnipotence works as we see no evidence that God rules in creation, tyrannically or otherwise. However, evidence is lacking and scarce at best to support self-limited omniscience, and seems unnecessary for Polkinghorne's argument. God from time to time has acted in creation providentially and more than likely will continue to do so.

Christology

Truly, Jesus was divine and human which the early church got right in the councils through Chalcedon 451.[14] Jesus stood at the center of controversy from the very beginning and throughout his life. He was not the Messiah the Jews expected and threatened their leadership. He upset cultural expectations by proclaiming that the poor were rich, the rich poor. He associated with those the culture considered as sinners and chose to violate the Sabbath which he pointed out was made for man and that man was not made for the Sabbath. He argues for the outcast as the neighbor and for compassion illustrated by way of parable.[15] Anyone familiar with Hebrew prophecy would suspect the appearance of the Messiah might make a difference politically. The Jews expected a Messiah who would restore the Davidic monarchy which would threaten Roman rule. The Jews did not expect a Messiah like Jesus, particularly a crucified Messiah which went against Jewish thought that believed anyone hung on a tree was under God's curse (Deut 21:23). Nonetheless, God became flesh and blood in the incarnation and faced the condemnation of the world.

God kenotically suffered the abuse, pain, and humiliation of the cross with Jesus. As he stood alongside Jesus, he stands alongside us. Friedrich Wilhelm Joseph Schelling argued that God is revealed in his opposite, in the godlessness, in the abandonment of the cross,[16] and in the horrific death of crucifixion. God stands out in the innocence of Jesus above the roar of the crowd to crucify him. The crowd called for the crucifixion of God, a folly that they did not understand, and Jesus stood above his accusers in death.

When we experience God through Jesus, we experience something larger than we are. In his coming, the world gained new understanding of what it meant to be human, and his crucifixion enlarged that rather than diminish it.

13. Ibid., 396–97.
14. Lohse, *Short History*, 94.
15. Ibid.
16. Moltmann, *Crucified God*, 26–31.

Eschatology

Kathryn Tanner pointed out that Christianity does not concern itself with either how the world began or how it will end.[17] Instead, Christianity concerns itself with human destiny. Zoroastrian Apocalypticism featured the battle between good and evil through veiled disclosure which carried over into Judeo-Christian Apocalypticism.[18] The apocalyptic reassures through veiled disclosure that good prevails, and 1 Thess 4:15 reassured Christians facing martyrdom in the early centuries of the church, a bleak time in the early church. The interpretation of *parousia* in 1 Thess 4:15 as presence suggested that Jesus is present with those facing martyrdom. This interpretation makes for a far more nourishing statement for God than the far-off picture of Jesus' coming again. Further, it reassures us for Jesus' presence today as it must have reassured the early Christians, despite the bleak future described by Mark.

Hill remarked that the apocalyptic literature was the most accurate for present events and represented the prophetic in a particular time frame.[19] Following his reasoning, he associated Daniel with Antiochus IV and the erection of the temple to Zeus in the Jewish temple in 167 BCE; he associated Revelation with Caesar Domitian.[20] The apocalyptic as noted addressed the issues of the present. It seems unlikely Daniel referred to events 200–250 years later and that Daniel and Revelation referred to events in the contemporary period. Instead their eschatology reassured Israel and the early Christians that God would prevail, which aligns with Brueggemann's discussion of the mission of the prophet.[21]

Moltmann, whose work strongly influenced Polkinghorne, argued for eschatological hope beginning in the cross. Only there can we find the purpose of God for humankind as well as hope for future destiny. Moltmann insisted that Christianity is really an eschatology which looks forward and transforms the present.[22] Moltmann avoids dismissing the cross to concentrate on the resurrection. Too often the church dwells only on the resurrection and misses the point which Paul argues so well in Romans that God paid the price, a huge one, and a price which gifts life to us on the merit of Jesus' sacrifice.

17. Polkinghorne, *God of Hope*, 98–100.
18. Hart, "Death," 484–85.
19. Hill, *In God's Time*, 99–100.
20. Ibid., 110–11.
21. Brueggemann, *Prophetic*.
22. Moltmann, *Theology of Hope*, 16.

Polkinghorne argued in his eschatology that creation "must be redeemed from transience and decay."[23] Any other position is not reasonable. Further, Christians, if loved by God, must also find fulfillment in the purposes of God. There must be continuity/discontinuity to assure Christians that they do not go through cycles of rebirth. The love and faithfulness of God support this eschatological hope.[24] Polkinghorne argues it does not make sense to say that God will desert creation and thus not redeem it as well. Unfortunately, we do not know what God ultimately plans for creation. The important point for humankind is that the earth will not survive for more than another five billion years or so. That is far more relevant than the fate of all creation. Moreover, our eschatological hope rests in the promise of our being with God for all eternity. These points remind us that theology and doctrine do not result in salvation. Response to Jesus' invitation and commitment to God through him save us, which is the core message of evangelism.

Polkinghorne's eschatology fits well for the contemporary message of evangelism. It coheres with Moltmann's thought and offers the contemporary world purpose and future destiny with God, calling the world to life in the kingdom. Eschatological hope begins in the present and is not merely the promise of a far-off event.

The Kingdom of God

Jesus began his mission declaring the presence of the kingdom which had begun to make itself felt, and immediately in Matthew in the Sermon on the Mount, he explained the content for the kingdom. As noted in the Beatitudes, people happily share in kingdom life. In the kingdom, God stands alongside, and in the kingdom, the Christian can call him alongside at a moment's notice with the expectancy he will be present and make a difference.

Abraham adds regarding the relationship of evangelism and the kingdom of God:

> Whatever evangelism may be, it is at least intimately related to the gospel of the reign of God that was inaugurated in the life, death, and resurrection of Jesus of Nazareth. Any vision of evangelism that ignores the kingdom of God, or relegates it to a position of secondary importance, or fails to wrestle thoroughly with its content is destined at the outset to fail.[25]

---

23. Polkinghorne, *God of Hope*, 148–49.
24. Ibid.
25. Abraham, *Logic*, 17–39.

Jesus' announcement and explanation of the kingdom in the beginning of his ministry illustrate how important he, and God as well, consider the kingdom. Evangelism cannot ignore the proclamation of the kingdom. It should invite everyone to the kingdom and into a relationship with God through Jesus Christ for kingdom life.

Resurrection

Polkinghorne began with the examination of the evidence for the resurrection in the Bible remarking that the stories emerged for their distinctly memorable description of the events.[26] The descriptions varied from gospel to gospel. N. T. Wright reminded us that variation in detail did not mean the events never happened.[27] People tend to remember the events that affect them significantly throughout life which we can argue occurred in the resurrection stories.

As we have seen in the instance of wave/particle duality, the lack of understanding does not deny the occurrence, and Polkinghorne points out we do not require prior explanation and understanding for something to be true. At the same time we may also seek for explanation and understanding.[28] Physicists like Christians cannot explain everything they experience, but lack of explanation does not disprove the experience. Jesus as both human and divine mattered. As human he physically suffered the crucifixion. As divine he suffered that we might live. As resurrected, he provides resurrection for all who come to him.

Polkinghorne presented a nuanced account for the factual and circumstantial evidence supporting the resurrection of Jesus. The strongest evidence came in the various appearances of Jesus following the resurrection beginning with his appearance to Mary who mistook him for the gardener. Those who saw him did not immediately recognize him. That and the fact that he appeared randomly and could go through walls in locked rooms indicated a change in his physicality. Finally, the tomb stood empty. As Wright remarked, only the burial clothes would have remained.[29] The circumstantial evidence strongly argued that something happened beginning with Jesus' burial in the tomb of Joseph of Arimathea. It would have been highly unlikely that either Nicodemus or Joseph of Arimathea would have been unaware should either the Jews or the Romans removed his body.

26. Polkinghorne, *Way the World*, 38–42.
27. Wright *Surprised*, 53–58.
28. Polkinghorne, *Meaning in Mathematics*, 90–92.
29. Wright *Surprised*, 58–62.

Additional circumstantial evidence included the early Christian adoption of Sunday for worship, the transformation of the disciples, and the fact early Christians would not have been willing to die for something that had not happened.[30] Those to whom Jesus appeared following the resurrection provided the acceptable testimony of that day for the resurrection. The varying descriptions further suggest the reality of their witness. Had they all told the story in the same detail, it would have seemed they manufactured the story and memorized the details.

Second, something happened which empowered them, and that something continued to empower those who responded to God through Jesus over the centuries. Polkinghorne in his defense of the resurrection has provided a strong evangelistic message for the faithfulness of God to creation.

While the strong message from Polkinghorne emerges in his discussion of eschatological hope, he demonstrates his strong, eloquent presentation for the facts supporting the resurrection, a discussion that stands out in his work. His argument for the resurrection greatly serves the evangelistic effort to commend Christian faith in contemporary culture.

Foundation for Hope

Crucial to the import of any religion is its sense of expectancy. For Moltmann, the resurrection represented the heart of Christian hope. He points out it was never seen as a private miracle that occurred in isolation.[31] It represented God's eschatological transformation as well as the beginning of eschatological hope for all humanity with which Polkinghorne agreed. The early Christians understood God had stood alongside Jesus as he would stand alongside them, and through eschatological hope, they no longer saw death as something to be feared.

Polkinghorne pursued Aristotle and Aquinas' discussions of the soul to develop his extension to the soul as the "information-bearing pattern" that represented the real me, the person. This "information-bearing pattern" carries the information that God remembers following death, that "information-bearing pattern" identifies each one to God, and in new creation, God will transform the person of the old creation to the one in new creation. He will not do so *creatio ex nihilo*.[32] Eschatological hope rests in the trust in a faithful, loving God. However, instead of replacing the soul with "information-bearing pattern" pattern, it has better congruence when

30. Polkinghorne, *Way the World*, 84–85.
31. Moltmann, *Crucified God*, 162–63.
32. Polkinghorne, *Belief*, 22–24.

"information-bearing pattern" is identified as one of the characteristics of the soul which enables its identification to God. Yet, this position falls back on human opinion regarding the character of God. To an extent, the requirement for the character of "information-bearing pattern" denies God's omniscience. We do not have the means to understand how omniscience works for God. I doubt God requires the pattern for which Polkinghorne argues. In conclusion, all we need to remember is that God retains us in divine memory in both the present and in death. I doubt God requires the pattern for which Polkinghorne argues. In conclusion, all we need to remember is that God retains us in divine memory in both the present and in death.

God as the source of all in the physical world and the world of the spirit can freely gift eternal life. He gifted life to us from the beginning and calls us to decide for residence with him for now and for eternity. We experience eternal life in the present world through the indwelling of the Holy Spirit and infusion of God's love within us. As we do so we experience the fruit of the Holy Spirit in our lives of love, joy, peace, patience, kindness, generosity, faithfulness, gentleness, and self-control (Gal 5:22–23).

Meaning

Hope for the future without meaning in the present lacks fulfillment. Experience, not reason, empowered the early disciples as it does us today. Kushner notes religion offers meaning and hope in life. Otherwise, it cannot be religion.[33] Viktor Frankl in *Man's Search for Meaning* (1968) also observes the importance of meaning for survival here and now.[34] Finding meaning enables one to live a life that makes a difference, and Christian faith provides that meaning and purpose.

Polkinghorne insists that a religious worldview must address the issue of meaning and the unfolding purpose observed in creation. The material world does not satisfy humankind's quest for satisfaction, contentment, and joy in this life. He notes that hope empowers one in the midst of uncertainty and disaster. In the liturgy, he points out that the prayer "Christ has died; Christ is risen; Christ will come again" imparts belief in past, present, and future.[35] Polkinghorne reminds us of the importance for worship. In worship we celebrate what God has done for us, and the liturgy reminds us of our hope, and that experience reminds us that despite all the success in the contemporary world, the accomplishments of science in its many areas

---

33. Kushner, *When All You've Ever Wanted*, 18–29.
34. Frankl, *Man's Search*, xiii.
35. Polkinghorne, *God of Hope*, 100–101.

cannot give us that hope. While I enjoy my work in physics, physics does not sustain me nor promise anything for the future. Only my relationship with God does that.

Religion, Kushner says, should call us to grow. It is not a system of do's and don'ts which Jean Piaget in *The Moral Judgment of the Child* (1932) considers religion for children (in Kushner, *When All You've Ever Wanted*, 127–28). True religion enables one to find one's path and does not dictate what the path might be. For such a path, God tells us to go forward and be the best that we can be and leave behind all those things which restrict us such as the tyranny of the dream.[36] God has the role when one suffers to stand alongside. Nothing is sadder at that time than the person who does not have someone's hand to hold. Evangelism has the task to offer the hand of God.

Eschatological Hope

With the emergence of consciousness came the fear of death, and no one had an answer for that fear, let alone assurance for anything comforting. Nothing is sadder than the task of burying someone who denies the reality of God. That all changed with the early Christians who found hope in the resurrection and no longer feared death. In death, I will look forward to resting with my loving God.

Polkinghorne explains that transformation occurs *ex vetere*, as may be seen in 1 Cor 15:51–54. Polkinghorne contends that transformation in the new creation involves process and temporality,[37] an observation with which I do not agree. He does say that new creation contains a different kind of matter and energy. However, evidence seems lacking in support of his argument here. The only support I see for a different kind of matter comes in the apparent change in the body of Jesus following the resurrection where he was able to enter locked rooms and appear randomly in various places. Also in John 20:17, Jesus' words to Mary indicated a change in his body. While Jesus has a body which those around him following the resurrection could experience through the senses, that does not support the same change for humans in their resurrection. Since Paul argues strongly in 1 Cor 15 for an imperishable spiritual body, I conclude the body in new creation is not material. Also, since Paul says in the same chapter that the transformation occurs instantly, I see no support for process after death.

---

36. Kushner, *When All You've Ever Wanted*, 151.
37. Polkinghorne, *God of Hope*, 116–18.

Polkinghorne states that hope does not involve optimism or wishful thinking.[38] Nor does it involve resuscitation; instead, it addresses future human destiny with God, with both present and future character. It delivers the Christian from the fear of death in order to live meaningfully in the present. Life in new creation does not repeat life here. It turns to intimate relationship with God always when our bodies change from the perishable to the imperishable.

Yet, as Wright pointed out, our bodies have significance. Significance occurs in their providing the substance for transformation in new creation.[39] As Paul said, flesh and blood cannot inherit eternal life, requiring transformation of our bodies as well. Clearly, this position raises the question of what happens to a dismembered body or one wracked by disease; the answer is that the body destroyed by dismemberment, disease, or otherwise receives a new immortal body from our God of love who remains faithful to his promises.

Polkinghorne expresses the important opinion that eschatological hope does not mean we look entirely to the future, ignoring the present and events like the Holocaust.[40] Instead, the church must decry the horrors of moral and natural evil and proclaim hope that provides meaning and reassurance in the present. Religion which has only a future event to look forward to fails to provide one meaning throughout life, whereas true religion enables one to be all one can be in the present, to find meaning and fulfillment, and to live a life which makes a difference. Life lived in the kingdom in the expectation of hope does exactly that and acknowledges the immanence of God.

Christian hope rests solidly on the knowledge for God as immanent within creation, as Polkinghorne rightly says.[41] In that knowledge, one sees God active through evolution and through the miracles of the everyday. Hope, he remarks, empowers one in the midst of disaster and uncertainty. It requires faith in God, faith that will see one through. Otherwise, he points out that Paul says: "Now hope that is seen is not hope. For who hopes for what is seen (Rom 8:24)?"[42] Hope then begins in our knowing that God is active and involved in creation. Eschatological hope calls us to place our faith in God as trustworthy and faithful to his promise, and in hope, we rest in God's hand.

38. Ibid., 28–30.
39. Wright *Surprised*, 189–205.
40. Polkinghorne, *God of Hope*, 94–96.
41. Polkinghorne, *Science and Providence*, 95–99.
42. Polkinghorne, *God of Hope*, 46–48.

Polkinghorne said that Christians who clasp hope reside in the hand of God who holds the open future which requires complete commitment to God, the focus that assures us we can pursue a path without always knowing where it leads. He quoted the apocryphal saying attributed to Martin Luther which says, "If he knew that tomorrow the world would end, he would plant an apple tree today."[43] Assurance that we rest in God's hand today and for all time invites us to deeper relationship with him today, a relationship which we gain through the operation of the Holy Spirit within us.

Polkinghorne has built on his strong argument for eschatological hope on resurrection, using his bottom-up approach to the examination of the evidence. As he does so, he clarifies the instances when God kenotically self-limits his activity in creation. He counters the problem of evil and the question for why an omnipotent God does not intervene to prevent suffering. His argument is threefold. First, he argues a world where God always intervenes would not have nearly as much interest. Second, that position would label God as the tyrannical puppet-master. Third, his argument for free-will and free-process relieves God of any responsibility for moral or natural evil. His argument commends Christian faith in the contemporary world, answers many questions that science cannot, and thus provides useful material for evangelism.

Theodicy

Polkinghorne says a totally risk-free world would be bland.[44] Instead, he argues for free-will and free-process as the cause of moral and natural evil in the world, but not God as cause.[45] God created a world that creates itself and self-limited his activity to not overwhelm humans nor creation. Yet, this position does not suggest that all that occurs does so within the will of God.[46] In this instance, God willed free-will and free-process omnisciently knowing the result. In that sense, all that happens occurs in the will and providence of God.

Polkinghorne says that the other option of God as tyrant or puppet master is unacceptable as characteristic of God. Moreover, it would not lead to the observed creativity and novelty in the world.[47] Instead, creation shares as cocreator with God, a claim which entirely relieves God from the respon-

43. Ibid., 102.
44. Polkinghorne, *Science and Theology*, 94–95.
45. Polkinghorne, *Reason and Reality*, 42–48.
46. Polkinghorne, *Faith, Science & Understanding*, 106.
47. Polkinghorne, *Scientists as Theologians*, 50.

sibility for evil.⁴⁸ He remarks that the recent awareness for the emergence of *Homo sapiens* only two hundred thousand years ago dismisses the free-will defense for many instances other than morality. However, it does not eliminate the free-will defense in the contemporary period.⁴⁹ God created a world which guided by the natural laws creates itself. Moreover, God gifted humankind with wonderful freedom in creation with the knowledge that it might lead to horrific times of suffering.

Polkinghorne remarks that free-will and free-process occur in God's plan for freedom in a world that creates itself, and that free-will and free-process relieve God the responsibility for moral and natural evil in the contemporary world. The alternative where God creates a world and intervenes to prevent moral and natural evil sets God up as a tyrant and removes the ability for humans to freely act in creation.

Divine Action

Polkinghorne argues divine action is hidden and God's activities are veiled.⁵⁰ Polkinghorne relates divine action to human action in commenting that when a human acts, that human's entire being acts, and God does similarly.⁵¹ Polkinghorne suggests divine action as the continuous input of information into creation without saying how that works. The unpredictable character of chance and necessity in creation contributes to the hiddenness of divine action. God must be consistent in divine action which requires he treat all similar events in the same fashion. In conclusion, Polkinghorne contends God acts temporally and self-limits his knowledge of the future.⁵² God must act temporally in order to act in a temporal creation. However, his temporal activity does not require any self-limitation with respect to omniscience. Otherwise, we risk projecting human values on God who far exceeds anything one can imagine.

Polkinghorne's argument for divine action as information input works well. He argues that God acts in creation through the input of information. Yet how God inputs information is not clear. I suggest one way God might do so is through natural law. In conclusion, Polkinghorne's argument here provides very helpful material for evangelism to answer questions of how God acts in creation.

48. Polkinghorne, "Kenotic Creation," 96–98.
49. Polkinghorne, *Reason and Reality*, 42–48.
50. Polkinghorne, *Quarks*, 72–74.
51. Polkinghorne, *Belief*, 54–60.
52. Ibid., 72–74.

Trinity

Polkinghorne says the crucifixion resulted in a new theological paradigm.[53] Further, something must have gone on in the life of Jesus for the crucifixion and resurrection to receive so much attention in the early church.[54] Polkinghorne focuses on the economic and immanent Trinity and says the church explored the Trinity in order to understand its experience of the divine nature. The Trinity, three persons in one, assists our understanding of the transcendent God as also personal and expands our view of God as love.[55] Polkinghorne remarks that Rahner made a good move in identifying the immanent Trinity, God in the Godhead, with the economic Trinity, God known through creation and soteriology.[56] The Trinity does not give a blueprint for God. Instead, it describes the richness in the divine revelation.[57] The church handled the development of trinitarian thought well beginning with Council of Nicaea (325) and continuing through the 451 Council of Chalcedon (451). The Trinity speaks powerfully to me in that I can understand God, Jesus, and the Holy Spirit as relational. Second, the Trinity describes the profound nature of God's relationship with creation.

Conclusion

This work addressed the problem for how one would interpret and commend Christian faith in the contemporary world.

Polkinghorne's inclusion of self-limitation for omniscience is unnecessary, and insufficient evidence exists for its inclusion. Similarly, process does not occur in new creation with God, and new creation does not have temporal character. While we do not understand the eternal picture, evolution and biological process do not continue beyond the new creation. Otherwise, we might argue God as changeable over time in eternity.

Shortcomings in Polkinghorne's arguments do not diminish the importance of his work. Instead, these shortcomings call for additional work in the subjects of omniscience, temporality, kenosis, intermediate state following death, psychosomatic human person, and soul as pattern. Polkinghorne could be useful here with the pursuit of further intellectual work to clarify his positions where shortcomings occur.

53. Polkinghorne, "Inbuilt," 48–50.
54. Polkinghorne, *Exploring Reality*, 88–89.
55. Polkinghorne, *Science and Christian Belief*, 154–56.
56. Polkinghorne, *Science and the Trinity*, 100–102.
57. Polkinghorne, *Way the World*, 98–101.

Evangelism has not only the crucial task to spread the message, but it also has the task to assure that those making a new or renewed commitment are linked into the church through discipleship and catechesis. At the forefront, evangelism not only announces the message of the kingdom, but evangelism spreads the message of expectancy and eschatological hope, both present and future, and invites everyone to meet the risen Lord. Polkinghorne's work invites everyone to eschatological hope and reminds the church of the future destiny for those committed to God in the present.

Free-process for Polkinghorne in his argument for eschatological hope led to his position of creation as *creatio continua* and a world that makes itself. He built on this point to suggest creatures as cocreators, co-sharers, and co-sufferers.

Polkinghorne presented a strong examination of the resurrection and covered the factual aspects as well as the circumstantial beginning with the gospel record. The points that stood out in his argument included the strong witness of the various stories despite their differences, the necessity for Jesus as both human and divine, the appearances of Jesus following the resurrection, and the fact that something happened and continues to happen in the empowerment of the disciples and those that have followed through the centuries. In the crucifixion and resurrection, God vindicated himself, Jesus, and us as well and made the promise of eschatological hope possible, another place where Polkinghorne's work commends Christian faith in the contemporary world. Polkinghorne provided a strong defense for the resurrection as foundation for his argument in eschatological hope, and his argument strongly commended his work for evangelism in the contemporary world.

Polkinghorne grounds eschatological hope in his argument for "information-bearing pattern" as soul and the real me. Instead of replacing the soul with "information-bearing pattern," it has better congruence when "information-bearing pattern" is identified as one of the characteristics of the soul which enables its identification to God. While Polkinghorne presented an interesting picture with "information-bearing pattern," the argument lowers God to the human level through imparting human recognition on the omniscience of God. God's omniscience far exceeds anything one can humanly imagine. All we need to remember is that God retains us in divine memory in both the present and in death. More important, eschatological hope gives assurance for human destiny in the hands of our faithful, trustworthy God. As such, eschatological hope does not deny the reality of death, but death does not have the last word. Polkinghorne argues for matter-energy in another form in new creation which he considers consistent with Jesus' appearances following the resurrection.

From these comments in this chapter, I conclude Polkinghorne's work responds to Leslie Newbigin's concerns in *Foolishness to the Greeks* (1986), commends Christian faith in the contemporary world, and satisfies the contemporary world's rational approach to the questions of meaning. His education, achievements, and approach to important theological questions has broad acceptance in today's world, and evangelism can take advantage of his work in support of its mission as well as for catechesis. Important subjects for catechesis include the modified anthropic principle, theodicy, creation as the footprint of God, kenosis, creatures as cocreators and co-sharers in creation with God, time, *creatio continua*, dual aspect monism, eschatology, the kingdom of God, the resurrection, meaning, hope, continuity/discontinuity, soul, new transformed body, theodicy, divine action, and the Trinity, all of which emerge from Polkinghorne's bottom-up approach and cohere with Scripture. Clearly, Polkinghorne offers much to those of us concerned with evangelizing the world. What remains is the working out of a coherent program for evangelism, which while important, lies beyond the scope of this work. I leave such development to scholars to come.

Bibliography

Abraham, William J. "Eschatology and Epistemology." In Walls, *Oxford Handbook of Eschatology*, 581–90.
———. *The Logic of Evangelism*. Grand Rapids: Eerdmans, 1989.
Adams, Marilyn McCord. Foreword to *Evil and the God of Love*, by John Hick, xviii-xxii. New York: Palgrave MacMillan, 2007.
Arias, Mortimer. *Announcing the Reign of God*. Eugene, OR: Wipf and Stock, 1984.
Arnold, Bill T. "Old Testament Eschatology and the Rise of Apocalypticism." In Walls, *Oxford Handbook of Eschatology*, 23–39.
Augustine. *Confessions*. Written ca. 397–400. Translated by Henry Chadwick. Oxford: Oxford University Press, 1998.
Ayala, Francisco J. "Darwin's Devolution: Design without Designer." In *Evolutionary and Molecular Biology*, edited by Robert John Russell et al., 101–16. Vatican City State: Vatican Observatory, 1998.
———. *Darwin's Gift to Science and Religion*. Washington, DC: Joseph Henry, 2007.
———. "Evolution by Natural Selection: Darwin's Gift to Science and Religion." *Theology and Science* 7 (2009) 323–35.
Barbour, Ian G. "God's Power: A Process View." In Polkinghorne, *Work of Love*, 1–20.
———. *Issues in Science and Religion*. New York: Harper Torchbook, 1966.
———. "John Polkinghorne on Three Scientist-Theologians." *Theology and Science* 8 (2010) 247–64.
———. "Remembering Arthur Peacocke: A Personal Reflection." *Zygon: Journal of Science & Religion* 43 (2008) 89–102.
Barrow, John D., and Frank J. Tipler. *The Anthropic Cosmological Principle*. Oxford: Oxford University Press, 1986.
Bloch, Ernst. *The Principle of Hope*. 3 vols. Translated by Neville Plaice et al. Cambridge: MIT Press, 1995.
Bonhoeffer, Dietrich. *The Cost of Discipleship*. New York: MacMillan, 1973.
Born, Max. *Einstein's Theory of Relativity*. New York: Dover, 1965.
Bosch, David J. *Transforming Mission*. Maryknoll: Orbis, 1991.
Boyd, Craig A., and Aaron D. Cobb. "The Causality Distinction, Kenosis, and a Middle Way: Aquinas and Polkinghorne on Divine Action." *Theology and Science* 7 (2009) 391–406.
Brown, Callum G. *The Death of Christian Britain*. London: Routledge, 2006.
Brown, Francis, et al. *The Brown-Driver-Briggs Hebrew and English Lexicon*. Peabody: Hendrickson, 1997.
Brown, Raymond E. *An Introduction to the New Testament*. New York: Doubleday, 1997.

Brueggemann, Walter. *Biblical Perspectives on Evangelism*. Nashville: Abingdon, 1993.
———. *The Prophetic Imagination*. 2nd ed. Minneapolis: Fortress, 2001.
Carnegie, Dale. *How to Win Friends and Influence People*. New York: Simon and Schuster, 1943.
Clouse, Robert G. "Fundamentalist Theology." In Walls, *Oxford Handbook of Eschatology*, 263–79.
Collins, John J. "Apocalyptic Eschatology in the Ancient World." In Walls, *Oxford Handbook of Eschatology*, 40–55.
Crutchfield, Larry V. *The Origins of Dispensationalism*. Lanham, MD: University Press of America, 1992.
Daley, Brian. "Eschatology in the Early Fathers." In Walls, *Oxford Handbook of Eschatology*, 91–109.
Darwin, Charles. *The Origin of Species*. New York: Signet Classic, 2003.
Di Liscia, Daniel A. "Johannes Kepler (1571–1630)." In *The Stanford Encyclopedia of Philosophy*, edited by Edward N. Zalta. Summer 2014 ed. http://plato.stanford.edu/archives/ sum2014/entries/kepler.
Donovan, Vincent J. *Christianity Rediscovered*. Marknoll: Orbis, 1987.
Eaton, Kent. "Beware the Trumpet of Judgment! John Nelson Darby and the Nineteenth-Century Brethren." In *The Coming Deliverer: Millennial Themes in World Religions*, edited by Fiona Bowie, 121–52. Cardiff University of Wales, 1997.
Eden, R. J., et al. *The Analytic S-Matrix*. Cambridge: Cambridge University Press, 1966.
Frankl, Viktor E. *Man's Search for Meaning*. New York: Washington Square, 1968.
Gilkey, Langdon. *Maker of Heaven and Earth*. Garden City, NY: Anchor, 1965.
González, Justo L. *The Story of Christianity*. 2 vols. New York: HarperCollins, 1984.
Gould, Stephen Jay. *Rock of Ages*. New York: Ballantine, 1999.
Bauer, Walter. *A Greek-English Lexicon of the New Testament and Other Christian Literature*. 4th rev. ed. Translated by William Arndt and F. Wilbur Gingrich. Chicago: University of Chicago Press, 1952.
Hall, Douglas John. *Lighten Our Darkness*. Lima, OH: Academic Renewal, 2001.
Halvorson, Hans, and Helge Kragh. "Cosmology and Theology." In *The Stanford Encyclopedia of Philosophy*, edited by Edward N. Zalta. Fall 2013 ed. http://plato.stanford.edu/archives/ fall2013/entries/cosmology-theology.
Happel, Stephen. "Divine Providence and Instrumentality: Metaphors for Time in Self-Organizing Systems and Divine Action." In *Chaos and Complexity*, edited by Robert John Russell et al., 177–203. Vatican City State: Vatican Observatory, 2000.
Hart, David Bentley. "Death, Final Judgment, and the Meaning of Life." In Walls, *Oxford Handbook of Eschatology*, 476–89.
Harvey, Van A. *A Handbook of Theological Terms*. New York: Touchstone, 1997.
Haught, John F. *God and the New Atheism*. Louisville: Westminster John Knox, 2008.
Hick, John. *Evil and the God of Love*. New York: Palgrave MacMillan, 2007.
Hill, Craig C. *In God's Time*. Grand Rapids: Eerdmans, 2002.
Hunter, George G., III. *Church for the Unchurched*. Nashville: Abingdon, 1996.
Koehn, Daryl. *The Nature of Evil*. New York: Palgrave Macmillan, 2005.
Kushner, Harold. *When All You've Ever Wanted Isn't Enough*. New York: Pocket, 1987.
———. *When Bad Things Happen to Good People*. New York: Schocken, 1981.
LaHaye, Tim, and Jerry B. Jenkins. *Left Behind*. Carol Stream, IL: Tyndale, 1995.
Latourette, Kenneth S. *A History of Christianity*. 2 vols. New York: Harper & Row, 1975.
Lewis, C. S. *The Great Divorce*. New York: MacMillan, 1976.

———. *The Problem of Pain*. SanFrancisco: HarperSanFrancisco, 2001.
Lindsay, Hal, and C. C. Carlson. *The Late Great Planet Earth*. Grand Rapids: Zondervan, 1970.
Lohse, Bernhard. *A Short History of Church Doctrine*. Philadelphia: Fortress, 1985.
Losch, Andreas. "On the Origins of Critical Realism." *Theology and Science* 7 (2009) 85–106.
Machamer, Peter. "Galileo Galilei." In *The Stanford Encyclopedia of Philosophy*, edited by Edward N. Zalta. Spring 2014 ed. http://plato.stanford.edu/archives/spr2014/entries/galileo.
Martin, David. *Pentecostalism: The World Their Parish*. Oxford: Blackwell, 2002.
May, Gerald G. *The Dark Night of the Soul*. New York: HarperSanFrancisco, 2005.
McGrath, Alister, "Tweaking the World for Life." *Science & Theology News* 6 (2006) 18.
McGrath, Alister E., and Joanna Collicutt McGrath. *The Dawkins Delusion?* Downers Grove: IVP, 2007.
McKim, Donald K. *Westminster Dictionary of Theological Terms*. Louisville: Westminster John Knox, 1996.
Meacham, Jon. "Heaven Can't Wait." *Time* 179 (2012) 30–36.
Messiah, Albert. *Quantum Mechanics*. Vol. 1. Amsterdam: North-Holland, 1958.
Migliore, Daniel L. *Faith Seeking Understanding*. Grand Rapids: Eerdmans, 1991.
Moltmann, Jürgen. *The Crucified God*. Minneapolis: Fortress, 1993.
———. "God's Kenosis in the Creation and Consummation of the World." In Polkinghorne, *Work of Love*, 137–51.
———. "Is There Life After Death?" In Polkinghorne and Welker, *End of the World*, 238–55.
———. *Theology of Hope: On the Ground and the Implications of a Christian Eschatology*. 5th ed. Translated by James W. Leitch. New York: Harper & Row, 1965.
———. *The Way of Jesus Christ*. London: SCM, 1990.
Monod, Jacques. *Chance & Necessity*. New York: Vintage, 1972.
Palen, Stacy, et al. *Understanding Our Universe*. New York: Norton, 2012.
Paley, William. *Natural Theology*. Edited by Matthew D. Eddy and David Knight. Oxford: Oxford University Press, 2006.
Pannenberg, Wolfhart. "Modernity, History, and Eschatology." In Walls, *Oxford Handbook of Eschatology*, 493–99.
Partridge, Christopher. "The End Is Nigh: Failed Prophecy, Apocalypticism, and the Rationalization of Violence in New Religious Eschatologies." In Walls, *Oxford Handbook of Eschatology*, 191–93.
Peacocke, Arthur. "The Cost of New Life." In Polkinghorne, *Work of Love*, 21–42.
———. *From DNA to Dean*. Norwich: Canterbury, 1996.
———. *God and the New Biology*. Gloucester, MA: Smith, 1986.
———. *Theology for a Scientific Age*. Minneapolis: Fortress, 1993.
Perkins, Pheme. "The Gospel of Mark." In *The New Interpreter's Bible*, edited by Leander E. Kick et al., 511–733. Nashville: Abingdon, 1995.
Peters, Ted. "Constructing a Theology of Evolution: Building on John Haught." *Zygon: Journal of Science & Religion* 45 (2010) 921–37.
Peterson, Eugene. *The Message* Bible online (March 4, 2014). http://www.biblestudytools.com/msg/.
Peterson, Michael L. "Eschatology and Theodicy." In Walls, *Oxford Handbook of Eschatology*, 518–33.

Polkinghorne, John C. *The Archbishop's School of Christianity and Science.* York, England: York Courses. 2003.
———. *Belief in God in an Age of Science.* New Haven: Yale University Press, 2003.
———. *Beyond Science.* Cambridge: Cambridge University Press, 1998.
———. "Comments on Sanborn Brown's 'Can Physics Contribute to Theology?'" *Zygon: Journal of Science & Religion* 40 (2005) 513–15.
———. "Creation and the Structure of the Physical World." *Theology Today* 44 (1987) 53.
———. *Encountering Scripture.* London: SPCK, 2010.
———. "Eschatology." In *The End of the World and the Ends of God,* edited by John Polkinghorne and Michael Welker, 29–41. Harrisburg, PA: Trinity International, 2000.
———. "Evolution and Providence: A Response to Thomas Tracy." *Theology and Science* 7 (2009) 317–22.
———. *Exploring Reality.* New Haven: Yale University Press, 2005.
———. "Faith in Christ." In *Faith in the Living God,* edited by John Polkinghorne and Michael Welker, 40–59. Minneapolis: Fortress, 2001.
———. *Faith, Science & Understanding.* New Haven: Yale Nota Bene, 2001.
———. *From Physicist to Priest: An Autobiography.* Eugene, OR: Cascade, 2007.
———. *The God of Hope and the End of the World.* New Haven: Yale University Press, 2002.
———. "The Hidden Hand of God." *Science & Theology News* 6 (2005) 29–31.
———. "The Inbuilt Potentiality of Creation." In *Debating Design,* edited by William A. Dembski and Michael Ruse, 246–60. Cambridge: Cambridge University Press, 2007.
———. Introduction to *Work of Love,* x–iv.
———. "Kenotic Creation and Divine Action." In *Work of Love,* 90–106.
———. "The Laws of Nature and the Laws of Physics." In *Quantum Cosmology and the Laws of Nature,* edited by Robert John Russell et al., 429–40. Vatican City State: Vatican Observatory, 1999.
———. *Living with Hope.* Louisville: Westminster John Knox, 2003.
———, ed. *Meaning in Mathematics.* Oxford: Oxford University Press, 2011.
———. "The Metaphysics of Divine Action." In *Chaos and Complexity,* edited by Robert John Russell et al., 147–56. Vatican City State: Vatican Observatory, 2000.
———. *Models of High Energy Processes.* Cambridge: Cambridge University Press, 1980.
———. *One World.* Princeton: Princeton University Press, 1987.
———. "Opening Windows onto Reality." In *Faith in the Living God,* edited by John Polkinghorne and Michael Welker, 101–10. Minneapolis: Fortress, 2001.
———. *The Particle Play.* Oxford: Freeman, 1981.
———. "Physical Processes, Quantum Events, and Divine Agency." In *Quantum Mechanics,* edited by Robert John Russell, 181–90. Vatican City State: Vatican Observatory, 2001.
———. *The Polkinghorne Reader.* Edited by Thomas J. Oord. West Conshohocken, PA: Templeton, 2010.
———. *Quantum Physics and Theology.* New Haven: Yale University Press, 2007.
———. *Quantum Theory.* Oxford: Oxford University Press, 2002.
———. *The Quantum World.* Princeton: Princeton University Press, 1989.

———. "The Quantum World." In *Physics, Philosophy, and Theology*, edited by Robert John Russell et al., 333–34. 3rd ed. Notre Dame: University of Notre Dame, 1997.
———. *Quarks, Chaos, and Christianity*. New York: Crossroad, 2004.
———. *Reason and Reality*. Valley Forge, PA: Trinity International, 1991.
———. *Science and Christian Belief*. London: SPCK, 2002.
———. *Science and Creation*. Boston: New Science Library, 1989.
———. *Science and Providence*. Boston: New Science Library, 1989.
———. "Science and Religion: Bottom-Up Style, Interfaith Context." *Zygon: Journal of Science & Religion* 42 (2007) 573–76.
———. *Science and Religion in Quest of Truth*. New Haven: Yale University Press, 2011.
———. *Science and Theology*. Minneapolis: Fortress, 1998.
———. *Science and the Trinity*. New Haven: Yale University Press, 2004.
———. *Scientists as Theologians*. London: SPCK, 1996.
———. *Searching for Truth*. New York: Crossroad, 1996.
———. *Serious Talk*. Harrisburg, PA: Trinity International, 1995.
———. *Theology in the Context of Science*. New Haven: Yale University Press, 2009.
———. *Traffic in Truth*. Minneapolis: Fortress, 2002.
———. *The Way the World Is*. London: Triangle, 1994.
———, ed. *The Work of Love: Creation as Kenosis*. Grand Rapids: Eerdmans, 2001.
Polkinghorne, John, and Nicholas Beale. *Questions of Truth*. Louisville: Westminster John Knox, 2009.
Polkinghorne, John, and Michael Welker, eds. *The End of the World and the Ends of God*. Harrisburg, PA: Trinity International, 2000.
Rabin, Sheila. "Nicolaus Copernicus (1473–1543)." In *The Stanford Encyclopedia of Philosophy*, edited by Edward N. Zalta. Fall 2010 ed. http://plato.stanford.edu/archives/fall2010/entries/copernicus.
Rahner, Karl. *Theological Investigations*. Translated by D. Bourke. Vol. 14. London: Darton, Longman & Todd, 1976.
Robinson, Paschal. "St. Francis of Assisi." In *The Catholic Encyclopedia*, vol. 6. http://www.newadvent.org/cathen/06221a.htm.
Rowland, Christopher. "The Eschatology of the New Testament Church." In Walls, *Oxford Handbook of Eschatology*, 56–72.
Russell, Robert John. "Cosmology and Eschatology." In Walls, *Oxford Handbook of Eschatology*, 563–80.
———. Introduction to *Quantum Mechanics: Scientific Perspectives on Divine Action*, edited by Robert John Russell et al., i–xxvi. Vatican City State: Vatican Observatory, 2001.
Smith, George. "Isaac Newton (1642–1727)." In *The Stanford Encyclopedia of Philosophy*, edited by Edward N. Zalta. Fall 2008 ed. http://plato.stanford.edu/archives/fall2008/entries/newton.
Smith, Huston. *The World's Religions*. New York: HarperOne, 1991.
Soskice, Janet Martin. "The Ends of Man and the Future of God." In Polkinghorne and Welker, *End of the World*, 78–87.
St. John of the Cross. *The Collected Works of St. John of the Cross*. Translated by Kieran Kavanaugh and Otilio Rodriguez. Washington, DC: ICS, 1991.
Strassberg, Barbara Ann. Review of *Religion-and-Science as Spiritual Quest for Meaning: Proceedings of the Sixth Annual Goshen Conference on Religion and Science*, by

Philip Hefner, edited by Carl S. Helrich. *Zygon: Journal of Science & Religion* 45 (2010) 523–24.

Swinburne, Richard. *The Existence of God.* 2nd ed. Oxford: Clarendon, 2004.

Tanner, Kathryn. "Eschatology without a Future?" In Polkinghorne and Welker, *End of the World,* 222–37.

Thucydides. *History of the Peloponnesian War.* Translated by Rex Warner. Middlesex, UK: Penguin, 1985.

Tillich, Paul. *Dynamics of Faith.* New York: Harper Colophon, 1957.

Tilling, Chris. "Engaging Science in the Mode of Trust: Hans Küng's *The Beginning of All Things.*" *Zygon: Journal of Science & Religion* 43 (2008) 201–16.

Ulanowicz, Robert E. "From Pessimism to Hope: A Natural Progression." *Zygon: Journal of Science & Religion* 45 (2010) 939–56.

Viviano, Benedict T. "Eschatology and the Quest for the Historical Jesus." In Walls, *Oxford Handbook of Eschatology,* 73–90.

Walls, Jerry L., ed. *The Oxford Handbook of Eschatology.* Oxford: Oxford University Press, 2008.

Ward, Keith. "Cosmos and Kenosis." In Polkinghorne, *Work of Love,* 152–66.

———. Review of *The Intertwining of Science and Religion,* by John Pokinghorne. *Science & Theology News* 6 (2006) 55.

Weber, Timothy P. "Millennialism." In Walls, *Oxford Handbook of Eschatology,* 365–83.

Welker, Michael. "Romantic Love, Covenantal Love, Kenotic Love." In Polkinghorne, *Work of Love,* 127–36.

Wessel, Walter W. "Mark." In *The Expositor's Bible Commentary,* edited by Frank E. Gaebelein, et al., 603–793. Grand Rapids: Zondervan, 1990.

Whitehead, Alfred North. *Science and the Modern World.* New York: Free Press, 1967.

Wilkinson, David. *Christian Eschatology and the Physical Universe.* London: T. & T. Clark, 2010.

Wisdo, David. "Michael Ruse on Science and Faith: Seeking Mutual Understanding." *Zygon: Journal of Science & Religion* 46 (2011) 639–54.

Wright, N. T. *Surprised by Hope.* New York: HarperOne, 2008.

Index

Abraham, William J, 6–17, 84, 95–99, 182: rule of life, 11; Spong, John Shelby, 16
Adversus Haereses (*Against the Heresies*), 83
advocate, *See* Holy Spirit
Agrippa, 67
analogy, principle of, 68
anonymous Christians, 137
Anthropic Principle: Final Anthropic Principle (FAP), 141; Moderate Anthropic Principle (MAP), 142; Strong Anthropic Principle (SAP), 141; Weak Anthropic Principle (WAP), 141
anthropocentric view, 22
Antiochus IV, 93
Antichrist, 88
apocalypticism: amillennialism, 95; apocalyptic, xxin8, 79–101, 82n8; Darby, John Nelson, 89; devas, 81; dispensationalism, 89, 89n28; eschatology, xxin9, 79–101; eschatological hope xiiin12, 79–101, 168–75; Gog, 91; Hill, Craig C, 84; IndoIranian Aryan culture, 81; *The Late Great Planet Earth* (Lindsey), 90–92; Lindsey, Hal, 90–92; LaHaye, Tim, 92; Jenkins, Jerry, 93; Mazdaism, 82; metaphor, 105; millenarian, 93–94; millennium, 93; New Jerusalem, 144; parousia, 167–68; postmillennialism, 93, 93n43; premillennial, 93–94; pretribulation premillennialism, 89n27, 91; Persia, 81; prediction after the fact, 88; rapture, 89n27, 89n28, 90–94; *vaticinium ex eventu*, 87; second coming, 143–67; seven-year tribulation, 90–92; signs, 90; signs of the times, 90; thousand year reign, 88n26, 94n43, 93–94; tribulation, 89n28, 90–91, 167; Zarathustra, 81; Zoroastrianism, 81–82; Zeus, 82n8, 93, 212; Zurvanism, 82
Aprocrypha, 106, 171, 201
Aquinas, Thomas: primary cause, 56; secondary cause, 40, 56
Arias, Mortimer, 13
Aristotle: Aristotle's God, 69; unmoved mover, 69; cause, 30n1; causality, 30n1; causal nexus, 56; telos, 96
armageddon, 90–91
Augustine, 58, 82–83, 89n28, 94–95, 108, 163, 192–97
Auschwitz, 70, 111–14, 157, 195

Barbour, Ian G: *Issues in Science and Religion* (Barbour), 5, 33
beauty, *See* Polkinghorne, John C
blasphemed, 73
Bloch, Ernst: *Cabbala*, 146; Dostoevsky, Fyodor, 68; *The Demons* (Dostoevsky), 68; forward dawning, 146; Goethe, Johann Wolfgang von, 147; Joachim of Fiore, 147; liberation, 14, 109, 146; Neo-Marxism, 128, 145–46;

Bloch, Ernst *(continued)*: Not-Yet-Conscious, 146; pre-appearance, 146; promised land, 147; ruling class, 147; secular hope, 139–40, 145–48; slavery, 147; utopia, 145–48; utopian hope, 145–48; values, 148
Bosch, David J: radical reorientation, 11–12
bottom-up, *See* discovery
Brueggemann, Walter: metaphor, 96

Caesar Domitian, 88, 93, 212
Camus, Albert, 138
canonical texts, 201
Cappadocian Fathers, 82n10: Basil of Caesarea, 82; Gregory of Nazianzus, 82; Gregory of Nyssa, 82
carbon-based life, 80, 141
Carnegie, Dale: *How to Win Friends and Influence People* (Carnegie), 7
carpe diem, 170
cartesianism: cartesian dualism, 127n63, 180; cartesian rationalism, 3n7, 154
cause, *See also* Aquinas, Thomas; Aristotle
CERN, xii, xiin6
chance and necessity, *See* Monod, Jacques
Christology: abandonment of the cross, 210; body of Christ, 17, 127; *en Christo*, 75; theology of the cross, 67–70, 166–67; crucifixion, 66–76; Davidic lineage, 116; Emmanuel, 67; genealogy, 4n12, 116; historical Jesus, 62; incarnation, 48–61; King of the Jews, 73; Messiah, 4, 73n33, 74, 90, 112, 116, 119; mind-body substance dualism, 85; miracles, 89, 113, 118, 193, 200; Son of God, 29, 63, 74–75; suffering servant, 143
Clement of Alexandria, 89n28
co-creators, *See* creation

comforter, *See* Holy Spirit
complexity, *See* evolution
contingent (contingency), *See* Monod, Jacques
continuity, *See* soul
Copernicus, Nicolaus, 3, 3n8
cosmological constant, *See* physics
Council of Chalcedon 451, 125, 133, 187, 211
Council of Nicaea, 221
creatio continua, *See* creation
creation: co-creators, 48–52, 196, 207, 209–10; co-sharers, 207–10; co-sufferers, 222; *creatio continua*, 18–19, 49–61, 199–208; *creatio ex nihilo*, 49, 49n9; creation as the footprint of God, 45, 223; design argument, 23n26, 27, 140; designer, 140, 152; Earth, 49, 49n8; intelligent design, 23; intelligible, 26, 151, 154; intelligibility, 151, 154; shared creation, 193
creeds: Athanasian, 203; Nicene Creed, 125; *Quicunque Vult*, 203
critical realism, *See* epistemology
cross: promise, xiiin12, 70, 83, 97, 105, 117, 128, 181–84

Dead Sea Scrolls, 87, 129
Descartes, Réne, 2–3, 152: *See* cartesianism; modernity, 3n7, 16n43, 16–17; rationalism, 2–3, 3n7, 16n43; reason, 1, 2n5, 3n7, 26, 32, 150
design argument, *See* creation
determinism (indeterminism), *See* physics
dialectic, 68
discipleship, *See* evangelism
discontinuity, *See* soul
divine action, *See* God
divine agency, *See* God
divine memory, *See* soul
Donovan, William J: *Christianity Rediscovered* (Donovan), 7–11; Masai 7–11; Kenya, 7–11

double-aspect (mental/physical) dualism, *See* God
dual aspect monism, *See* God
dualism, *See also* cartesianism; Christology

Einstein, Albert: general relativity, 4, 4n11, 23, 54n27; proper time, 21n17; special relativity, 4n11
emergence, *See* evolution
empty tomb, *See* resurrection
enlightenment, *See* epistemology
Enoch, 87
epistemology, 30–32: discovery, 34–53; analogical, 68,117; bottom-up, 37–38; critical realism, 33n62, 33–36; enlightenment, 2, 2n5, 30n53; fact-laden, 35–36; falsifiability, 116; indeterminism, 43; knowledge, 35–36; *kritischer realismus*, 33, 33n62; logical positivists, 20; metaphysics, 43, 153, 202, 203; Occam's Razor, 194, 198, 208; ontology, 25, 35, 76, 130, 185; ontological, 20, 86; potentiality, 20; reality, 19–26, 34–45, 81, 103, 106, 108, 115, 153, 155, 171, 178; *Sitz em liben* (situation in life), 29, 116; theory-laden, 32–37, 39, 42n89; top-down, 38–40; truth, 41–45, 154; unseen reality, 21, 21n15, 86–87; verifiability, 116; verisimilitude, 36, 36n68
errancy (inerrancy), *See* scriptural authority
eschatological hope, *See* apocalypticism
eschatology: *See* apocalypticism; ultimate human destiny, 79, 140
eternal life, *See* hope
evangelism, 1–17: discipleship, 1, 12–13; doing the text, 12; Matthean commission (Matt 28:18-20), 14
evil: moral, 24n28, 48–50, 94–111, 192; natural, 48n4, 47–60, 156, 165, 190–98; nature of evil, 194; fellow-sufferer, 193, 196, 203; free-will, 24n28, 48–60; free-process, 48n4, 48–60; God's will, 51; Holocaust, 111, 182–192, 207; oppression, 79, 145–47; pain, 69, 112, 184, 190–96; Satan, 63, 75, 89; suffering, 8, 29–30, 57, 59, 64, 67–72, 98, 139, 160, 166, 178; theodicy, 190–98
evolution: Darwin, Charles (Darwinism), 16; *Origin of Species* (Darwin), 1,4 4n10; complexity, 18, 25–26, 38n75, 39, 50–61, 142; emergence, 38n75; *Homo sapiens*, 22, 80, 156–57, 192; mutations, 49; natural law, 49, 53–55; natural selection, 4n10, 27, 39; Scopes, John T, 6, 6n15
ex vetere, *See* soul
Ezra, 87

fact-laden, *See* epistemology
Feynman, Richard, xii, xiin5, 20, 114
fine-tuning, *See* physics
footprint of God, See creation
St Francis of Assisi, 28n45
Frankl, Viktor, 150, 157
free-process, *See* evil
free-will, *See* evil

Galilei, Galileo, 1, 3, 3n8, 6, 6n15, 36, 44
gentiles, 78
Gilkey, Langdon, 150, 154–56
God: atemporality, 58, 60; deism, 51; deists, 51; divine action, 39, 55, 198–201; divine agency, 39, 46, 153, 198–201; divine purpose, 98, 191; hidden divine action, 200; double-aspect (mental/physical) dualism, 85; dual aspect monism 153; duality of light, 40, 153; God's faithfulness, 101, 127, 164; God of the gaps, 31, 173, 191; God of love, xxii, 6n14, 190; Godlessness, 68, 211; guarantor, 21, 104n5, 110, 151; immanent, 39, 57, 69, 143; immutability, 19, 197; impassibility, 69, 197; kenosis, 47–61; kenotic thought, 47–61;

God *(continued)*: kenoticism, 47–61; omniscience, 51–61, 198; omnipotent, 23n26, 50, 54, 59–69, 108, 195–97; omnipresence, 57, 74, 137; panentheism, 46n100, 56; pantheism, 46n100; self-limited, 49, 57, 60; self-limits, 56, 60–61, 198; suzerain covenant, 104, 104n5; temporality, 21n17, 51, 55–60; theism, 55, 143; time, 4, 21n17, 23, 23n24, 51, 55, 57–60; timeless, 55; timelessness, 55; transcendent power; transcendent (transcendence), 57, 69, 83, 143, 156, 169, 202; veiled presence of God, 199; veiled disclosure, 212, 220
God of the gaps, *See* God
Gould, Stephen J: non-overlapping magisterial (NOMA), 31, 31n56
grace, *See* salvation
Gründman, Adolf, 9

hades, 113, 172
Hartshorne, Charles, 197
Haught, John F: atheists, 16, 28; new atheists, xxin5, 16, 28
Hill, Craig C, *See* apocalypticism
Holy Spirit: advocate, 8–10; comforter, 10; Pentecostals, 11; Pentecostalism, 11
hope: despair, 12, 17, 117, 144, 182–84; eternal life, 79, 100, 106, 130, 137, 143, 151, 172, 176, 180; expectancy, 1, 10, 138, 169; hope within, 137; theology of hope, 70, 138–39, 185–86; nihilism, 144, 183; optimism, 77, 129, 143, 144–45, 169, 183; pessimism, 144, 183; *sub specie aeternitatis* (in the light of eternity), 170
Hoyle, Fred, 22
Hubble, Edwin, 4, 4n12
Hippolytus, 83, 88

Ignatius, 129

immortal (immortality), *See* soul
imperishable (imperishable body), *See* soul
Irenaeus, 83, 89n28, 94–95, 112–13, 129, 190, 193–95: Christian perfection, 198
Isaiah, 74, 87, 103, 181

Jung, Carl, 157–58

Kant, Immanuel, 33, 153
kenosis, 47–61
Kepler, Johannes: planetary motion, 3, 3n8
kingdom of God, 13–15, 72n31, 79, 81n6, 83–84, 100: kingdom of heaven, 102–9; reign of God, 10–14, 72, 108; Sermon on the Mount, 102, 106–7, 150–51
kingdom of heaven, *See* kingdom of God
Kuhn, Thomas: scientific revolutions, 201
Kushner, Harold: meaning, 5–6, 6n14, 8, 34, 125, 136, 150–61; tyranny of the dream, 159

Lactantius, 83
Lonergan, Bernard, *See* Polkinghorne
lukewarm Christian, 12
Luther, Martin: *theologia cruces* (theology of the cross), 67; Protestant Reformation, 3, 3n6, 152;*theologia gloria*, 113–14

Martyr, Justin, 83, 89n28
meaning, *See* Kushner, Harold
metaphor, *See also* apocalypticism; Brueggemann, Walter
millennium, *See* apocalypticism
Moltmann, Jürgen: *The Crucified God* (Moltmann) 66–72; prisoner of war, 72, 186; existential writing, 188; romanticist writing, 188; self-estrangement, 188; self-realization, 188; Third Reich, 72, 139; word of the cross, 68
Monod, Jacques: *Chance and Necessity* (Monod), 27, 27n39, 157;

INDEX

contingent (contingency), 22, 27, 39, 142, 155, 191
More, Thomas, 147
Moses, 47, 64, 70, 85, 103, 171, 182

natural theology, *See* Paley, William
new creation, *See* resurrection
new transformed body, *See* resurrection
Newbigin, Leslie, xix, 1
Newton, Isaac: *Principia* (Newton), 3, 3n8, 30n53, 43
NOMA, *See* Gould, Stephen J
non-overlapping magisterial, (NOMA), *See* Gould, Stephen J

observer, *See* quantum physics
ontology, *See* epistemology

Paley, William: natural theology, 44–45, 152
Papias, 83–84
pattern, *See* soul
Paul, 67–76, 112, 129–30, 130n73, 133, 134: Pauline corpus, 26, 32, 75, 110, 116, 125, 201
physics: chaos, 39; constants of, 21–22, 22n19, 27, 53, 58, 140; Copenhagen school, 20, 20n10; cosmology, 54, 79; cosmological argument, 140; cosmological constant, 21, 21n17, 142; dark energy, 21n17, 142; determinism (indeterminism), 39, 43; fine tuning; geocentric, 3n8, 6n15; heliocentric, 1, 3, 3n8, 6n15, 16; gluons, 45; grand unified force, 21n17, 142; Laplacian view, 198
Pilate, 66, 123
Plato, 65, 68, 131, 165, 172: logos, 64–65; Platonists, 129
Polanyi, Michael, 41
Polkinghorne, John C: Advent, 143; Anglican Priest; beauty, 26, 151–52; brain damage, 176; Polkinghorne's Christian conversion, xi; Christology, 23, 72–76; Dean of Trinity Hall Chapel, xii; Director of Theological Studies, xii; idealism, 43; Lonergan, Bernard, 34; President of Queens' College Cambridge, xiii; professorship of mathematics, xi–xii; religious experience, 42, 45, 86, 115; religious worldview, 152; The Royal Society, xiii; scientific worldview, 26, 184; 2002 Templeton Prize, xiii; theodicy, xxiiin11, 50, 60, 190–93; trinity, 26, 201–3; worldview, 25–29, 119, 153
post-Christian, 4
potentiality, *See* epistemology
Peacocke, Arthur R, xix, 1, 5, 5n13, 39, 75, 113, 121, 133, 157, 195
Philippi, 67
Popper, Karl: Popper-Wittgenstein event, 117
postexilic Judaism, 82
premodern, 16, 16n43
postmodern, 3n7, 16, 16n43
process theology, *See* Whitehead, Alfred N
providence, 51, 54, 56, 132, 198–99
psychosomatic human person, *See* soul

quantum physics: Heisenberg, Werner, 3, 3n9, 19n8, 20, 20n10; observer, 19n8, 20; probability, 20, 43; Schrödinger, Erwin, 3, 3n9, 19n8, 21; wave function, 19n8, 20–21

Rahner, Karl: *See* anonymous Christians
rapture, *See* apocalypticism
real me, *See* soul
reality, *See* epistemology
relativity: *See* Einstein, Albert
religious worldview, *See* Polkinghorne, John C
repentance, *See* salvation
resurrection, 29, 66–72, 82–99, 110–35, 137–39, 143–46, 162–85: Day of Preparation, 66; empty tomb, 76–77, 121–22; Golgotha, 66;

resurrection *(continued)*: Herod, 63, 66, 123; high priest, 73, 73n33; matter-energy, 174; Maundy Thursday, 114; metaphor, 112; metonymy, 112; new body, 86, 106, 121, 127, 129–35, 137, 142, 173–79; new creation, 71, 99, 126, 129–32, 144, 169–83; new transformed body, 120; paradise, 118, 130, 130n70; Pharisees, 119, 172; resuscitation, 71, 119, 137, 175; Sabbath; Sadducees, 85, 103, 105–6, 109, 119, 129, 171; Sanhedrin, 73; transformation, 23, 63, 83, 118–19, 126, 128–39; Yahweh, 74, 76, 181; YHWH, 74, 76, 167

resuscitation, *See* resurrection

Roman Empire, 91, 167

Russell, Robert J, 79–80

Sadduceean lawyer, 103, 105, 109

salvation: Christian; The Fall, 190, 190n1; grace, 14, 70, 107, 110, 126, 134, 136–37, 144, 151, 171, 177, 199; liberation, 14, 109; redeemed, 96, 98, 131; redemption, 52, 131; repentance, 9–10, 100, 102; sanctification, 46, 149, 198; sin, 2, 50, 55, 65, 65n12, 66, 68, 78, 102, 103, 109, 125, 162, 163–65, 179, 191–92, 197; soteriology, 12n35, 202, 221

sanctification, *See* resurrection

scientific worldview, *See* Polkinghorne, John C

scriptural authority, 58, 88, 118: divine dictation, 32n58; errancy (inerrancy), 32, 32n58; literalism, 89

second coming, *See* apocalypticism

secular Christianity, 4, 11

Smith, Huston: Bharata, 81; Buddhism, 136; Confucius (Confucianism), 8, 136, 136n3; Hinduism, 136; Islam, 6, 82, 136; Israel, 9, 32, 54, 72, 78, 83, 87, 90, 91, 97, 103–4, 104n5, 119, 136, 143, 151, 160, 163, 171, 181, 182; Jews, 63, 74, 111, 123, 127, 180, 183, 195; Jewish Temple, 91; Judeo-Christianity, 83, 136, 147, 154, 156, 160, 171; Muslim, 136; Taoism, 136; *The Torah*; Wise Lord (Ahura Mazda), 81

soul: Aristotelian, 215; characteristic of the soul, 176–77; continuity, 86, 98, 106, 130, 132, 173–75; death of the body (*mors corporalis*), 165; eternal death (*mors aeterna*), 165; death of the soul (*mors spiritualis*), 165; decay, 98, 131; discontinuity, 86, 98, 106, 130, 132, 173–75; divine memory, 137, 171, 176–77; evolving soul, 176; *ex vetere*, 130, 130n73, 131; *ex nihilo*, 131, form, 85, 113, 127, 131, 144, 175; God's remembrance, 175; immortal (immortality), 129, 163, 165, 171–77; imperishable (imperishable body), 129, 130n73, 174, 177, 180; information-bearing-pattern, 175–78; information carrying entity, 175; information input, 199, 220; intermediate state following death, 94; pattern, 38, 131, 143, 173, 175–76; psychosomatic human person, 127, 127n63, 173, 175; real me, 175–77, 175n35; static, 176, 196; Thomistic, 43, 50, 175

Standard Model: Quark, 20–21, 21n15, 26n37, 43, 45

Swinburne, Richard: principle of credulity, 115, 115n15

temporality, *See* God

Tertullian, 83, 88, 112–13, 130

theodicy, *See* evil

theology of the cross, *See* cartesianism

theology of hope, *See* hope

theory-laden, *See* epistemology

transformation, *See* resurrection

trinity: economic trinity, 201–3; essential trinity, 202; immanent trinity, 201–2; trinity of love, 26; Trinitarian Model of Kenosis (TMK), 208
Tyconius, 82

United Methodist Church, 9
Ussher, James (Bishop), 4, 4n12

Weisel, Eliezer, 111, 186
Wesley, John: classes, 13; Frazier Memorial Methodist Church, 13, 17; societies, 13; Wesleyan model, 13
Whitehead, Alfred N: process, 5, 18; process theology, 5, 18, 19, 39–40, 126, 195, 196–97; *Science and the Modern World* (Whitehead), 5
worldview, *See* Polkinghorne, John C
Worship: Eucharist, 110, 113, 169; liturgy, 153
Wright, Nicholas T: Wittgenstein, Ludwig, *See* Popper, Karl